English Literature of the 1920s

David Ayers

Edinburgh University Press

For Margaret

First published in hardback by
Edinburgh University Press in 1999.

© David Ayers, 1999, 2004
Edinburgh University Press
22 George Square, Edinburgh

Typeset in New Baskerville
by Koinonia, Bury, and
printed and bound in Great Britain by
the University Press, Cambridge

A CIP record for this book is available
from the British Library

ISBN 0 7486 2025 7

Contents

Acknowledgements

THIS WORK WOULD HARDLY have been possible without the helpful staff and well-organised facilities at the British Library and the Templeman Library at the University of Kent. I am grateful to the School of English at the University of Kent for giving me teaching relief at a crucial stage, and I am indebted to colleagues and students at Kent for the many forms of exchange which I have had with them. In particular, I would like to thank Thomas Docherty, Rod Edmond, David Ellis and Jan Montefiore, who gave generously of their time and expertise in commenting on sections of the typescript, and Leon Boardman, Howard Booth, Caroline Rooney and Paul Russell for our helpful and informative discussions. Special thanks are due to Drew Milne for our many invaluable conversations and for his assistance with the typescript in the final stages. Finally, my thanks and love to Margaret Geraghty, for her commitment and support.

A version of part of Chapter 1 has previously appeared in *English*.

Introduction

THIS BOOK SITUATES THE fiction of the 1920s in its social and political context, with some reference to the literary journals of the period. It has previously been usual to examine the literature of this period as part of the era of international or high Modernism and to stress the importance of its formal innovations. Modernism is an indispensable category, especially if we agree to talk about Modernisms in the plural,[1] but the use of the Modernist model as a periodising device in the English context has tended to conceal as much as it reveals. Much of the work produced in the 1920s can only be considered Modernist in a vague sense – even some of the best-known authors of the period sit uneasily outside or on the margins of the Modernist canon. In what sense can Forster's *A Passage to India* be considered Modernist? How can the apparent modernity of Lawrence's *The Plumed Serpent* be compared to the routinely acknowledged Modernism of Joyce or Proust? How are slightly less well-known authors, such as Aldous Huxley or Sylvia Townsend Warner, to be accommodated to this model? What can the Modernist paradigm tell us about popular fiction? These are not questions without answers, but the answers are more complicated than a formalist account of Modernism can provide.

The paradigm of international Modernism, which does successfully encompass a range of phenomena, needs to be supplemented by a more localised map to describe the literature of the 1920s. Studies of Faulkner have returned him to his context in the American South, while recent work on Joyce has stressed his Irish context and argued for his place in Irish literature. Modern Irish literature in particular is well established as a relatively autonomous field of study, and more recently the case has been made for considering twentieth-century Scottish literature in relation to the project of cultural and political nationalism. Cairns Craig has argued that the works of the Scottish Literary Renaissance of the 1920s in particular 'will go down as major contributions to the total literary achievement of Scottish culture', even though at this time in Scotland 'there remained only the vestiges of the once powerful Scottish publishing industry'.[2] Hugh MacDiarmid (Christopher Murray Grieve), Edwin Muir and Neil Gunn are the central figures in this Renaissance. Craig's claim suggests that there may also be a case for making a more careful map of English literature which will be true to recognisable local contours, even though the pre-eminence of London as a centre of publication certainly conditioned the activities of Irish, Scottish and Welsh writers in the 1920s, whether because they sought to publish there or to avoid doing so. London as capital of the British State was at the same time the centre to which English writers had to look, and disentangling the fictions of Englishness which this centre fostered is one result of focussing on London as the English literary capital. This is not to argue for a parochial or nationalistic model of English literature: it is simply to note that, while we long ago developed a category for literature of the 1930s which has proven more flexible than its narrowly conceived inception seemed to promise,[3] we have been slow to build a corresponding model for literature of the 1920s, one which should remain flexible and not become periodising in a stilted fashion. I do not believe that the theoretical arguments for the cultural meaning of Modernism – especially in the form of the famous 'torn halves' model elaborated by Adorno – can simply be overcome or bypassed by reference to a national model. Indeed, one of the principal advantages of looking at English literature of the 1920s as a quasi-sociological category is that it highlights in one specific cultural frame of reference the emergence of the modern capitalist state and its culture against which the autonomous art of Modernism is considered to be a reaction. It seems likely that the separation of the component strands of British and Irish literatures will prove to be a strategic move which can enable a more confident return of these literatures to their European and international contexts. There is at least some hope that, as a consequence of this process, early twentieth-century English literature will cease to be regarded as a subset of American literature, the mid-Atlantic model which, whatever its origins, seems now to be most vigorously promoted by those academic publishers in Britain who feel – I would hope wrongly – that a book with an Anglo-American focus will generate more sales.

I have taken the 1920s as beginning with the end of the war. War poetry unsurprisingly fell out of fashion with the end of the war and is excluded: some of the fiction which features the war as its background or its content is of course included. My remit includes works published in England but not translations or English issues of American books, although no nationality check has been applied. I had originally intended to produce a study of both fiction and poetry, but have decided to exclude poetry both for reasons of space and because, while we still need a fuller account of the poetry of the 1920s, I have come to the conclusion that a quite different and separate full-length study is required. The aim here has been to produce an account of a selection of texts of the 1920s which reviews some of the better-known work alongside popular and less-known works. In concentrating on sustained readings of a selection of texts, there have inevitably been notable omissions and I hope that these will be excused. My intention has been to avoid the pitfalls of a reductively empirical historicising in order to foreground the complexity of textual dynamics.

In what follows, I have sought to distinguish between those aspects of a text which are related to or which confirm contemporary ideology, and those which contradict normative values, formulate critique and seek to project, in however flawed a fashion, a utopian alternative to the present. Both of these approaches are present, in a contradictory and usually confused fashion, in most of the works in question, although popular works mainly emerge as bastions of ideology and regression. While the popular has its vocal advocates in our own time as an alleged site of counter-cultural endeavour, I have found little to affirm in those mass-circulation novels of the 1920s which I have discussed, nor, I might add, in those which I do not mention. Although these mass-circulation novels were read by literally millions and fulfilled the role of the television soap opera in our own time as a guide to 'being oneself' in the context of general submissiveness, I do not pretend, as it might be convenient to do once one has gone to the trouble of studying them, that they give us a privileged access to the contemporary popular mind. With their diet of, variously, moralism, escapism and titillation, they do, however, attempt to sustain a climate of general acquiescence and incuriosity in a time of great uncertainty and potential for massive change, and are examined in that light. Their continued ability to exercise a certain kitsch fascination may have outlasted whatever contribution they made at the time to ideological propriety. There is a small number of works, one of which I discuss here, which attempt to harness the popular romance form to progressive ends: these novels did not run to the innumerable reprints of their conservative or escapist rivals.

Although some of the concerns of the decade prove to be localised, others seem to anticipate the concerns of our own time: unsurprisingly so, since the 1920s is the decade which heralded the arrival of late capitalism, with its armoury of mass media, its attempted consolidation of global hegemony (which was, however, powerfully interdicted by the success of the Russian Revolution) and its dialectic of promise and refusal in which a great many social alternatives are systemically closed down while new human possibilities are tantalisingly glimpsed. It is also at this time that sex, sexuality and gender relations attained the kind of mediatic ubiquity which pertains again in the present. The 1920s also saw English emerge as a modern University subject, and it is appropriate that a study of the English literature of the period should concern itself with the literary and ideological formations which shaped the discipline as it still knows itself. Finally, this decade, which witnesses the beginning of the end of British colonial domination, begins at least to wonder what alternatives this phase of world history has eclipsed, and whether the English subject of the British Empire can cast off the mutual shackles of colonialism and enter into any kind of dialogue or exchange with colonised cultures.

Throughout I have brought a variety of critical modes into contact with the range of texts I have selected for discussion. Each chapter combines contextualising information with a series of readings of individual texts. While my approach admits that texts can be viewed as the products of particular social and ideological configurations, I have not argued for anything like a rigorous reduction of texts to a narrative of history which determines their form and content. One effect of this has been that a construction of authorial intention is at times freely invoked to supplement the more obviously formal analyses. Another more important theoretical consequence is the use of the concept of the utopian to suggest, following Adorno, the negation within art of existing conditions which serves to indicate the space of a different if unarticulated social dispensation, even where the form of this futurity cannot be positively described.[4] In accordance with this model, I will suggest that the utopian moment in a work can be located and disentangled from other of the work's more obviously ideological or simply 'wrong' components. It is this privileging of negativity and critique which has led me to give most attention to the works of Woolf, Lewis and Lawrence, the latter analysed across several chapters in order better to grasp the variety of contexts which his work addresses. In the case of Woolf, where I have found existing accounts to be excessively affirmative, this has involved elaborating the dystopian pessimism of her work and the manner in which this pessimism is articulated in a symbolic framework which in many ways refuses the optimism of the feminist accounts of its own time and ours with which it has been most generally identified. In the case of Lewis I have attempted the perhaps more difficult task of creating a space for the acceptance of Lewis's negativity – and the brilliant but still comparatively neglected oeuvre which it produced – by articulating with some specificity the react-ionary nature of Lewis's stance in order, as I see it, to make Lewis tractable and available again to non-specialised or otherwise uncommitted readers. My belief is that Lewis is better served by this approach than by the kind of apology and obfuscation which once almost completely surrounded the politics of Pound and Eliot. A similar consideration applies in my accounts of Lawrence, which again confront the semblance of reaction in his work to suggest that, as with Lewis, this critical negativity serves at least to negate or inter-dict a series of complacent assumptions about the nature of progress in capitalist society.

The effect of taking an extended decade as my object has been to encapsulate neatly the most important moment in certain literary careers – Woolf, Lewis – and to subdivide others in ways which I hope will not prove objectionable. It has seemed to me fruitful to analyse and bracket together, for example, the later Lawrence of the works after *Women in Love* and the early Huxley of works before *Brave New World*, along with more obviously 'period' works which are rarely referred to in the context of single-author studies but which are mutually illuminating. Some of the exclusions entailed by period-isation are pragmatic. I have not considered Katherine Mansfield as a 1920s author although some of her work does belong to this decade. Other decisions reflect my opinion about where critical attention might be better bestowed, so, for example, I have allowed Evelyn Waugh to slide off the end of the decade because Lewis and Huxley are in this context more interesting. Decisions about authors who fairly decisively belong to the period are equally both critical and pragmatic. That is, I have dedicated extensive space to Woolf and neglected Richardson simply because I believe that Woolf has more of importance to tell us than does Richardson. In the case of the popular works I have made a selection based on what I have found to say, and in including Warwick Deeping's *Sorrell and Son* and excluding parallel works such as A. S. M. Hutchinson's *If Winter Comes*, for example, I have preferred the insights yielded by a giving a more sustained account of a single work to the effects of more obviously sociological summary. The popular works which I have selected are part of an informal canon of such works which are frequently mentioned as such by contemporary commentators.

The discussion is organised so as to present a series of social and political themes as the context for the discussion of particular texts. Chapter 1, 'Men and Masculinity: The Response to Social Change', describes the background of uncertainty for men and masculinity stemming from social changes brought about by the war, and examines the complex mediation of these issues in works by Ford Madox Ford, Richard Aldington, D. H. Lawrence and Warwick Deeping. Chapter 2, 'Ideals and Realities of the English Woman', finds that, despite a background of official optimism about the actual and future social role of women, women's writing struggled to find any ground for unequivocal affirmation. This is shown to be so in the works of Rebecca West and Sylvia Townsend Warner, which celebrate motherhood and spinsterhood in ways which have a limited social purchase, and in the works of Virginia Woolf, which offer only a limited affirmation of female possibility in the context of their resolutely critical modelling of ruling-class culture as patriarchal. Chapter 3, 'Mass Civilisation and Minority Culture', complements the account of gender politics which determined the ideological nature of so much fiction of the 1920s by detailing the class politics of the period. Although gender rather than class forms the ideological topos of the work examined in the first two chapters, this chapter shows how class confrontation in the years leading up to 1926 contributed to the development of the notion of a divided culture and a disabled literary public sphere. This pessimistic view is examined in an account of a series of important literary journals which created the context for the emergence of the discipline of English literature as a response to cultural crisis, as exemplified in key arguments of Q. D. Leavis. This is followed by an examination of two of the few works of the period to take the new mass politics as their principal focus: Ellen Wilkinson's novel of the General Strike, *Clash*, and D. H. Lawrence's prophetic modelling of the new world order of mass politics in *Kangaroo*. Chapter 4, 'Sex, Satire and the Jazz Age', shows how and on what terms sex became a central topic of the 1920s, and examines work by Radclyffe Hall, Wyndham Lewis, Michael Arlen and Aldous Huxley and, finally, the socio-political genesis of *Lady Chatterley's Lover*. Chapter 5, 'England and its Other: Seduction and Friendship, Bodies and Ghosts', outlines the context of Imperial decline with reference to the British presence in Ireland and India. Against this background, the chapter discusses the modelling of the Oriental other in popular desert romance and the utopianism of Lawrence's *The Plumed Serpent*, and concludes with some theoretical speculation about the underestimated concern with post-imperial friendship of Forster's *A Passage to India*.

Notes

1. Peter Nicholls, *Modernisms: A Literary Guide*, p. vii, shows how the pluralisation of this term serves to maintain its continued validity in the face of recent critique of an earlier, monolithic use of the term.
2. Cairns Craig (ed.), *The History of Scottish Literature. Volume IV: Twentieth Century*, pp. 2–5.
3. For a recent revaluation of this period, see Janet Montefiore, *Men and Women Writers of the 1930s*.
4. For a summary account of Adorno's 'utopian negativity', see Simon Jarvis, *Adorno: A Critical Introduction*, pp. 7–8.

1

Men and Masculinity

The Response to Social Change

THE WAR POETRY OF Wilfred Owen and Siegfried Sassoon has established an image of the First World War in which the futility of combat and death remains the most outstanding impression. One of the most famous of the war memoirs, Robert Graves's *Goodbye to All That* (1929), conveys a similar impression inasmuch as it concentrates on the realistic description of trench warfare, but the male poets and memoirists of the war only address its social aspects to a limited extent.[1] They refer to the inability of civilians to understand the plight of soldiers, and go on from this to doubt the social mechanism that has begun the war, or that has sought to prolong it.[2] Lyric poetry, which addresses the actions and feelings of single moments of experience, and the memoir, which is mainly valued for its representation of particular experience rather than abstract social analysis, have become the privileged literary forms through which the war is imaged and imagined. However, although the experience of fighting was very widespread, it is misleading to think of the war only in terms of fighting and the trenches. After the introduction of conscription in 1916 it became the lot of perhaps one-third of the adult male population, of increasingly unsuitable age and degree of fitness, to be sent to the front and experience combat. Yet the war had an impact not only on the combatants but on the population as a whole. Although the war brought about the increased centralisation of power in the hands of the government, its effect on the social structure was to achieve a level of perceived democratisation. This worked in two ways: closing the gap between social classes as workers' wages rose in relation to middle-class salaries[3] and the creation of unprecedented opportunities for women to perform work which had hitherto been open only to men. The effects of these changes were immense. Women of all classes came to feel more confident and many experienced financial independence for the first time in their lives. In a parallel development, the working class grew in confidence, both because it became more wealthy as a consequence of the war, and because, in spite of attempts to curb it, trade union organisation had grown in efficiency. While the confidence of women and the working class grew, the middle class came to feel less sure of its own relative position of dominance, while men of all social classes felt threatened by the new-found independence of women. Against a background of severe unemployment, men lower down the social scale, especially returned soldiers, frequently had reason to resent the impression that women were taking male jobs. At the top end of the social scale, the war served merely to confirm the domination of the continuously rising industrial and commercial classes over long-established land owners.

Women's war work had been a major factor in female emancipation and generated changes which the suffrage movement had been unable to create and which the male-dominated Labour movement had largely never even contemplated. Before the war working-class women had mainly been employed in low-paid work such as dressmaking or as domestics. Now the professions were beginning to open to upper-class women, but few were in a position to grasp the opportunities.[4] The war brought a demand for female labour in a variety of areas, most notably in munitions after the Munitions War Act (1915) allowed women to undertake skilled work from which they had previously been banned as lacking both training and aptitude. As a consequence of this Act, especially after the introduction of conscription in 1916, women were employed in many forms of skilled labour outside munitions as a process of 'dilution' began to take place, in which previously skilled assembly jobs were broken down into a series of separate tasks to enable a hastily trained worker to perform them adequately. This process of substituting cheap semi- or unskilled labour for expensive skilled labour was to continue after the war and was partly responsible for the continued demand for women's labour.[5]

The confidence and independence of women in work previously barred to them grew measurably. These women often earned more money than they had done previously, and in many cases they were earning independently of men who were away fighting. Others left home themselves to work, again often for the first time. The general effect was to contribute to rising expectations among women, especially inasmuch as their new lives began to confirm theories of independence and emancipation which had been long explored in feminist literature of the pre-war – from Sarah Grand's *The Beth Book* (1897) to H. G. Wells's *Ann Veronica* (1907).[6] Journalists, propagandists, feminists and politicians agreed in glorifying the efforts of women workers and in anticipating a new role for women after the war.[7]

Changes in women's behaviour had their roots in the war and were the cause of much male anxiety both during the war and after. Even during the war conservative Trade Unionists had treated women workers with suspicion and hostility.[8] The men fighting at the front were not separate from or indifferent to shifting social patterns back home and some of the most significant fiction about the war written by men represents the trenches and combat itself as a moment in a broader social process. Much of this fiction was not produced in the immediate aftermath of the war and therefore tends to refract it through the concerns of the 1920s. Consequently, it is difficult to be sure to exactly what extent the carefully cultivated public anxiety about the role of women which was a feature of the 1920s retrospectively influenced accounts of the war and the pre-war. While Chapter Two looks at the effects on women and women's writing, this chapter begins by looking in some detail at Ford Madox Ford's *Parade's End* and Richard Aldington's *Death of a Hero*, works which share the project of exploring the war in relation to social change and which strikingly associate the demoralisation of the war with the accelerating revolution in gender relations. This is followed by an examination of some key works of D. H. Lawrence, showing them to form a project which I have termed 'masculinist', by analogy with the term 'feminist', which is only in part rooted in simple male defensiveness. The closing discussion concerns the immensely popular novel, *Sorrell and Son*, by Warwick Deeping, which is found to reflect the culture of male defensiveness in its smallest narrative detail.

The Feminist Toryism of Ford Madox Ford's Parade's End

Parade's End was the collective title which Ford Madox Ford gave to a sequence of four novels written between 1924 and 1928: *Some Do Not* ... (1924), *No More Parades* (1925), *A Man Could Stand Up –* (1926) and *The Last Post* (1928);[9] they are known also as the Tietjens tetralogy after the family name of their protagonist. *Parade's End* is among the most ambitious and best written fiction produced by and about the First World War. It combines social and psychological depth, naturalistic description of the war, conventional plot interest and a Modernist narrative technique involving complex time-shifts.

Ford was born in 1873 and was forty-two years old when he enlisted. Due to his age he never undertook front-line combat although he was often near the front, and the extended descriptions of army life and of shell-shock in the novel are based on his own experience.[10] However, his protagonist Tietjens is not a version of himself, but an idealised version of his friend Arthur Marwood.[11] *Parade's End* is much more than a documentary attempt to demonstrate war experience to the public: it is a complex examination of the passing of the Victorian and Edwardian England in which Ford had his roots. It is not a nostalgic evocation of the pre-war era but locates the war as the catalyst for a series of social problems which were already fully developed. Nostalgia is reserved for an older England. Tietjens's own values are rooted in an earlier and idealised England which is associated with probity and a corresponding verbal clarity. Ford called himself a 'suffragette' and was the author of a pro-suffrage pamphlet called *This Monstrous Regiment of Women* (1912), published by the Women's Freedom League, and expressed himself a 'Tory' on various occasions, although his relationship to this term was complex and ambivalent.[12] It is from these standpoints that *Parade's End* launches what I have called its feminist Tory critique of the condition of England and of its ruling class in particular.

Because its regrets are selective and critical, the tetralogy differs from Woolf's *To The Lighthouse* (1927) which similarly bridges the war and articulates the passing of old and imperfect social ideals and the imperfect emergence of new ones, but seeks to preserve the now neutralised pre-war world almost elegiacally. It differs too from Eliot's *The Waste Land* (1922) which is more frankly apocalyptic in its imaging of the post-war as a fallen world awaiting redemption. While *The Waste Land* is characterised by a fear of sexuality,[13] *Parade's End* is more subtle in its account of sexual repression in the English ruling class. The difficulty of divorce created intolerable situations: *Parade's End* shows that the supposed sanctity of marriage in the English ruling class was a question not of moral propriety but of property rights, in a society which tolerated infidelity as long as appearances were maintained. The narrative of *Parade's End* concerns the eventual decision of the protagonist to abandon his wife, thereby relinquishing his social status and much of his property, in order to go and live, unmarried, with another woman. Initially Tietjens will not seek a divorce, although he is given ample cause when his wife Sylvia runs away with another man, because he has stubbornly internalised the gentlemanly code which says that only a 'blackguard' (Ford, 1982: 6) divorces his wife. That the narrative begins before the war and ends immediately afterwards means that the pattern of the dissolution of the marriage, and the change in attitude as well as in fortune of Tietjens, are superimposed on the war itself. In its commitment to analytic social documentation, *Parade's End* insists on the profound connection between social anxieties and the experience of combat. The narration of the war experience represents combat itself as only part of the mental torment. One aspect of the new phenomenon of total war is that now not merely the army but the whole of society goes to war: insisting on the connection between the war and society in general, the novel shows how Tietjens's social and marital problems pursue him to the front.

Parade's End is not a threnody like *Death of a Hero*, but the two works share a structure which places a male experience of the war at the narrative and conceptual centre. While Aldington creates a vehicle for the investment of male anxieties about social change and especially feminine sexuality, Ford's approach is in a broad sense feminist. Not, however, that the female characters of *Parade's End* are portrayed in a uniformly rosy light. In one of his editorials for the *English Review,* which he founded in 1908 and edited for the first year of its existence, Ford had criticised the representation of women in the whole of English fiction, arguing that writers from Shakespeare to George Meredith had established an idealised form of woman. The idealised 'Woman of the Novelists' has denied men a recognition of women's reality, and failed to serve the cause of women by advancing their claims to social justice:

> She is always, this super-woman, gliding along some few inches above the earth [...]. She is a sort of Diana with triumphant mien before whose touch all knotted problems dissolve themselves. [...]
>
> Ah! The Woman of the Novelist – the Woman of the Novelist: what great harm she has done to the cause of women in these days and for centuries back![14]

Ford challenges the Victorian tendency to put women on a pedestal and argues for the right of the novelist to represent women whose motivation is less than virtuous without being accused of misogyny.

He felt that writers were constrained to represent women in a blandly affirmative light and wanted to open the way for a realistic approach to female character and, above all, to female sexuality in literature. His model is Flaubert who possesses 'The Critical Attitude' which this series of essays has set out to endorse, (Hueffer [Ford]: 1911 155) and who, in Emma Bovary, provides a distant archetype for Sylvia Tietjens.

However, *Parade's End* does not fulfil Ford's commitment to a new level of psychological and sexual realism in the representation of women to the extent that the two main female characters are present less as ends in themselves but as structural opposites, framing the existence of the male protagonist. Sylvia is the wife of Christopher Tietjens, and Valentine Wannop, the daughter of a progressive and accomplished mother, is his mistress. As a structure, the novel is organised as a triangle, with Tietjens at the apex. The novel arranges its conflict of values between the poles represented by the two women, invariably resolving these conflicts in favour of Valentine. Sylvia represents corruption, sexuality, property, propriety, the creeping disease of pre-war England now rampant in the period of its post-war decline; Valentine represents innocence and idealism, chastity, dispossession and disenfranchisement, a principled disregard for hypocritical propriety, and the robust health of an inner morality untainted by power. In other words, Sylvia is the villain of the piece and Valentine the chaste heroine. This essentially melodramatic struc-ture, although decorated with layers of psychological detail, remains in evidence throughout.

Tietjens, the son of a traditional country family from the North of England, is at the centre of the novel's value system. Hailing from Yorkshire, he is represented as stubborn, taciturn and completely honest, values which the novel associates with a North which is not yet entirely corrupted by Southern cynicism. His Tory outlook is characterised by a mystical love of the English countryside of what he calls, not without ironic ambivalence, 'God's England' (Ford, 1982: 106),[15] and a cultivation of 'the peculiarly English habit of self-suppression in matters of the emotions, [...] a habit of behaviour which he considered to be the best in the world for normal life' (178). Tietjens's taste in literature is for the verbal clarity of Eliza-bethan and seventeenth-century England – for the poetry of Herbert, Donne, Crashaw, Vaughan and Herrick and the word-setting of Purcell (564–7) – a growing taste for poets of the 1920s, in fact, but Tietjens is no Modernist: 'There has been nothing worth *reading* written in England since the eighteenth century', he claims, 'except by a woman' (19), a qualification which is important in terms of his eventual alliance with the suffragist, Valentine. It is this alliance which will lead him to revise his conservative views on marriage. Tietjens's wife has betrayed him in an affair which has become a public scandal. Chivalrously, he refuses to seek a divorce, instead preferring to sacrifice himself by giving Sylvia public grounds for divorce. His view early in the novel is that one must play by the rules – 'I stand for monogamy and chastity. And no talking about it.' (18) – but only because these *are* the rules and because he considers sex not to be immoral but to be merely a secondary consideration – 'Of course if a man who's a man wants to have a woman he has her. And again no talking about it. He'd no doubt be in the end better, and better off, if he didn't.' (18). Tietjens is a one-nation Tory who believes that class society depends for its justice and efficient functioning on the integrity of the system. As the ruling class becomes corrupted by commercial values, only the lower classes embody the integrity which his own class had once exemplified: 'They're the only people in this country who are sound in wind and limb. They'll save the country if the country's to be saved' (18). Tietjens is a limited hero,[16] who recognises that his self-consciously English values are themselves probably an ideological construction owing less to real history than to the idealised codes and artificial egalitarianism of the public school: 'I really am the English public school boy' (490). The ideals of his class as instilled by the public school system now inform only social appearance but no longer reflect actual social practice; his adherence to the rules is at odds with the pragmatism of the rest of his class. Tietjens's Englishness is therefore not an expression of contemporary values and does not blind him to the condition of contemporary England: rather, his Englishness is at odds with, and informs his ability to resist, the modern state.

Tietjens works in the 'Imperial Department of Statistics' where he is assured a brilliant career. As heir to a vast, coal-rich estate, an expert statistician and a person so knowledgeable that he tabulates the errors in the *Encyclopaedia Britannica* for his own amusement, Tietjens stands for intellectual and social order. The order represented by the quasi-feudal world of social relations implies fixed hierarchies, stability, and also, at least in the Tory vision, a one-nation view of social responsibility. The order implied by the administrative world of statistics, the rational form of order associated with industrial economics and progress which sent millions to their deaths in the first total European war, is of a quite different type. Tietjens is asked to put his statistical skills at the service of the state to produce propaganda to prove the ludicrous case that the war does no more damage to property than an average year of natural wear and tear. In a key decision not to compromise his integrity, he chooses to remove his mind from the public service and accept military service at the front as a less compromised activity. In this, Christopher Tietjens contrasts with his brother Mark, who remains intellectually committed to the war. Mark concludes the novel paralysed by a stroke at the Armistice, shocked or disgusted by the decision of the victorious allies not to invade Germany and hence, as he sees it, not to pursue the war to its rational conclusion. Tietjens eschews modern nationalism, which has been whipped by press and propaganda into a bloodthirsty aggression, and remains committed to the values of an English culture and heritage which England no longer embodies. By entering into an unmarried relationship while he is still married, he relinquishes his property to his wife: but this property, without the cultural context which created it, has no meaning for him as mere wealth. In an ironic and highly symbolic twist, Tietjens turns to making a living out of selling eighteenth-century English furniture to Americans, as if the whole nation were now no more than a giant antique shop. His renunciation of the English establishment is precipitated by the war, but it is essentially brought about by the progressive abandonment by his own class of the values on which it was established. Tietjens can only retain his own integrity and that of the older England by abandoning the class which has deserted him.

Parade's End establishes intricate connections between the war and society. In *No More Parades,* called in for an interview with the General, Tietjens is made to remark: 'Military operations sweep on. But my problem will remain the same whether I'm here or not. For it's insoluble. It's the whole problem of the relation of the sexes' (491). Aldington's *Death of a Hero* rehearses the embittered view, common among veterans, that the men at the front had been betrayed by the generals, by those back home and by their women.[17] *Parade's End* goes beyond this culture of male complaint but it retains a version of the same argument. Tietjens's domestic life intrudes constantly at the front, and all three strands of the betrayal scenario are embodied in the person of his superior, General Campion, who apart from representing the conniving and heartless military command structure also represents the social and political manoeuvring back home, as well as representing sexual betrayal: the

General has a sexual interest in Sylvia which she cultivates in order to get at her husband.

Tietjens's wife Sylvia sees herself as a type of 'man-mad' vamp (147), and is the novel's representative of the new sexuality. Her belief in sexual liberation is given a mocking treatment in the narrative which notes the comparative timidity of an upper-middle class which prefers, at most, mild bouts of promiscuity to recognisably improper affairs (147–8). This class is too bound up with property and inheritance to be able to neglect the institution of marriage. Sexual liberation is treated in the novel as a pre-war phenomenon rather than a merely disillusioned reaction to the war. It does not liberate sexuality but serves to highlight sexual repression. It is merely an expression of the bankruptcy of the English ruling class in which marriage is dominated by property considerations. However, while the novel rejects the surface culture of sexual liberation, it acknowledges the importance and legitimacy of sexual frustration. In fact, Sylvia does not obtain a healthy pleasure from sex by indulging in it. Rather, she obtains a distorted pleasure by encouraging and manipulating men's sexual interest in her. Tietjens is uninterested in sex to a degree that provokes Sylvia's fury and her brief affair. His reaction to her affair is to take her back almost without a word. This passionlessness is compounded by his increasing shell-shock, and his apparent indifference culminates in a memorable scene of domestic violence in which Sylvia throws her dinner at her taciturn husband, who barely moves to avoid the impact (156). So distorted is her framework of desire that Sylvia does not take the opportunity to divorce Tietjens when he begins a relationship with Valentine, in part to retain her claims on his property, but mostly in order to retain her claim on his person, which, now unavailable, becomes sexually desirable to her. In all of this, Tietjens is cast as an innocent victim, but his posture of martyrdom is also a provocation. Sylvia and others are so frustrated by his silent righteousness that they mockingly claim he has aspirations to be an Anglican saint. Correspondingly, Sylvia is characterised at certain points as the devil and as a snake. While she is certainly demonised by the narrative, she is not shown to be the sexually motivated devil which others believe her to be. Rather, her sexuality is itself shown to be distorted and frustrated by the class system.

If Sylvia negatively embodies the distorted sexuality of the modern woman, Valentine Wannop more positively embodies her intellectual independence. The novel thus structurally separates what it construes to be the two main facets of the modern woman. Valentine lives with her mother in genteel poverty, and has worked a period as a maid or 'slavey', a short-lived encounter with working-class experience which has radicalised her politics: she has become a suffragette. She meets Tietjens when she and a friend invade a golf course to dig up the turf as a suffrage protest, on the occasion of a visit to the course of a Government Minister. The incident is the occasion for an examination of the values of contemporary England. Chased by the golfers, Valentine's companion is cornered by two 'City men', who represent the world of banking and business and its values, the antithesis of the inherited wealth and tradition of the Tietjens family. The suffragette, Gertie, seems like a 'hunted rat': her blouse is torn, Tietjens sees her as 'an assaulted female', and one of the City men shouts 'Strip the bitch naked' (67). In this scenario, as he comes to the rescue, Tietjens stands for the older tradition of public spiritedness and chivalry, while the City men represent the ugly new values. The behaviour of these City men is a travesty, designed to highlight Tietjens's comparative virtues and the decline in modern moral standards. One of the men is so amazed at Tietjens's intervention, the narrative tells us, that 'It was as if the bottom of his assured world, where all men desire in their hearts to bash women, had fallen out' (67).

From the point of view of its own objectives this passage is highly effective. In part it serves to create an image of an England become brutal. Indeed, the novel arranges several images of social and domestic violence which anticipate and are parallel to the violence of the war, further reinforcing the impression of the war as an 'intensification' of peacetime trends. The apparent assumption of the City man that any other man would be complicit in violence against a woman who had gone 'beyond the pale' and thereby, according to a perverted logic, 'deserved it', is a psychological insight with a modern ring.[18] At the same time, his amazement that Tietjens could be different creates a sense of how isolated Tietjens's values are. Further, the scene manages to relate male resistance to female empowerment ('Why *don't* you give women the vote?' [69]) to a cultural nexus of misogyny in which sexual desire and violence are closely related ('Strip the bitch naked!'). That no one wanted to catch the women 'except the swine' (that is, the City men) locates brutal misogyny at the heart of the rising part of the British ruling class and conveniently enhances the image of the declining traditional wing. That the scene is such a striking and brilliantly contrived one does not conceal the manner in which apparently frank psychological analysis and special pleading for the traditional ruling class are blended into each other.

The passage also has other dimensions. By suggesting that the Tietjens' party behave in a chivalric manner towards the women, and indeed that they respect their daring and are at the same time attracted to their unconventionality and youthfulness (the Minister finds Valentine 'a ripping girl' [69]), the passage also suggests that suffragism in part is not as confrontational as certain of its more dramatic demonstrations may have made it seem. These women are of the same social standing as the ruling class: they are, in varying degrees, part of it, and can rely on a chivalric male response informed by unconcealed sexual interest (the Minister wishes to invite Valentine to the House). The response of Tietjens is carefully distinguished from that of the Minister and the others. The plot, which takes the High Tory Tietjens into an alliance with the suffragette Valentine is designed to illustrate a profound confluence of values. Tietjens, in a reversal of the more common response which would deplore violence and confrontation but recognise the case for suffragism, supports the actions of the suffragettes in attacking the government and state, but not their objective (114). Because he believes 'All the governing class' to be 'rotten' (106) he considers the democratic process to be useless; it had in any case yielded a Liberal Government and the 'social service state' in 1906, to which he is bitterly opposed. In the course of the narrative, Tietjens withdraws from the state in which it is his class inheritance to wield power, progressively refusing to recognise its legitimacy as his own values come into conflict with the social system.

With the outbreak of the war Valentine's suffragism is transformed into pacifism in a social world where pacifists are judged to be pro-German. In reality, the connection between suffragism and pacifism was tenuous.[19] Her pacifism links her to the Conscientious Objectors, few in number and vilified, who either would take no part in combat (and were found non-combat duties), or who would take no part whatsoever in the war (in which case they were imprisoned). In the climate of aggressive nationalism which swiftly took over the country in 1914, and which was constantly buoyed up by carefully calculated propaganda campaigns, pacifists and Objectors were harassed and occasionally imprisoned. Her pacifism is the mark of her intellectual independence. Tietjens considers Valentine to be 'the only intelligent soul I've met for years' (127). A Tory feminist,

Tietjens respects each of the women in his life: 'she and Sylvia were the only two human beings he had met for years whom he could respect' (128), the one as an ally, the other as an opponent, whereas male culture has decayed: 'He hadn't in years met a man that he hadn't talked down to' (128). 'Perhaps the future of the world then was to women? Why not?' (128) muses Tietjens, although the novel does not suggest that this future will necessarily be a rosy one. *Parade's End* does not belong to the same culture of male defensiveness and women-blaming as do the works of Aldington and Deeping outlined below. By dividing the feminine between two characters the novel is able to prefer certain values in the emergent culture and to reject others, rewriting as it does so the orthodox opposition between Old and New Woman. Tietjens's brother Mark dies at the end of the novel, immobilised after a stroke but believing himself a god, a symbol of the inflexibility and impotence of a modern English Toryism which has abandoned its better aspects and declined into mere reaction. Tietjens, the true inheritor of Toryism, is flexible: he begins a relationship where he accepts that he is not even the most competent partner and does not attempt to dominate, just as he accepts a life where his own small business skills rather than class prerogative must earn him a living. The novel concludes in the private sphere, with both Valentine and Tietjens abandoning the public and the political. They retreat together into private, unmarried life, although as the novel only implicitly acknowledges, their independence from the social order is flawed. In establishing a small business to sell furniture they still obey the market rules which have been responsible for the decline of English values: they enter into a form of only apparently private life and independence which the market itself makes possible.[20] Despite the ambivalence and necessary contradictions of its conclusion, *Parade's End* is virtually alone of the male writing of the 1920s in affirming the ascendance of women and advocating a course of graceful withdrawal from dominance for men.

The Proto-Fascism of Richard Aldington's Death of a Hero

Published in a mildly expurgated edition in 1929, and made available in 1965 with its few Anglo-Saxon terms restored, *Death of a Hero* presents a view of the war and of social change which is mocking and embittered. *Parade's End* negotiated some kind of future for lost values; *Death of a Hero* is scathing, vitriolic and thoroughly alienated in its vision of social collapse. The title is a savage rebuke, framed in crudely ironic terms, to the post-war slogan that England would be made, according to the rhetoric of Lloyd George, into 'a country fit for heroes to live in'. The irony is two-pronged. It refers to the truism that trench warfare had offered few opportunities for traditional forms of military heroism, despite exposing millions to death and wounding, and to the psychological effects of extreme combat fatigue known as shell-shock. Even if the survivors thought of themselves as heroes, after demobilisation they found themselves ill-received by a civilian society which was embarrassed by their presence, not least because it had actually enriched itself in their absence.[21] At the same time, the title refers the reader to the implicit thesis of the narrative that post-war England is now no longer a land fit for men of any kind, let alone for men recognised in public rhetoric, but in no practical sense, as heroes. *Death of a Hero* is content to frame its protagonist as a more or less helpless victim – in fact, as a victim more of women, and of feminine sexual desire, than of the politics of war.

Death of a Hero sees the war not as the cause of change, but as a further blow to English society, and above all to English men, driving its limited hero, George Winterbourne, to deliver himself to death before the bullets of a German machine gun only one week before the Armistice. His death is unnecessary because the war is effectively over. Since it was the unbearableness of his domestic life which motivated George Winterbourne to join the army in the first place, we can assume that it is the unbearable thought of return which drives him to deliberately expose himself to death. This at least is the thesis of the narrator who intrudes upon his narrative at frequent intervals, whether to comment on the action or to deliver himself of general theories about pre-war society, the effects of the war, or, indeed, on the post-war society in which the embittered narrator considers himself unlucky to be still living. Aldington creates a narrator which the reader will assume to be the author speaking in person, in order to better assert a point of view which he believes has been silenced in the post-war; that is, that of the now thoroughly alienated war veteran. Aldington was an experienced writer, but not of novels, and chooses in his brief introduction to claim that he has simply disregarded novelistic conventions.

> This book is not the work of a conventional novelist. It is, apparently, not a novel at all. [...] To me the excuse for a novel is that one can do any

damn thing one pleases. [...] Whether I have been guilty of Expressionism or Super-realism or not, I don't know and don't care. I knew what I wanted to say and said it. And I know I have not tried to be 'original'.

The technique of this book, if it can be said to have one, is that which I evolved for myself in writing a longish modern poem [...]. Some people said that was 'jazz poetry'; so I suppose this is a jazz novel. You will see how appropriate that is to the theme.   (Aldington, 1968: 7)

As a poet Aldington had been associated with H.D. and Ezra Pound as an Imagist, a school which professed ideals of classical control and economy. Even after the war Aldington remained pro-classical and anti-romantic when, in a hostile review of Joyce's work in 1922, he accused *Ulysses* of being undisciplined – as well as disgusting and obscure – akin to Dadaism in its idealisation of expression.[22] Eliot's well-known defence of Joyce, '*Ulysses*, Order and Myth', written in reply to Aldington's article, did not diverge from Aldington's position as much as might be thought, for Eliot chooses to find in Joyce's use of myth – which he calls 'the mythic method' and deploys himself in *The Waste Land* – a deep structure which can give form to 'the immense panorama of futility and anarchy which is contemporary history'.[23] Although Aldington criticised Joyce for lack of form, his own poetry had moved away from the ideal economy of Imagism to a more loosely framed prose poetry or *vers libre*, which culminated in the 'jazz poetry' of *A Fool i'the Forest* (1924).[24] In the years immediately following the war, Aldington seems to have remained a committed classicist, but by the end of the 1920s, by which time he was resident in Paris, any claim to classicism, or indeed to any variety of programmatic Modernism is gone. With *Death of a Hero* Aldington aimed to start a career as a novelist, and indeed did so successfully. However, his abandonment of classicism was not simply the result of commercial motives, but stemmed from the desire to create an expressive literature that would be free from the evasions, preciosity and irony of Modernism.

Death of a Hero is, therefore, essentially modern, even if its Modernism takes a new tack. The novel represents an attempt to create an aesthetic which would be true to the nature of experience and to the communicative function of literature. Aldington's novel might seem to be a 'conventional' novel in its avoidance of complex structures of representation, its only unconventional gesture being the device of a prologue which relays the whole action, a device of classical tragedy, as is the narrator's commentary which can be related to the chorus of classical drama, hints at a connection with Euripides, whom Aldington was translating at this time. However, his matter has forced a new approach on him, and while he deliberately avoids claiming association with any modern school, his guesses about which school others might choose to associate him with present us with a thumbnail sketch of the aesthetic climate at the end of the 1920s.

Jazz, Expressionism and Surrealism (Super-realism as it was then known) were all aesthetics associated with romantic self-expression, and each earned the opprobrium of figures such as T. S. Eliot and Wyndham Lewis who represented themselves as classicists. They were also quite distinct from each other, associated with different arts and even nations, and the careless fashion in which Aldington associates them suggests a continued classicist hostility to the mode of self-expression, even though *Death of a Hero* is clearly more about emotion than about classical ideals of restrained expression and cultivated form. Aldington is linking his novel to an age of which he knows it to be a part, yet which, as the novel will make abundantly clear, he despises: the jazz age. He considers his novel to have a 'jazz age' theme: the change in sexual mores which began to take place before the war. The change in gender roles is represented as a major part of the suffering caused by the war. In the 'Prologue' in particular, which outlines the story, the narrator – who cannot in effect be distinguished from Aldington – is content to blame women for the breakdown of the relationship between the sexes, even if at times in the narrative which follows the treatment is slightly more even-handed. The narrator has faith not in women but in non-sexual male bonding, of the kind which many men learned during the war. German war veterans, feeling themselves unwanted and uncom-prehended in post-war society, had, in the decade or so after the war, formed veterans groups which fed directly into the rise of Nazism in Germany. Although in England the comparable phenomenon was less widespread, and Fascist politics had less purchase at all social levels, Aldington's novel, in its bursts of misogyny, its faith in male friendship, its distrust of and hatred for the established power, and in its self-proclaimed role as a 'threnody, a memorial in its ineffective way to a generation which hoped much, strove honestly, and suffered deeply' (7), is perhaps the nearest thing to a proto-Fascist novel which the war produced in England. At the time it was linked to Robert Graves's autobiographical *Goodbye To All That* (1929) with which it shared unsparing descriptions of trench life and combat, while in 1930 Aldington himself highlighted a parallel between the satirical element in his own novel and that of Wyndham Lewis's *Apes of God* (1930), for which he wrote a spirited review.[25]

As the 'Prologue' is more extreme in its misogyny than the main narrative it is worth separate discussion. The Winterbournes are a lower-middle-class family, at a time when the lower professional classes are still very clearly distinguished from the working class. George Winterbourne, a friend of the narrator who has been killed in the war, depended on four people: his father, mother, wife and mistress. The prologue of the novel describes how they have all lost interest in him and betrayed him in accounts of their reactions when they hear about his death. Although it concerns particular, fiction-alised individuals, this account must also be read as an allegory of the betrayal of a whole class and generation of men. Nevertheless, much of the novel is deeply personal to its author. Winterbourne, with his desire to become a writer and his attempt to enter London art circles, is modelled on Aldington himself, although he is distinct from the narrator who also functions as an Aldington surrogate. Winterbourne's parents are cruel, comic portrayals of Aldington's own parents. The two women in Winterbourne's life, Elizabeth and Fanny, are suitably disguised portraits of H.D. (the poet Hilda Doolittle) who married Aldington in 1913, and Dorothy Yorke, who began a relationship with Aldington in 1917. The problems in Aldington's relationship with H.D. are reflected in Winterbourne's problems with Fanny and Elizabeth, and Winterbourne's method of suicide is one which, on his own account, tempted Aldington.[26] Four of the figures on the London arts scene are thinly disguised versions of four men closely associated with Aldington: Upjohn is Ezra Pound, while Shobbe, Bobbe and Tubbe are Ford, Lawrence and Eliot respectively. With regards to her marriage to Aldington, H.D. later gave her own version of events in *Bid Me To Live* (1960), and an earlier version of the relationships in this circle is found in Lawrence's *Aaron's Rod* (1922). Given the intimacy of each of the main portraits, the vitriolic tone of the narrator and the frequently brusque treatment of the feelings and motives of the characters might seem surprising, but the cultural critique advanced by the narrator goes well beyond the particular history which it transforms into cultural allegory.

In the prologue, George Winterbourne senior is presented as a Christian sentimentalist who has retreated into a 'drivelling religiosity' (13) which shields him from his wife's sexuality, which takes the form of numerous affairs, and incidentally from the reality of the war. The narrator states bluntly that his weakness has 'messed up his wife's life', meaning that a more active response to his wife's desire for affairs might have restored their relationship rather than allow it to be destroyed. The main narrative does not, however, take a traditionalist view of marriage, even though the prologue seems to assert a traditional view of male independence and domination, inasmuch as it mocks male weakness. The news of George's death reaches Mrs Winterbourne while she is with her most recent lover – she finds the news sexually stimulating, much to the discomfort of her conventional young man. The narrator draws some general conclusions from this:

> But the effect of George's death on her temperament was, strangely enough, almost wholly erotic. The war did that to lots of women. All the dying and wounds and mud and bloodiness – at a safe distance – gave them a great kick and excited them to an almost unbearable pitch of amorousness. Of course, in that eternity of 1914–18 they must have come to feel that men alone were mortal, and they immortals; wherefore they tried to behave like houris with all available sheiks – hence the lure of 'war work' with its unbounded opportunities. And then there was the deep primitive physiological instinct – men to kill and be killed; women to produce more men to continue the process.   (18–19)

The hostility to the figure of the woman combines anger at the parent who failed to save the child from the danger of the war, and resentment at the lover who has transferred her emotional cathexis to another. The archetype of this is, of course, the Oedipus complex, as Aldington, who read Freud early and with conviction, would undoubtedly have known. On George Winterbourne's behalf, the narrator murderously attacks the masculinity both of the father, who is in any case already displaced, and of the lover who is facetiously termed a 'sheik'.[27] The jibe about the 'safe distance' conflates erotic anxiety with the widely shared perception of veterans that those who had not experienced the war had ideas of it which were false to the extent of being fantasy, a perception aided by the climate of hysterical propaganda which prevailed throughout the war. The image of women exulting in the deaths of men evokes the archetype of the *vagina dentata*, woman as the creator of man's life, but also as its consumer.[28] The passage does not dwell on the psychology but moves on to another myth of the war: the notion that people adopted a more *carpe diem* approach to sex – seizing the day because there may well not be another – and it is certainly true that after 1916 the rate of illegitimate births grew, with the moral climate itself adjusting to accommodate the increase.[29] This idea determines one of the central events in Ford's *Parade's End* when Tietjens and Valentine decide to spend the night together as lovers before he goes away to the war. With the demise of so many other attitudes and values, Valentine Wannop supposes that chastity too is a thing of the past: 'Chastity: napoo finny! Like everything else!' (Ford, 1982: 266). However, the narrator's sardonic reference to war work, while it correctly identifies an important element in female emancipation, is concerned both to belittle women's work and to suggest that sex itself outside of a relationship is the single female goal. The final sentence introduces a further strand in the form of popular Social Darwinist assumptions that the war was one of population adjustment (it was not), and that nations clashed like species seeking the 'survival of the fittest'. This account shares with the others the same anxiety concerning the contingency of (male) existence. An existence once given significance by the love of mother, lover or God is now neglected by all three. Through the use of the persona of the narrator, Aldington creates a figure whose various hatreds and resentments are rooted in a configuration of fear and anxieties clustered around women and the war.

Mrs Winterbourne and her lover of the moment are stigmatised for making love after hearing the news of George's death:

> He rose – if the expression may be allowed – powerfully to the situation. He, too, found a certain queer, perverse satisfaction in honeying and making love over a nasty corpse; while, if he had been capable of making the reflection, he would have realised that Mrs. Winterbourne was not only a sadist, but a necrophilous one.   (Aldington, 1968: 20)

The brutality and explicitness of this portrayal of sexual psychology is motivated at the narrative level by the narrator's general hostility to romantic love, which he represents as 'cant', and to women's autonomous sexual appetites. At the same time it is informed by Aldington's understanding of Freud, certainly in its general pessimism about the nature of psychosexual behaviour, and perhaps specifically in its repetition of the brutal Oedipal scene in which the symbolic son (this lover is George's age) makes love to the mother over the corpse of the symbolic father (now George himself, dispossessed of his mother by death). Although it is the woman whose 'necrophilous' satisfaction is emphasised, the lover might on further reflection have found the root of his own erotic impulse in the death of his rival. The scenario represents a profoundly pessimistic version of received readings of Freud and Darwin, in which war deaths are merely the stimulus to more breeding, while the monuments which memorialise the dead represent a hypocritical veiling of a deep-seated sense of satisfaction.

From this perspective we can map out the complex dynamics of the relationship between narrator and narratee. The author's introduction expresses the desire to create a 'memorial [...] to a generation' (8). The opening pages of the narrator's prologue discuss memorialisation: 'The casualty lists went on appearing for a long time after the Armistice [...]. Of course, nobody much bothered to read the lists. Why should they? The living must protect themselves from the dead, especially the intrusive dead' (11). The 'intrusive dead' are the returned combatants, collectively unwanted, but unable to be forgotten because they are not yet dead. The feeling of being displaced and unwanted was a common one for returning veterans,[30] and was certainly felt by Aldington himself.[31] The 'intrusive dead' are now living ghosts, returned to haunt the nation in whose name, and for whose fantasy life, they have fought. I stress the notion of fantasy life because *Death of a Hero* does so. The narrator is keen to emphasise the way in which soldiers at the front rapidly unlearnt domestic propaganda about the nature and purpose of the war, coming to disbelieve especially the patriotic elements and the outrageous attempts to present the Germans as sub-human, especially the famous *canard* about Germans recycling human corpses.[32] The war hysteria of those who did not fight was a fantasy, and a vicious one at that. The prologue to *Death of a Hero* adds the charge of willing credence in an implausible fantasy of England to the alleged necrophilia of Mrs Winterbourne: English women might well advocate war – as the conversion of suffragism into the infamous white feather campaigns showed – but they never experienced it directly, and Aldington's narrative is one of the few places where hostility against non-combatants is directed frankly against women, making them at a certain level responsible for the war itself in the male psychic economy.

The portrait of Mrs Winterbourne deploys a stereotype which belongs more properly to the 1920s. Although her lover is a soldier and has even been respectably wounded, he is not portrayed as a virile alternative to her husband: he is young and naïve, with a 'capacity for being gulled by females', mockingly termed a 'sheik' by the narrator. The figure of the Sheik had widespread currency in novels and films of the 1920s. Brought to life in E. M. Hull's *The Sheik* (1919), which was first filmed in 1921 with Rudolph Valentino, the Sheik occupied a central place in women's romantic and sexual fantasies. The narrative of *The Sheik* concerns the abduction and rape of a white woman by a desert prince with whom the woman consequently falls in love. The Sheik was interpreted by some male writers at the time as an effeminate figure and a threat to Western manhood,[33] but the image also harbours the opposite notion: that a generation of women whose indigenous men were mainly dead, wounded or psychologically scarred (the 'lost generation') were looking elsewhere for sexual satisfaction – even if that elsewhere were mainly a romanticised and fictional Other rather than any more imminently rivalrous real thing. Thus, the figure of the Sheik need not be interpreted simply as undermining Western manhood through the apparent effeminacy of his clothing and make-up. On the contrary, he represents a fantasy stereotype of enhanced masculinity who, as far as the male is concerned, confronts the native with his own sexual inadequacy. In *Death of a Hero* the Sheik is a further element, actually anachronistically deployed, in the pattern of male anxieties.

Masculinity is given a complex treatment in this book, however, and it would be a mistake to see the novel as merely a reassertion of traditional values. The ideal of male friendship which the narrator advances[34] is not simply a reassertion of the *status quo*, but reflects a desire to escape sexuality altogether. The narrator is insistent that male friendship at the front had no sexual content whatsoever, but rather was disinterested. This is an idealisation of the situation which *Parade's End*, in its examination of the connections between domestic society and the machinations on the front, laboured hard to discount. The main narrative of *Death of a Hero* explores the fate of the new values which both George and Elizabeth represent, representing their ideas as an honourable alternative to those of their parents, but as flawed by naïvety and based on a lack of realism about sexuality which, in this novel, often means female sexuality. Winterbourne junior turns to writing and the art world as an alternative to the institutionalised forms of masculinity represented by his father, whose hunting lessons George finds merely brutal, and his school, which fails to make him into a 'really manly fellow' (82) in spite of the best efforts of its Officers' Training Corps. These institutions were, and in some cases still are, the bodies at public schools for boys designed to equip them for leadership in general, and in some cases for a military career. The war provided the opportunity for many eager ex-public schoolboys to exercise the leadership roles as junior officers to which their class origins entitled them, resulting on the one hand in a vastly disproportionate number of deaths among junior officers compared to the ranks, and on the other in a resentment towards these officers from the ranks who felt that this 'leadership' too frequently amounted to a type of stagey heroics which generated unnecessary risks. Lord Wellington apocryphally claimed that the Battle of Waterloo was won on the playing fields of Eton. One hundred years later, British public school culture continued to play a key role both in the formation of nationalistic pro-war attitudes, and in the actual conduct of combat. That he rejects the nationalistic public school culture in favour of unwarlike 'WRITING' (61) is held by the narrator to be in George's favour, even though the narrator's cult of male friendship at the front is intolerant of non-combatants and conscientious objectors.

The figure of Elizabeth is modelled on H.D. and represents the modern woman and the new sexual morality, in contrast to the old values represented by Mrs Winterbourne. Her flat chest and cigarette smoking make her a prototype of the stereotypical flapper of the 1920s. As with George, her desire to break with those values is represented sympathetically, but she is satirised inasmuch as her behaviour is made to represent a covert continuation of the old values. The narrative defends the new sexual experimentation in the middle classes, which seems not to have been widespread, but in the case of George and Elizabeth involves, unusually at that time, an open relationship. They have a sexual relationship without marriage, and continue to live separately. The narrator offers critical support:

> They had seen in their own homes the dreadful unhappiness caused by Victorian, and indeed Edwardian, ignorance and domestic dennery and swarming infants. So far, good. But they failed to see that in the way they went about it they were merely setting up another tyranny – the tyranny of free love.

However, the right to experiment with alternatives is vigorously defended:

> It is an interesting comment on the sadism latent in communities that the cruelty and misery of the Victorian home are legally protected and held up as shining examples of behaviour, whereas any attempt to make people a little more natural and happy and tolerant is supposed to be wicked. [...] Think of the insane delusion of female chastity which holds

that any woman who has 'had' more than one man is 'impure', whereas in fact many women soon come to dislike profoundly their first lover, and most are really only happy and satisfied with a fourth or sixth or tenth. (164)

The idealism of the couple is shattered in two ways, first when Elizabeth has a phantom pregnancy and rushes George into marriage, revealing a degree of fragility in the free love experiment, and again when subsequent to the marriage each of them takes a second lover, a situation which proves too emotionally stressful – George's lover is Elizabeth's best friend Fanny, and is the main cause of George's suicide (just as the parallel events in Aldington's own life led him to almost suicidal depression).[35]

> With the whole world collapsing about him, it seemed quite logical that the Triumphal Scheme for the Perfect Sex Relation should collapse too. [...] Unfortunately, they [Elizabeth and Fanny] did not realize the strain under which he was living, and did not perceive the widening gulf which was separating the men of that generation from the women. How could they? The friends of a person with cancer haven't got cancer. They sympathize, but they aren't in the horrid category of the doomed. (227)

In its pessimism about the 'lost generation' and collective 'doom',[36] this passage is close in tone to the comprehensive cultural pessimism of T. S. Eliot and other conservative radicals influenced by French 'classicist' and royalist idealists, such as Wyndham Lewis. *Parade's End* espoused a vision in which an integrated and rational male self could in some degree survive by retreating from the collapsed public sphere into the private sphere. Aldington's novel repudiates the old sexual values but finds men to be merely the victims of the new ones. It evokes a nostalgic version of male camaraderie without claiming this as a genuine alternative to the present. The work of D. H. Lawrence goes much further in its utopian examination of a new masculinity.

Men Alone and Men Together: The Masculinist Project of D. H. Lawrence

The protagonist of *Parade's End* thought that women might be the future, a position which reflected the author's pre-war commitment to women's suffrage. *Death of a Hero* gave full vent to the cynicism and frustration of the returned soldier in an emasculated, 'feminised' world, but although it was Aldington's first novel it did not in any way represent a *volte face* with respect to his pre-war position. In contrast, the work of D. H. Lawrence effects an extraordinary shift from an idiosyncratic sympathy for feminism in the pre-war to a 'masculinist' and tendentially anti-feminist position in the post-war. Against the more customary emphasis on anti-feminism in Lawrence's work, this section describes the nature and function of what I have termed his 'masculinist' programme.[37] The shift in Lawrence's position owed nothing to combat experiences as he had been rejected by the military authorities and was in any case scornful of the war. Moreover, the trajectory of his fiction and polemics is more than a reaction to the social changes which we have described, although it clearly reflects them. The Lawrence of *The Rainbow* (published in 1915 and promptly suppressed) appeared to be the friend of the feminist. However ambivalently, the novel presents women in their successive destinies as standing for a life-creating matriarchy and for a femininity which in the early years of the twentieth century finds itself in a stark contrast with the brutalised and masculine world of industry, and with what Lawrence sees as a type of will to power which is involved in the masculine project of dominating nature. In *Women in Love* an exploration of male friendship and of the limits of femininity is instigated, but it is only in the post-war fiction, examined here in an account of *England, My England* (1922), which bridges the Armistice, and *Aaron's Rod* (1922), that a rejection of the feminine and re-examination of the possibilities of masculine values is initiated.

Emasculated Englishmen: England, My England

Of the stories published in *England, My England*, six were written between November 1918 and July 1919. Of the rest, only 'The Primrose Path' belongs to the pre-war, while the title story and 'Samson and Delilah' belong to the middle phase of the war. Although in principle 'England, My England' is one of the earlier stories of the volume, it was substantially revised for publication in 1922, at the same time that Lawrence was working on his novel *Aaron's Rod* (1922) so that, in effect, its ideological concerns post-date the other stories in the collection and correspond to those of the novel.

The dates are important because we would expect to be able to model from these stories an account of Lawrence's response to the war and its immediate aftermath. Since we are accustomed from his self-portrayal in the novels to expect the author of these stories to be a determined preacher of his own point of view, such as Rupert

Birkin in *Women in Love* or Rawdon Lilly in *Aaron's Rod*, the temptation to read the stories in terms of a schematic ideological template is almost overwhelming.

It is important in reading Lawrence, however, to distinguish between the various levels of authorial concern and of textual commitment, and this is especially so in relation to these stories where ideology critique proves a blunt instrument. It is especially important in relation to these stories which are surrounded in time by other of Lawrence's works on a Dostoevskyan scale, as well as by historical events which tend to eclipse not only the stories but the very world they seek to embody. Ideology critique, and its avatar discourse analysis, tend to produce an account of these stories in terms of Lawrence as a sexual ideologue and the stories as mere exemplifications of a 'discourse' of sexuality which Lawrence sought to maintain.[38] Lawrence is the pre-eminent author of the English working class since the Industrial Revolution, as well as being the chief literary exponent of the vernacular of Northern England, and at their best his stories about working-class and lower-middle-class life owe more to an attempt to document the reality of that life, including its sexual ideologies, than to any programmatic attempt to advance a sexual utopia.

Lawrence's central interest in these stories is courtship and marriage, and the configurations of unexamined and articulated desire, interpersonal understanding and misunderstanding, practical consideration, and social expectation which frame the individual destiny of a series of characters highly particular to the social situation of the North of England. The relationships depicted are all based on a profound disequilibrium in which necessity, desire and understanding only partially overlap and correspond; Lawrence is acutely aware of the mosaic of compromise, aspiration and inarticulacy which frames the lives of the common people he depicts. It is important to recognise where the centre of gravity of the collection lies because, although several of the stories deal with the impact of the war on courtship and marriage, several do not, and although the title of the volume with its ironic evocation of nationalism[39] seems to reflect Lawrence's rejection of England and his departure from there in 1919, these stories should not be read exclusively as an anticipation of those events.

Of the stories which deal with the war, 'England, My England' [1915] is the first, but I shall treat it in its revised 1922 form as the last. 'Samson and Delilah' [1916] only indirectly deals with the theme of the returning soldier, since its male protagonist has not returned from the war but from the USA. After deserting his wife sixteen years earlier and going to the USA to make his fortune, William Nankervis returns unannounced and unrecognised to the public house which his wife runs to support herself. The title is designed to manipulate the reader's expectation that Nankervis will fail to assert his masculinity, and this seems to be confirmed when his wife has him tied up and thrown out by the soldiers who stay in the pub as lodgers. However, this is merely the prelude to his return after the soldiers have gone to bed. His wife now accepts his return and the story finishes as he slides his hand between her breasts. So, at the conclusion of the story, it is the model of Odysseus returning as a stranger and routing the suitors before resuming his marriage which is uppermost. It is quite important that Nankervis is not a soldier, however, for the central section suggests not only Samson and Delilah, but Gulliver in Lilliput, as the diminutive sergeant and his youthful group of soldiers seek to subdue and tie the broad-shouldered giant Nankervis. The Gulliver element is present as an emblem of the fate of individuality in the Lilliputian British war state, in which the *ressentiment* of the mediocre mass is given expression. This element corresponds to the reaction to the war which Lawrence would later describe in the famous 'Nightmare' section of *Kangaroo*. The retrospective title 'Samson and Delilah' confirms the idea of the wife as attempting symbolically to emasculate her husband and failing – as did Delilah in her initial attempts. The Odysseus element seems to suggest a reading of the story in terms of the assertion of the masculine prerogative in marriage. Moreover, an element of animal magnetism suggested by Nankervis's ability to finally seduce his wife into taking him back suggests that the story is simply concerned with a fantasised version of masculine sexual prowess. However, the mythical and realistic elements of the narrative exist in an uneasy tension and the story does not simply decode into ideological expression. The theme of women's war work is not yet uppermost in Lawrence's mind, but he is very interested in the dynamic of marriage. It would be a mistake to see this story as merely the expression and justification of the husband's right and magnetic ability to assert himself within the contract of marriage. The original title of the story was 'The Prodigal Husband', suggesting a different focus altogether, for the prodigality of the husband lies in his desertion of his wife. Like Aaron Sisson, he has simply opted out altogether of marriage in particular and English society in general. It is important not to take it for granted that Nankervis returns simply to assert his prerogative. More fundamentally, the story revolves around his decision to return at all. For while his wife slowly becomes sexually drawn to him, helplessly 'losing her self control' (Lawrence, 1995: 121), Nankervis himself is seduced by the appearance of her breasts, and his final action of slipping his hand between them as much confirms his resubmission to the marriage which he has so long avoided as any simple assertion of prerogative. Thus the story is implicitly concerned with the process in which Nankervis surrenders his independence for the second time. The narrative emphasises the sparks that fly between the two from the moment Nankervis returns anonymously, as if to show how the strength and independence of each character had contributed to their original relationship and even now resurfaces to assert an elective bond between them. Nankervis, indeed, is seduced also by his wife's strength, by the fact that she has overcome him, so the final seduction is not one way, even if it is Nankervis who has the last word. Unlike Aaron, who must learn to resist women, Nankervis cannot stay away: it is in this sense that he resembles Samson, whose passion for women was his downfall.

Two of the later stories in the collection portray the additional psychological imbalance brought to the already fraught dynamics of courtship by the creation of new employment for women, as bus conductresses in 'Tickets Please' [1918] and as farm workers, or 'Land Girls', in 'Monkey Nuts' [1919].[40] Each of these deals with situations involving women who are emboldened by their new social roles, wear short skirts (practical for work but also sexually suggestive) and begin to take an active role in courtship. 'Monkey Nuts' is a social comedy set in England in the immediate post-war and depicts the anxiety and discomfort of a young man who does not know how to react to the attention of a Land Girl who actively courts him. 'He felt maddened, but helpless. Her arm was round his waist, she drew him closely to her with a soft pressure that made all his bones rotten.' (71) It is an astonishing image of the debilitation of manhood. The young man Joe passively acquiesces and starts walking with the unusually pro-active 'Miss Stokes', formally so called throughout the narrative. Joe sees Miss Stokes against his will, and it can be inferred that he is put off by her taking the active role. However, it is also clear that Joe is young and shy, and the comedy of the tale stems from the juxtaposition of his shyness and inexperience with Miss Stokes's confidence. He finally drives her away with a show of infantile disrespect which merely confirms his social inadequacy.

The acuteness of his confusion is confirmed by the conclusion of the story:

> They were reassured, however, when they found that Miss Stokes came no more with the hay. As far as they were concerned, she had vanished into oblivion. And Joe felt more relieved even than he had felt when he heard the firing cease, after the news had come that the armistice was signed. (76)

In this story, the nuanced depiction of a particular case opens out on to the general situation of the post-war, but not in a dogmatic fashion. The disappearance of Miss Stokes generically represents the disappearance of women from their wartime jobs after the armistice. That they were removed from these jobs should have alleviated male anxiety, and in this story the young male protagonist is 'relieved'. Like Tietjens and Winterbourne, young Joe discovers that the anxiety caused by what is conceived here as a change in the balance of the relationship between the sexes is a greater source of anxiety than the war itself.

This is more than the case in 'Tickets Please', another comically conceived story which opens out on to a situation of profound psychological unease. More schematically than in 'Monkey Nuts', this story is an emblematic representation of the new dilemmas of masculinity. Here, several women working as bus conductresses decide to take revenge on the male ticket inspector, a womaniser who bears the overtly symbolic name John Thomas. He is physically assaulted by the women, in a scene which recalls a Bacchanalian orgy and identifies the protagonist with Pentheus, torn to pieces by the orgiastic women. The reader might expect a fatal outcome, but the violence stops and the women shape a more conventional demand: that he must choose one of them as his 'girl'. That women collectively offer violence against men already suggests the theme of emasculation and castration, but the demand of the women harks back to a traditional desire which is understood in the story as fixed, a desire which makes competition for a man more important than female solidarity. The unease in the story therefore turns out to be not that of the man, who can recover from the attack, but that of the women, uneasily remorseful about their collective act of violence, which suddenly brings their war work within the frame of the war in an unexpected way, and destabilised by the sense of their new-found collective strength, as if suddenly nothing need ever be the same again, although their demand that he 'choose' is a superficial attempt to act not only as if nothing has happened, but as if the huge psycho-logical and symbolic change which has occurred were reversible. It is not, and Annie, the girl he chooses, and who initiated the violence against him, cannot accept his choice. In this imbalancing of the courtship process, then, the man emerges wounded but defiant, while the women, individually, are shown to have lost something indefinable:

> He rose slowly, a strange, ragged dazed creature. The girls eyed him from a distance, curiously, furtively, dangerously.
> 'Who wants him?' cried Laura roughly.
> 'Nobody', they answered, with contempt. Yet each one of them waited for him to look at her, hoped he would look at her. All except Annie, and something was broken in her. (45)

In the narrative mode of these stories, which imply complex and ambivalent states without ever making them explicit, it is not said what is broken in Annie, but it may be nothing less than her whole sense of her place in the social order which has changed. Like 'Monkey Nuts', this tale concludes with an ambiguous epiphany, but unlike the epiphanies of Joyce's *Dubliners*, which are epiphanies rooted in continued self-delusion and do not look beyond the general paralysis, Lawrence places the small moment of change on the part of people who are young and as yet unilluminated within the wider cultural context of psychological and sexual adjustment which remains implicit, describing the micrological stages of an incipient social change which is likely to prove actual and overwhelming.

The first version of 'England, My England' was composed in 1915 but was substantially revised before publication in the collection. The revised version suggests the new agenda which Lawrence developed in *Aaron's Rod*, the agenda of male separatism. It is concerned not with the question of the changing role of women, but with the role of a man who is unwilling to subscribe to the expectations of collective society – work, reproduction and family. There is a significant connection with Lawrence's unpublished essay, 'Education of the People' [1918], which eventually appeared in *Phoenix* (1936). This essay argues against modern materialism, the 'craven terror of poverty' (Lawrence, 1967: 591) which drives the modern world, and against the democratic ideals of equality and fraternity on the grounds that 'men are not equal, neither are they brothers. They are themselves.' (603). Individuality is denied by the system of education which begins in the family with the role of the mother. The essay argues that modern motherhood has become perverted: it is based on a conscious attempt to manipulate and engage the child rather than let her or him grow separately and individually. And so the modern mother unwittingly initiates the process of standardisation desired by the state and continued by the education system. The essay is certainly anti-feminist in that it makes no allowance for female liberation from the process in which the existence of the individual is instrumentalised by industry and the state. However, its advocacy of a form of male separatism, and of a new male sociality which respects difference and does not presuppose an ideal of equality or sameness which is state driven, contains a significant utopian moment and has continued contemporary resonance, even though it builds on sexist stereotypes:

> Let the men scout ahead. Let them go always ahead of their women [...]. And between men let there be a new, spontaneous relationship, a new fidelity. [...] There, in these womanless regions of fight, and pure thought and abstracted instrumentality, let men have a new attitude to one another. [...] Let there be again the old passion of deathless friendship between man and man. Humanity can never advance into the new regions of unexplored futurity otherwise. (664–5)

'England, My England' does not produce a realised version of this agenda, but depicts an example of its failure, examining in the process contrasted versions of masculinity and their root in a common Englishness. The protagonist of the first version is called Evelyn, and his masculinity is juxtaposed with that of his father-in-law. The name Evelyn is highly suggestive, but in the revised version Lawrence retracts any hint that he is examining an androgynous or feminine alternative to the paternalism and patriarchy of the father-in-law by renaming his protagonist Egbert. Like Evelyn, Egbert is 'living on his father-in-law' (Lawrence, 1995: 11), unwilling to involve himself in the world of work which will sustain his family. In an arbitrary attempt to provide an alternative tradition of masculinity for Egbert, he is given an interest in the 'savage England' of the Saxons (5), living in a 'timbered cottage' said to belong to 'the old England of hamlets and yeomen' (6). Egbert is described as a rose, and generally associated with flowers, as always in Lawrence a metaphor for an existence in and for itself, which is not determined by the externally imposed necessities of work. It is not work in general which is repudiated, but the modern world in which labour is alienated, performed for money and not for its own sake. Egbert is committed to what he conceives as being an older version of Englishness: he collects folk-songs.

His wife Winifred is depicted as a modern mother who dutifully looks after her children rather than loving them. Winifred's dutiful and protective attitude to her children contrasts with the *laissez-faire* approach of Egbert, which commands his children's affection but makes him appear an unsuitable parent. The narrative opposes the 'love' which motivates Egbert to the 'duty' which motivates his wife in the care of their children: 'he had kept, and all honour to him, a certain primitive dominion over the souls of his children, the old, almost magic prestige of paternity.' (16). Egbert's 'magic prestige' is affirmed by the narrative, but the story is concerned to explore its limitations. Egbert's version of fatherhood is juxtaposed with that of his father-in-law whom he cannot displace from the centre of his wife's affections:

> Let the psychoanalysts talk about the father complex. It is just a word invented. Here was a man who had kept alive the old red flame of fatherhood [...], a great natural power. And till his children could be brought under some other great authority as girls [...] Godfrey Marshall would keep his children. (16)

Because Egbert is protective to neither his wife nor his children, he cannot fulfil the logic of the family romance and displace his father-in-law, and his relationship to family life, and thereby to the collective social life, is consequently tenuous. One set of nature imagery associates Egbert with the individuality and separateness of the flower, and links him to the wild plants of old England: but the flower is isolated and vulnerable, and his father-in-law is associated with another English symbol, the oak, representative of family strength and generational continuity. 'Different as the two men were, they were two real Englishmen, and their instincts were almost the same.' (28). The narrative claims that each tradition of paternity has historical roots in cultural Englishness. However, the narrative dramatises the problems of the male separatist ethos advanced in 'Education of the People' in the face of a materialist ethic which is itself rooted in tradition and in the 'father complex' of women who demand a strong male in the image of a father. (Compare the goading remarks of Mrs Nankervis: 'Do you call yourself a *man?*' [121].) The dilemma for men is thus rooted in the demands of women. Egbert's version of masculinity is consequently unable to take hold, and when his daughter is injured in an accident due to his neglect, he finally becomes completely occluded from his own family. When the war begins, Egbert joins up, not out of patriotism but out of indifference and because his role as an organic part of his family has now come to an end. When he goes out to Flanders, 'he seemed already to have gone out of life, beyond the pale of life' (30), and as he dies from a wound he experiences merely the futility and isolation of his own unconnected consciousness.

While *The Rainbow* (1915) presented the feminine as an alternative to industrial and collective values identified in the text as masculine, 'England, My England' is typical of Lawrence's post-war work in reversing this polarity by attempting to blame women. The dutiful wife now passively binds her husband to the world of work through simple biological reproduction; further elaboration of her character and motives serving only a cosmetic role in an attempt to disguise the schematic nature of the narrative's central thesis. She does not want her husband to work for money – her role in his oppression is not a deliberate or malevolent one. At the same time, in terms of the psychoanalysis which the narrative itself invokes, the protagonist is unable to take the place of the father in his wife's affections, and the father's emotional authority remains absolute with her. From the protagonist's point of view this represents an inability to effect the Oedipal substitution (of himself for the symbolic father) which would allow him to create an adult, social space for himself in the world, so the industrial world, through the agency of the demands of women and children, effects a psychic emasculation which displaces the protagonist from the social world in which he can no longer assume any symbolic role. The theme of masculinity emasculated is a characteristic strand of post-war male anxiety, here given a representation which is fully cognisant of the basic principles of psychoanalysis. As for the protagonist of *Death of a Hero*, the war is represented as an escape from psychosexual confusion. Yet Lawrence's map is fundamentally different from that of Aldington. Lawrence now begins to represent heterosexual love as impossible not as a result of a change in the disposition of women towards men, but as a result of women's inability to follow men in a process of self-liberation which will involve the disruption of the whole symbolic order.

Declaration of Independence: Aaron's Rod

It is a useful corrective to have this analysis of the carefully organised gender politics of 'England, My England' in place before passing to the better known treatment of male separatism in *Aaron's Rod*

(1922). The best recent account[41] of this novel rightly evokes its 'subversive intent' towards the contemporary pieties, but goes on to reiterate a number of these pieties in their contemporary form, following earlier accounts in finding male separatism to have its roots merely in male anxiety – about being 'engulfed' by women,[42] the 'bizarre' conspiracy of woman and the war to undermine masculinity,[43] and the 'hysterical' loss of masculine identity ensuing from combat fatigue (shell-shock).[44] While we may well concur with a Freudian reading that emphasises Lawrence's ambivalent relationship to his mother – a mainstay, after all, of the tradition of Lawrence criticism – it is important to note that 'England, My England' places a significant theoretical gloss on the rejection of family culture, using a psychoanalytical frame (which it simultaneously evokes and disavows: 'it is just a word invented') to claim a deep-seated psychological need as the principal factor in women's complicity in the conservatism of the family and thereby of the state. While *Death of a Hero* is merely reactive, *Aaron's Rod* cannot be understood simply in terms of an unanalysed reaction against women, although it certainly evidences such a reaction. Similarly, while these works do not exactly 'blame' women for the war, and although they certainly fail to acknowledge male responsibility, their reaction against women's role in the war is less bizarre if we recall both the use made by male and female war propagandists of the image of the mother,[45] and the female demands on stereotypical masculinity symbolised in Christabel Pankhurst's 'white feather' campaign. Moreover, it is simply clumsy to argue that Lawrence sought to restore the common pre-war ideal of masculinity when 'England, My England' so clearly seeks to show how that version of the masculine eclipses the possibilities of another kind which he wishes to explore. Nor can Lawrence as a non-combatant be rigorously connected to the phenomenon of combat fatigue, even if we agree reductively to conflate shell-shock and hysteria. Finally, the risk of invoking the Freudian framework is to imply that Lawrence simply needed to be normalised; that is, returned to a healthy relationship to women and to the reality principle of the family and its logic of reproduction. Whatever the distortions and incompletion of Lawrence's response to this problem, it seems to me better to acknowledge the fundamental logic of his reaction against the ideological and actual claims of masculinity, the family and the state, rather than to portray his work as the product of simple inadequacy.

Because sexual politics are very much to the fore in *Aaron's Rod*, it is usually remarked that Aaron leaves his wife and family at the opening of the novel, and that this occurs without explicit motivation. However, Aaron leaves not only his family but his job and community, and the description of him arriving home after work on Christmas Eve after the Armistice in the opening chapter makes the reasons for his unannounced departure very clear. Aaron is a miner, and his domestic situation is a common one of the period: he works while his wife maintains a 'scrupulously clean and perfect' house (Lawrence, 1995: 7). The violence of the war has erupted into general society. At work, where he is a Union official, there is a growing dispute about pay distribution which reflects the general growth of industrial unrest after the war, but also Lawrence's own analysis of the role played by general materialism. At home, this dispute is reflected in an argument between his daughters about Christmas tree decorations: unsatisfied by their beauty, they bicker about ownership and break one. Outside, the 'vocal violence' of boys carol singing is only ended when they are paid – in effect, to go away. Against the mass collective violence is juxtaposed the voice of Aaron's flute, to him a 'peace-music' (13), a source of beauty and individuality, but an annoyance to his children. This is not a specifically post-war crisis: 'The war over, nothing was changed' (12). Aaron is in general reaction against the life of the miner, not simply against the female space of the home but against the male spaces of work, and of the pub where he next goes. There the conversation revolves around the advantages of education, which Aaron rejects as being unable to change a society dominated by money and class division. Pub culture is represented as a further reinforcement of the *status quo*: drink and the attention of the 'fierce warmth' of the landlady whose sexual interest in him 'enveloped him' (22) threaten to reconcile Aaron to the existence which has been prepared for him. It is in this moment that he experiences the feeling of rejection of his surroundings, 'a hard core of irrational, exhausting withholding of himself' (22), which will drive his departure and motivate his wanderings in the rest of the novel. 'A woman and a whiskey, these were usually a remedy – and music' (22): these are the things which diminish Aaron's resistance to his involvement in the capitalist economy. Certainly, Aaron reacts against the engulfing woman, although the landlady too is engaged in business – she drinks only lightly to maintain her commercially necessary detachment – and it is against the instrumentalised role of female seductiveness, not simply against women, that Aaron reacts. He wants to feel 'rosy and loving and all that' (22), but he rejects the ideology of 'the common good' which others in the pub unreflectingly advance as a justification for the *status quo*, and this time the seductiveness of a woman, drink and company 'did not overcome him':

> There was a devilish little cold eye in his brain that was not taken in by what he saw. [...] He had drowned himself too often in whiskey and love. Now he floated like a corpse in both, with a cold, hostile eye. He became aware that he was deadly antagonistic to the landlady, that he disliked his whole circumstances. (22–3)

The dilemma of the working man is also that of the Anglo-Saxon. Aaron argues with the local Hindu doctor who defends the British Government in India on the grounds that it removes responsibility from the Indian and thereby serves the common good. This argument is structured around the Orientalist myth which associates the East and its religions with collectivism and loss of individual identity. It is this discussion which finally congeals Aaron's mood of resistance:

> The little oriental laughed a queer, sniggering laugh. His eyes were very bright, dilated, completely black. He was looking into the ice-blue, pointed eyes of Aaron Sisson. [...] They looked at each other in elemental difference. [...] He saw in the black, void, glistening eyes of the oriental only the same danger, the same menace he saw in the landlady. [...] Wise speech and good intentions – they were invariably maggoty with these secret inclinations to destroy the man in a man. [...] Even the infernal love and good-will of his wife. To hell with good-will! It was more hateful than ill-will. Self-righteous bullying, like poison gas!
> (24–5)

The novel here reproduces the ideology that mass society is feminised and orientalised. Western self-hood as represented by impossibly 'pointed' eyes contrasts with oriental self-surrender. The utopian impulse temporarily takes the form of a search for real masculinity, the discovery of the 'man in a man'. Moreover, it succumbs, as did 'England, My England', to the temptation of representing the lost individuality as a racial masculinity which has somehow become historically occluded. This rationale is later picked up by Rawdon Lilly in his remarks on 'flea-bitten Asiatics' and reverence for 'the Aztecs and the Red Indians' (97). The difficulty of acknowledging the logic of the novel's separatist agenda and disengaging an important utopian moment in the work is clearly hindered by these more obviously ideological claims.

41

Indeed, the tension between the model initially established by the narrative with a firm basis in the imbrication of class and gender and subsequent accounts which isolate heterosexual love as the core issue, accounts offered principally by Rawdon Lilly, the author's surrogate, is resolved by the subsequent narrative in favour of the latter. Once Aaron is detached from his class, although his economic existence is precarious compared to most of the people with whom he is subsequently brought into contact, class ceases to be an issue. The precondition of an independent existence becomes to live by one's art, and this involves contact principally with other artists who, with variable means, depending on class affiliation, have chosen the marginal Bohemian existence, and with potential patrons. When the writer Lilly speaks, and when Aaron assents, his preaching becomes the point of view of the novel. Lilly's preaching continues in the vein of 'Education of the People' – against women's will, marriage and mass society, and in favour of independent self-hood, the restoration of man as the seeker, and the possibility of a relationship between two men based on the spiritual authority of one and the assent of the other, an assent which Aaron is almost certainly at the point of refusing on the novel's closing page.

Although now commonly characterised as a picaresque,[46] the episodes in the narrative, which reflect Lawrence's own experiences in London, Florence and Capri, are the consequentially organised stops in a spiritual journey which sees Aaron casting off the mask of his old self and assuming an openness to a new existence. Shortly after his arrival at Novara in Italy: 'the mask split and shattered, he was at last quiet and free' (164). As alternatives to his former mode of existence, Aaron experiences a series of conditions: simple solitude; the brittle free-love ethos of a sophisticated Bohemian set (modelled on figures of Lawrence's acquaintance such as H.D. and Richard Aldington); the offer of binary homosociality in spiritual and intellectual submission to Lilly; the company of a gay expatriate group in Florence (based around versions of such figures as Norman Douglas); or the resumption of 'male passion-powers' in the relationship with a Marchesa.

Aaron finds the anti-feminism of the gay group congenial, and joins in their denunciations of women and marriage, but it is Lilly who offers a more moderate alternative designed to conserve independence and openness to human possibility by preserving solitariness and independence while entering into marriage and friendships. As with much of the dialogue of this novel, the terms of the discussion seem jejune, a kind of earnest public school debate at a level which is alienating certainly for Aaron and probably for the author. However, as I have indicated, *Aaron's Rod*, in its inception at least, has framed a coherent question about how to live socially in a society run on the basis of what Lawrence and Lilly call 'bullying', a playground word designedly chosen to assign an infantile and regressive character to a variety of modes of social domination. Tentatively, the novel shows that certain modes of evasion if not of escape are available, although all represent a compromise which must be carefully negotiated: the free love of the Bohemians is rejected as being continually rooted in the ethos of love and marriage; complete detachment can be experienced only as a moment; the homosociality of the pseudo-couple, which acknowledges the body not in self-abandoned heterosexual intercourse but in non-sexual touching is shown to be an important stage; the company of gay men who act as a mutual support network is also important for Aaron, although homosexuality is not an option for the protagonist of this novel; a form of heterosexuality based on indifference and command is not exactly valorised by the narrative (Aaron restores his separation from the demands of the Marchesa by apparently penetrating her anally so as to deny her pleasure), but dramatises Aaron's continued dilemma of independence *vis-à-vis* women; finally, the spiritual submission of one man to another remains an open possibility, and the mainstay of what remains of the novel's tracking of a way out. *Aaron's Rod* does not present a blueprint for a new form of masculinity, and is certainly not an attempt merely to reinstate the old version. The solutions it examines are recognisably flawed and the terms which the dialogue and narrator privilege are clearly inadequate to the potential scope of the questions which it opens, an inadequacy which Aaron's continuing resistance to Lilly is designed to dramatise.[47] It is, however, important to acknowledge the force of its strategic rebuttal of any form of political correctness, its some-times heavy-handed negotiation of its own anti-feminism, and the stringency of its demand that available modes of collective political solution to the contemporary dilemmas of men be rejected.

New Family Values and Anti-Oedipal Fantasy in Warwick Deeping's Sorrell and Son

Warwick Deeping's *Sorrell and Son* (1925) is an eminently consumable novel of sentiment which maintained its popularity throughout the inter-war period and beyond.[48] Deeping had been publishing with Cassell since 1907, and was considered a reliable producer, with a safe product, who yielded a modest profit and made a modest living. *Sorrell and Son* broke this pattern and became a national, and eventually international, bestseller. On the surface it has nothing in common with the complex, idea-fuelled creations of committed highbrows like Lawrence and Aldington. Its lasting appeal might also lead us to suspect that its popularity is not merely connected to local features of the 1920s. As a novel of sentiment written by a man and constantly highlighting the perspective of the eponymous male protagonists, there is also an ambiguity about the readership: does the novel make its sentimental appeal to men, whose feelings are its central subject, or is it aimed more at a female readership more interested in matters of the heart, while male readers might be supposed at this period to prefer the ubiquitous thrillers of Edgar Wallace and the westerns of Zane Grey? Any answer to this question is necessarily speculative as factual information about the readership or distribution of the novel is lacking in this case as for so many others. Internal features of the novel suggest that it is set up to appeal to either sex.

There is a kind of populism at work in the study of recent English literature which claims to discover that differences between élite and popular culture are socially constructed and do not conform to the objects in question. The popular novel might easily be as 'well written' as the highbrow, it is claimed, and the highbrows are defending simple social prestige, like capitalists defending their right to property ownership. This argument goes right back to the period of the 1920s in which popular culture first became a visibly autonomous, commercial entity, and questions about the difference between the élite and the popular – or, in the language of the period, between the highbrow and the lowbrow – can be fruitfully addressed through an analysis of a huge popular success such as *Sorrell and Son.*

There is no question that *Sorrell and Son* is 'well written' in the restricted sense that it is well presented, absolutely clear, and skilfully creates narrative interest. This is the type of efficient writing which A. C. Ward comments on as a feature of the novel-writing of the period which he does not welcome. Its very artistic 'efficiency' limits the notion of art and is to be contrasted unfavourably with the stylistic risk-taking of D. H. Lawrence who deliberately avoids the cultivation of a homogeneous 'good style' in favour of a restless prose style which might occasionally express something new. As Ward noted of Lawrence in 1930:

> He was a professional author who tried to preserve the mark of the amateur. 'He despises fine writing even where it would best suit his purpose,' but though this resulted sometimes in an apparent want of care and finish in his books, it did at the same time preserve him from that bugbear of smooth and almost absentminded competence which is the bane of present-day traditional novelists.[49]

What is true of the style is also true of the narrative ideology. The highbrow fiction which we have examined so far has been shown to contain ideological elements, especially in relation to the largely male collective myth of femininity which characterises fiction and journalism of the period. At the same time, each of these works operates at a critical and reflective distance from the general ideology, and represents an attempt to create an account of the post-war reality which that reality had so far proved incapable of producing. What typifies a work such as *Sorrell and Son* is its lack of reflexivity, the fact that, far from attempting to analyse existing conditions, it seeks merely to negate unhappiness with fantasy.

Sorrell and Son is an escapist fantasy, although its narrative content is realistic and socially contemporaneous. This is clearly a different order of escapism than that provided by Zane Grey or Edgar Wallace. The escapism of the novel lies in the manner in which it traces a thoroughly idealised social trajectory, and the manner in which it seeks to reconcile both real and imagined social conflicts. The narrative suggests meaningful continuity of social purpose and provides a happy ending, in a world which feared for such continuity and suspected that the world which it had created for its youth was altogether worse than the one which it had itself inherited.

At the centre of the narrative is the relationship between a father and his son. The father, a demobilised officer, is impecunious and socially unconnected. He is forced to take a job as a porter which has no social prestige, and considers that he has failed to transfer his quality and worth as an officer into a civilian equivalent. Of course, the whole of the 1920s was beset by a guilty sense that the nation had failed to transform itself into that land fit for heroes which the politicians had promised, and Sorrell is one among millions who returned from the war to little thanks. As Douglas Goldring later noted of the effects of the social dislocation created by demobilisation, 'ex-officers in particular were reduced in many cases to the [sic] direct misery and ex-officer organ-grinders, cabmen and railway porters became familiar objects of compassion'.[50] However, the figure of Sorrell is set up not simply as a figure of compassion, but as a moral lesson to the returned soldiers that if they only knuckle down and work hard their value shall be recognised and rewarded. Manuals discussing the principles of self-reliance were extremely popular in the immediate post-war period and advertisements for them appeared regularly and prominently in the press. Robert Graves and Alan Hodge remark sardonically on the ideological role of the widely advertised Pelman method: ' "There is plenty of room at the top" was the catchword. Once the revolutionary crowd-spirit had thus been canalized into a million streams of individual ambition, the representatives of Law and Order could be easy at heart.'[51] Content to improve more slowly and unmethodically, Sorrell is overworked, but remains a loyal and uncomplaining employee. He is finally rewarded by being made a full partner in the hotel business by his employer who, it transpires, has had an eye on him the whole time. Sorrell finishes the novel relatively wealthy. This rags to riches fantasy might appeal to anyone involved in menial labour who could wish that one day their commitment to work would be rewarded by a benign employer.

The novel seeks to create an image of social justice based around an idealisation of individual effort which precisely challenges the socialist ideas of the Labour Party and the Trade Unions. Trade Union thought emphasised the use of collective bargaining to obtain fair pay and conditions. Sorrell, who is overworked and badly paid, does not complain about his conditions even when they become almost insufferable. Instead, he tacitly accepts that any reward beyond subsistence level is entirely at the discretion of the employer. The reward that he receives – a major stake in the business – is one that would never be given by any employer to a junior employee, however long-serving. In this fantasy, it is not work done which is rewarded so much as Sorrell's moral commitment to hard work as such, with no expectation of reward. Hard work is compensated beyond its wildest dreams because its dreams are tightly circumscribed by unquestioning deference to the economic *status quo.*

At best an escape from the worsening employment conditions of the mid-1920s, at worst an ugly apology for the *status quo,* the novel also addresses two of the key perceived areas of social conflict of the period – the 'sex war' and inter-generational conflict.

Sorrell and Son beautifully exemplifies the manner in which male anxieties were displaced from the war and the state of domestic politics and economics on to women. Sorrell is returned from the war to disillusionment at home. The narrative encapsulates the nature of his disillusion in the opening pages: 'Women! How through he was with women!' (Deeping, 1984: 11). Here the breakdown of the relation between the sexes is represented as affecting only the ex-combatants:

> Two years ago his wife had left him, and her leaving him had labelled him a shabby failure. [...] And all that scramble after the war, the disillusionment of it, the drying up of the fine and foolish enthusiasms, the women going to the rich fellows who stayed at home, the bewilderment, the sense of bitter wrong, of blood poured out to be sucked up by the lips of a money-mad materialism.
> He looked at the face of his boy.
> 'Yes, its just a scramble,' he thought, 'but an organized scramble. The thing is to keep on your feet and fight, and not to get trampled on in the crush.' (11)

The novel which follows will have nothing further to say about the conduct or causes of the war, or about the widespread sense of betrayal felt by many returning soldiers. It will concentrate on two simple lessons for men: that they must work hard without expect-ation of reward, and that they must avoid being corrupted by women's sexuality. Sorrell is therefore first employed in a menial hotel job by a landlady who appears to exult over his loss of social status in a display of an unnatural, 'brutal and laughing vitality' (24). This situation is designed to resonate with that of all those men who felt socially humiliated in the post-war in their inability to re-assume economically dominant, bread-winning positions – a complex hum-iliation in which the inability to protect wife and children was channelled into a hostility against women themselves, as male self-blame was projected outwards on to the female other. Sorrell has already been made to feel his inadequacy by his wife's leaving him; now he is made to feel it again at the hands of the landlady. The general culture, in its tirades against women's usurpation of male roles and their sexuality, served to legitimise male hostility against women, and to direct anger at the post-war situation away from capitalism and government and on to women in general. *Sorrell and Son* creates the same mechanism of psychic discharge inside its own closed fictional world. Thus, the landlady Mrs Palfrey, although not an androgynous flapper, is described as a Circe, running a hotel of which the 'sly filthiness' (31) not only recalls the pigs of *The Odyssey* but is held to reflect her lack of character – that is, her lack of the disciplined capacity for work which the meticulous Sorrell possesses in abundance. She has usurped the functions of her husband who has become very ill, perhaps as a consequence of her domination, and her power over Sorrell also has a psychologically corrosive effect.

> She saw the white teeth under the little black moustache, and she understood how he was feeling. He hated her. He could have struck her in the face, and his suppressed passion gave her the sort of emotion she found pleasurable. She liked using her claws on men, driving them to various exasperations, and not for a long time had she had such a victim.
>
> (29)

The narrative provides a framework in which hostility towards women is legitimised, and it is only masculine self-control allied to chivalric instincts (which might now, it seems, be misplaced) that prevents an eruption of violence. One function of this passage is to establish that the humiliation felt by the economically marginalised male is consciously caused and relished by the female. The implied reader will not assume from a reading of this passage that all women are like this, although he or she will imagine that some are; it is as a scapegoat, a hate figure for male and female readers, that the figure of Mrs Palfrey functions. She does not represent all women, but all women might be subliminally associated with her. This two-dimensional character reaches the nadir of evil when she attempts to seduce Sorrell while her husband is dying in another room.

It turns out that Mrs Palfrey has been only an appetiser, however, when the former Mrs Sorrell arrives on the scene. This occurs only after the passage of a number of years in which the young Sorrell is seen through school and on to University in spite of economic circumstances so adverse as to have made such an outcome highly unlikely. During the period of the son's education the bond between father and son has become close and strong. The relationship between two males is portrayed as the intimate human heart of the novel. This male friendship at one level draws less on the idealisation of male friendship to be found in the war novels such as *Death of a Hero* than on the ethos of Edmund Gosse's *Father and Son* (1917). The idealisation of father/son friendship goes further than the homosociality of Aldington's novel, although each is predicated on the exclusion of and resistance to corrupting female encroachment. The father/son relationship resists the phenomenon of inter-generational war which Wyndham Lewis describes in *Doom of Youth* as less a reality than an invention of 'Big Business' and propagated by the press as part of a divide-and-rule policy aimed at creating social divisions.[52] Although the press was clearly influential in spreading the idea of a lost generation of doomed youth which had been betrayed by its elders, it is clear that the war went a long way towards dissolving the tradition of respect for the elders and betters who had presided over a conflict widely perceived as folly. In addition, the idea of generational conflict now had a psychological theory all of its own, one which had again received a certain amount of press advertisement: the Oedipus Complex. In its insistence on the bond between father and son, *Sorrell and Son* is fully cognisant of the psychoanalytic account of conflict, which it explicitly resists:

> Sorrell had dipped into Freud, and his inclination was to laugh at Freud [...]. As for the so-called 'Oedipus complex,' it did not appear to exist in Kit [the son]. Nor had it existed in Sorrell. And yet it did not seem to him that either he or his son were abnormal. He rather thought that the abnormality could be looked for on the Continent and in the mental make-up of a certain sort of Continental youth who grew up to be a professor. (167)

Sorrell and Son aims not only to seal the generational rift with a gloss of fantasy, but also to combat the findings of Freud, who was felt by many at this time to have dehumanised love by representing it in terms of a mechanics of desire. The novel tackles the question of desire and father–son rivalry directly in terms of the second major female personage which it introduces: the mother. The mother returns to her ex-husband and son two marriages later, for motives which are allowed to remain mildly ambiguous. It is therefore the suspicion of Sorrell and not the narrative voice which sees her as a vampiric revenant setting out to seduce the son away from the father.

> In his mental diary he wrote her down a vampire, a woman, who, having had all the satisfactions she desired from men and sex, was seeking other satisfactions. That red mouth of hers was ready to feed upon the young vitality of her son. (199)

Her own actions appear to confirm this interpretation, however, and the narration refers to her aim as the 'seduction' (214) of her son. The issue for Sorrell and son is whether the mother can come between them and disrupt not only their relationship of love and trust but also their collective economic and social rise – a project which requires Christopher to complete his education undistracted by women. Sorrell writes to his son: 'I do not believe that she can come between us'. Christopher reads the letter in tears and reflects: 'His father was a great man. He loved him'. We have already noted that the assault on patriarchy is an issue in the 1920s, and one which this novel attempts crudely to address. More unusual here is the attempt to rewrite the Oedipus complex (as popularly understood) as a matter not of male but of female desire. The disturbing feature of Freud's theory of the Oedipus complex was the manner in which the male psyche was found to be rooted in a taboo desire for the mother. Because it was (and is) widely considered unnatural that a son should desire his mother, the theory proved very provocative, and its sensational nature made it the topic of widespread public discussion. Where the theory provoked male resistance it only appeared to be confirmed: the strength of the resistance could be attributed to the strength of the repressed, unacknowledged desire for the mother. *Sorrell and Son* attempts to break the vicious circle of denying the theory by attempting to write the Oedipus complex out of existence altogether. The narrative removes the element of competition between father and son over the mother, which Freud's theory predicts, and replaces the taboo desire of the son for the mother with the unnatural desire of the mother for the son. The mother's desire for the son is represented not as sexual but, euphemistically, as a desire for his 'youth'. The method of fulfilling this desire is to introduce her son to two attractive young women who, she hopes, will distract him from his studies and cause him to visit her more often.

> She decided it had been rather subtle of her to ask two charming girls to meet and amuse Christopher, and she included them in the furnishings and drapings of her temple of Venus. She thought that if she meant to get at the boy she would get at him most successfully through sex, not crudely, but by way of pleasant emanations of sex, by suggesting to him what a good time she could give him. (225–6)

The attempted distraction fails. The mother and younger women are seen off and the son goes on to complete his career, while the father finishes life comfortably as part-owner of a successful company, and can find time to garden and even, now, read a novel.

Sorrell and Son is characterised by an inability to reflect on social conditions or, indeed, on its own presuppositions. Instead of critical reflection, it addresses a series of social anxieties – about social status, employment, gender and familial relations – by resolving them through fantasy. Nothing which the novel narrates might not possibly happen, yet all of its resolutions are idealised, and the outcomes for Sorrell and son are singularly improbable. Its solutions serve as a salve to quite explicable anxieties, and encourage unreflective faith in an individual effort which can stave off hardship and social injustice through obedient hard work and resilience before a corrupting feminine onslaught. The re-writing of Freud in terms designed to redeem masculinity from the taint of 'unnatural' or taboo desires testifies to the role of new psychological theories in reinforcing the self-doubt of men by casting masculinity itself into doubt. That women get the blame connects this novel directly to the popular ideology encouraged by the press, and herein lies the most sinister aspect of the fantasy: that critical reflection on social conditions is discouraged, while a type of scapegoating of women which harnesses general male anxieties about women to other social anxieties is set in its place.

Notes

1. However, a number of recent anthologists have broadened our knowledge of war literature by including writings from a wider social base. See, for example, Catherine Reilly (ed.), *Scars Upon My Heart*; Martin Stephen (ed.), *Never Such Innocence*; Peter Vansittart (ed.), *Voices From the Great War*; Dominic Hibberd and John Onions (eds), *Poetry of the Great War*.
2. See Jon Silkin, *Out of Battle*, p. 148.
3. See Arthur Marwick, *The Deluge*, pp. 124–9.
4. See Marwick, *The Deluge*, p. 87.
5. Noreen Branson, *Britain in the Nineteen Twenties*, p. 210.
6. For a recent account, see Jane Eldridge Miller, *Rebel Women*.
7. Gail Brabon, *Women Workers of the First World War*, pp. 154–72.
8. See Brabon, *Women Workers*, pp. 67–82.
9. *The Bodley Head Ford Madox Ford* includes only the first three of these, but subsequent editions have included the complete tetralogy.
10. See Alan Judd, *Ford Madox Ford*, pp. 278–310, and the extensive account

in Max Saunders, *Ford Madox Ford: A Dual Life. Volume II*, pp. 1–41.

11. See Judd, pp. 104–7 and Saunders, pp. 201–4.

12. See Saunders volume I, pp. 266–7 and volume II, pp. 154–5 for a discussion of Ford's relationship to these terms.

13. I share this view of *The Waste Land* with Peter Nicholls who argues in *Modernisms* (p. 258) that 'nothing can redeem the blight of sexuality which afflicts the poem, and the equation of an unregenerate femininity chokes any kind of narrative or dialectical movement.'

14. Reproduced in Hueffer [Ford], *The Critical Attitude*, p. 160. Ford changed his name to Hueffer only after the war.

15. See Paul Fussell, *The Great War and Modern Memory* (pp. 231–69) on the English tendency to see the war in pastoral terms. Fussell makes especial reference to the work of Edmund Blunden, including his *Undertones of War* (1928). The musical analogue was Ralph Vaughan Williams's *A Pastoral Symphony* (first performed 1922): mistaken by contemporaries for a nostalgic rural tone poem, it was in fact a war symphony conceived on active service.

16. On Ford's 'limited heroes' see Norman Leer, *The Limited Hero in the Fiction of Ford Madox Ford*.

17. Fussell, *The Great War* (pp. 82–90) discusses the belief of those at the front in an 'enemy at the rear'.

18. The terms in inverted commas are not used at his point in Ford's text, but I paraphrase Ford in this manner to indicate the extensive use in this novel of class idioms to characterise the cultural outlook of the various components of the class system.

19. See, for example, Sheila Jeffreys, *The Spinster and Her Enemies*, pp. 147–8.

20. See Robert Graves and Alan Hodge, *The Long Week-End* (p. 37) on the American appetite for British heritage in the context of Britain's indebtedness to the USA after the war.

21. See Marwick, *The Deluge*, pp. 123–30.

22. Richard Aldington, 'The Influence of Mr. James Joyce', *The English Review* 32 (April 1921), 333–41.

23. See '*Ulysses*, Order, and Myth', first published in *The Dial* for November 1923 and reprinted in Eliot, *Selected Prose*, pp. 175–8.

24. For a further discussion of the classical/romantic paradigm, see Chapter Three.

25. Reprinted in part in Wyndham Lewis, *Satire and Fiction*.

26. Charles Doyle, *Richard Aldington*, pp. 64, 132.

27. For a discussion of the sheik in the context of popular fiction see Chapter Five.

28. See also p. 135 of the novel, on woman as Aphrodite the Devourer of men.

29. See the discussion in Marwick, *The Deluge*, pp. 105–13.

30. See, for example, Fussell, *The Great War*, pp. 82–90. Compare Part Three of *A Man Could Stand Up -: Parade's End*, pp. 645–74.
31. See Doyle, *Richard Aldington*, p. 69.
32. This is also mentioned in *Parade's End* where Tietjens's explanation is the correct one, which emerged eventually in the years after the war: that the Germans were recycling the cadavers of horse and cattle for their fat, and the English propagandists had simply mistranslated the word. It is perhaps a sign of the times that this story was considered absurdly improbable and unmasked as a fraud once the wartime hysteria had died down. See Marwick, *The Deluge*, p. 213.
33. See the discussion in Billie Melman, *Women and the Popular Imagination in the Twenties*, pp. 89–104.
34. An ideal which corresponds to Aldington's own views in the immediate post-war period. See Doyle, *Richard Aldington*, p. 54.
35. The relationship is documented in Caroline Zilboorg (ed.), *Richard Aldington and H.D.*
36. Journalistic clichés, the latter recalling Alec Waugh's *The Loom of Youth* (1917), a novel about school experience, and Wilfred Owen's poem 'Anthem for Doomed Youth', which Wyndham Lewis criticised in *Doom of Youth* (1932), a polemical attack on the ability of the press to manipulate popular ideas.
37. Compare Hilary Simpson, *D. H. Lawrence and Feminism* (p. 65): 'Lawrence develops in the twenties an explicit anti-feminism which is of a different quality from the more open-ended probings of love and power to be found in his earlier work. [...] Yet the very explicit historical relationship between the changing position of women in the war years and Lawrence's launching on his career as the prophet of male supremacy has rarely been discussed.'
38. Judith Ruderman, *D. H. Lawrence and the Devouring Mother* (p. 81) sees these stories in terms of a psychobiographical reading which privileges 'Lawrence's hostility toward the Magna Mater'; Simpson, *D. H. Lawrence and Feminism*, (p. 65) relates these stories to Lawrence's 'explicit antifeminism'; a rare caveat is offered in Kiernan Ryan, 'The Revenge of the Women: Lawrence's "Tickets, Please"', in *Literature and History* 7:2 (Autumn 1981), 210–22. Ryan's account shows that Lawrence's story does not so much express his own attitudes as those of others. Other accounts of the complexity and subtlety of these stories include Keith Cushman, 'The Achievement of *England, My England and Other Stories*, in Robert B. Partlow and Harry T. Moore (eds), *D. H. Lawrence: The Man Who Lived* (pp. 27–38); Lydia Blanchard, 'Lawrence on the Fighting Line: Changes in the Form of the Post-War Short Fiction', in *The D. H. Lawrence Review* 16:3 (Fall 1983), 235–46; Weldon Thornton, 'The Flower or The Fruit: a Reading of D. H. Lawrence's "England, My England"', in *The D. H. Lawrence Review* 16:3 (Fall 1983), 247–58.

39. Taken from W. E. Henley's patriotic poem, 'England' (1900).

40. Space precludes a discussion of the novella Lawrence began in 1918, *The Fox* (1923), which shares the war work theme.

41. Steve Vine, 'Introduction' to *Aaron's Rod* (1995: xv–xxxvi).

42. Following Ruderman, *D. H. Lawrence and the Devouring Mother* (pp. 10–11, 17–21, 90–103). According to Ruderman, Aaron is 'in flight from his wife because she is smothering him' (p. 97) and 'the emphasis on aloneness in *Aaron's Rod* is a reaction to the male's overreliance on the female for nourishment and support, life and health' (p. 98).

43. Following Tony Pinkney, *D. H. Lawrence*, pp. 11–18.

44. Following Sandra M. Gilbert and Susan Gubar, *No Man's Land. Volume II: Sexchanges,* p. 260, and Elaine Showalter, *The Female Malady*, pp. 170–4.

45. Compare Gilbert and Gubar, *No Man's Land II*, pp. 282–9.

46. See William R. Barr, '*Aaron's Rod* as D. H. Lawrence's Picaresque Novel' in *The D. H. Lawrence Review* 9 1976, 213–25.

47. See Paul G. Baker, 'Profile of an Anti-Hero: Aaron Sisson Reconsidered', in *The D. H. Lawrence Review* 10 1977, 182–92.

48. The edition which I have used is the forty-first edition, third impression, 1984, and the publisher, Cassell, remains unchanged.

49. A. C. Ward, *The Nineteen-Twenties*, pp. 112–13.

50. Douglas Goldring, *The Nineteen Twenties*, p. 5.

51. Robert Graves and Alan Hodge, *The Long Week-End*, pp. 64–5. See also John Collier and Iain Lang, *Just The Other Day*, p. 29.

52. See Wyndham Lewis, *Doom of Youth*, pp. 3–8, 73–81, 201–5 and *passim*.

2

Ideals and Realities of the English Woman

ALTHOUGH WOMEN GAINED IN the eyes of men, as emphasised in Chapter 1, employment gains in the working class at least were negligible. If the returned heroes of the war were recast as revolutionary villains, a similar ideological image change beset women who 'ceased to be splendid patriots serving their country, and became instead selfish vampires depriving men of jobs'.[1] Some firms dismissed women, others ceased recruiting them and replaced them with men. With the shrinking of middle-class households, the demand for domestic labour declined. In any case, domestic service was no longer regarded by women as a desirable option.[2] Female employment was probably only slightly higher after the war than before, and women continued to earn about two-thirds of the male rates for comparable work. The Government had made no plans for the women who would be laid off after the war.[3] However, employment of some kind became more normal among middle-class women, and the numbers of female undergraduates at Oxford and Cambridge, as well as at other universities such as London and Manchester, continued to rise, while the Sex Disqualification (Removal) Act of 1919 allowed women to the Bar for the first time.[4] Women also emerged as heroic figures accomplishing feats of endurance in the masculine mould: an American, Gertrude Ederle, swam the Channel in 1926 and set a record; Lady Heath flew single-handed from Capetown to Croydon in 1928; Amy Johnson flew alone from England to Australia in 1930.

Women's most tangible gains from the war were political. The suffrage movement had established the agenda of female enfranchisement long before the outbreak of the war. The National Union of Women's Suffrage Societies had grouped together existing organisations in 1897, and the Women's Social and Political Union had been founded in 1903 by Emmeline Pankhurst and her daughters Christabel and Sylvia. The WSPU had begun a campaign of direct action in 1905, which had extended to arson, bombing and assault, while prison sentences for those caught were fought by hunger strike. While Parliament stalled over women's suffrage, the increasing militancy of the WSPU served to alienate some supporters. The suffrage movement was dominated by the middle class, and conceived of itself in fundamentally nationalistic terms. When war broke out nearly every section of the movement suspended the struggle for suffrage and became patriotic or nationalistic, some-times to an extreme degree. Only Sylvia Pankhurst emerges from this period as an antithetical and independent figure, opposing the extreme nationalism of her mother Emmeline and the WSPU, and forming the Workers' Suffrage Federation, at one stroke broadening the franchise issue and creating a vehicle for undeviating opposition to the war.[5]

It was not, however, political organisation which finally gained women the vote, and neither did it come all at once but rather in two stages, with the passing of the Representation of the People Acts of 1918 and 1928. The first of these was a war measure designed to prepare for the immediate post-war election. Already certain anomalies meant that many men who had been at the front would be disenfranchised as they did not fulfil residence requirements. After a period of debate, it was decided to grant the vote to all men over twenty-one, although the majority of returning soldiers lost the vote in spite of a reform which seemed intended to benefit them. It was also widely recognised that, given the contribution that women had made to the war, it would be anomalous to exclude them completely from the electoral process, and the national franchise should therefore be extended to some women. Provision for women was less generous than for men, the vote being granted to women who were over the age of thirty and who were householders or married to householders. This meant that some 1.8 million women over thirty, as well as 3.5 million aged between twenty-one and thirty were excluded from the franchise in 1918.[6] The issue of votes for these women was to dominate political debate in England for the next decade and to create a climate sometimes characterised as a 'sex war'.

The 1918 solution represented not merely a compromise with traditionalists who opposed the vote for women, but also a widely felt unease among men that enfranchisement on equal terms would lead to political domination by women. Under normal circumstances, universal suffrage would have given a slight majority of votes to women. War losses meant that universal suffrage, when it did come in 1928, created an electorate of 14.5 million women to only 12.25 million men.[7] The 'sex war' consisted largely of newspaper editorials designed to vilify young women, especially the so-called 'surplus women', young women who might normally have married but were said to have been denied the opportunity by the shortage of males were therefore considered 'surplus' to male requirements. The newspapers, who feared above all that these women once enfranchised would prove to be socialists, criticised the dress and behaviour of young women, who were characterised as 'flappers', pointed out that they were a threat to men in various fields of employment, and tried to create a climate in which a general male fear of emasculation would prevent further enfranchisement.[8] The press campaign failed to deter the government of Stanley Baldwin from passing the Act, although the subsequent election which allowed the formation of the first Labour Government under Ramsay MacDonald might well have given Baldwin cause to regret it, and certainly seemed to confirm the view of those who had argued that the young female vote would be a 'Bolshevik' vote.

Contemporary accounts emphasise the changes in the dress and social habits of young women in the aftermath of the war which led to the journalistic creation of the flapper, a generic figure which indiscriminately blended the attributes of women of different classes for propaganda purposes.[9] The war brought about very apparent changes in women's clothing. Short hair had been an art school fashion before the war, a Parisian import. It was taken over by women workers in the war as a matter of convenience, and afterwards it became common among younger women. Trousers and shorter skirts were also common, and skirts and sleeves continued to become shorter. Under American influence, lipstick, rouge and eye make-up became popular, while, as if to mark the onset of androgyny, the pullover, which could in effect be worn by either sex, became a vogue. Indeed, it was an American author, F. Scott Fitzgerald, who gave the flapper her first literary incarnation with his opportunistically titled book of short stories, *Flappers and Philosophers* (1920: British publication, 1922), which with his following collection,

Tales of The Jazz Age (1922: British publication, 1923), set an American imprint on the whole decade. So the 'flapper' was actually a descendant of the factory worker, slimmed by rationing, and combining a taste for the new American fashions, including smoking and the new jazz dances, with a more confident approach to sexuality and an unwillingness to passively await the male approach. During the war the image of this plucky young woman had been approved by press and advertising: after the war, the image of the housewife once again became the ideal.[10] The invention of the flapper skilfully blended aspects of real changes in women's culture into an image of the young woman as pleasure-loving and irresponsible. The excited denunciations of flapper culture were designed to reinforce the attempt to persuade women to surrender their jobs to men and were central to the press campaign against the extension of the female suffrage, which was labelled the 'flapper vote'. Flapper culture was denounced in the name of a return to femininity: the flapper, like the career woman, was unlikely to marry and risked becoming a 'surplus woman', ending up as a 'spinster' – another target of anti-feminist hostility.

Feminism before the war had been characterised by two goals: equal rights with men and the reform of male sexuality. The 1920s saw a shift from the confrontational feminism of the pre-war to a more muted bureaucratic and constitutional version.[11] The 'old feminism' of equal rights was challenged by a 'new feminism', typified by the activities of Eleanor Rathbone, who glorified motherhood and argued for a state allowance for mothers.[12] Some 'new feminists' echoed the new interest in the joys of sex as advocated by Marie Stopes in *Married Love* (1918) and Dora Russell in *Hypatia* (1925). In the context of these accounts, in which (hetero)sexual pleasure was represented as healthy and biologically inevitable (although Russell stopped short of recommending marriage[13]), abstinence or spinsterhood became anathema.

The women's writing which this chapter examines does not reflect the degree of optimism which these social and cultural changes might lead us to expect. The work considered here is concerned with examining the domestic effects of the war, and the climate of anti-feminism and 'new feminism'. Despite the progressive feminist politics with which Rebecca West (the chosen name of Cicely Isabel Fairfield) had associated herself, her short and artful novel *The Return of the Soldier* (1918), which deals with the impact of the war in the phenomenon of the returning soldier, emerges as a fairly regressive defence of the ideal of motherhood. Sylvia Townsend Warner's *Lolly Willowes* (1926) is considered the pre-eminent example of the feminist novel designed to assert the figure of the spinster: that novel's connection of the feminine and nature in opposition to the ideals of urban society and culture which it locates as masculine is also found to fall short of a properly articulated progressive literary agenda. The final and longest section examines the complex aesthetic of Virginia Woolf's *Jacob's Room* (1922), *Mrs Dalloway* (1925) and *To The Lighthouse* (1927) in relation to her engagement with the war, the state and gender. This account uncovers problems with the structure of Woolf's analytic, but shows how she locates art itself as an androgynous territory in which the feminine can avoid the identification with teleological male culture, but equally with the ideal of motherhood, and the more insidious identification of the feminine with nature, which are privileged by West and Townsend Warner respectively.

The Fairy-tale of War: Rebecca West's The Return of the Soldier

Rebecca West's *The Return of the Soldier* (1918) is an early attempt to deal with the problem of reintegration faced by returning soldiers and their families, and the effects and treatment of shell-shock. The novel reflects psychoanalytic insight, both in the use of the idea of repressed memory, and in the role played by displacement in the novel's central *ménage à trois*, in which a woman's love for her cousin is deflected into an attachment to his wife. Formally, the novel emulates Henry James, the subject of West's first published book, and Ford Madox Ford's *The Good Soldier* (1915),[14] also greatly admired by West, in its use of an unreliable narrator, although the effects of this are generally muted, as the hidden situation is only thinly concealed.

The plot is a reworking of the fairy-tale 'Sleeping Beauty', in which the notion of awakening is cruelly reversed. Baldry Court is the idealised castle where Kitty, the wife of the absent soldier, and his cousin Jenny, wait for his return. At first it seems that Kitty must be the Princess awaiting her Prince. Kitty's snobbish love of fine things and her pristine appearance – 'she looked so like a girl on a magazine cover that one expected to find a large "7d." somewhere attached to her person' (West, 1980: 11) – conceal an emotional paralysis: she has lost her only son at two years of age. Baldry Court is 'the impregnable fortress of a gracious life' (121), a 'magic circle' (145), a buttress against loss as well as against the outside world, a 'little globe of ease' (15) into which the two women hope to rescue Chris from the war (16). The 'controlled beauty' (115) of the lands around the house is juxtaposed with the disorderly wilderness outside. The house is emotionally paralysed, a denial of nature, life and love, as well as death, and the nursery, kept as it was since the child's death, reflects the life-denying function of the whole house. The fields of Flanders represent death, a disordered world of mud which contrasts with the perfect order of Baldry Court, a 'dreary place of death and dirt' (18). The image of the house, Jenny hopes, will function as an enchantment, an 'amulet' protecting Chris from the disenchantment of war (18). As Jenny remembers him, Chris has retained his childhood optimism and sense of magic and the 'hopeless hope' of transcendence, of 'an experience that would act on his life like alchemy, turning to gold all the dark metals of events, and from that revelation he would go on his way rich with an inextinguishable joy' (20).

The enchanted spell of Baldry Court is broken by the arrival of Mrs Grey, a lower-class woman, 'furred with neglect and poverty' (25), an 'animal' and an 'insect' (31–2). The intrusion of the outside world is represented as a violation of class barriers, bringing the untidy outside into the ordered interior. This woman brings the news that Chris has been concussed by a shell. Mrs Grey, now married, is Margaret Allington, Chris's fiancé of fifteen years ago. Chris has amnesia, and has reverted in his mind to the person he was fifteen years previously, still in love with Margaret. The fairy-tale awakening scenario is now suddenly changed as the initial symbolic structure is abruptly transformed. Kitty will not be awoken by the kiss of the returning soldier. When he is brought back from the war he does not remember her and cannot kiss her (52). Now it is Chris who must be awoken from his amnesia. Kitty, angry at her husband, becomes an Ice Queen, her face, hands and bosom 'shining like the snow', radiant with 'the white fire of jewels' (57–8). She does not awake but Jenny does, realising that the new Chris exposes the old order of Baldry Court: 'we had all been living wickedly and he too' (59).

Jenny, seduced by Chris's description of his old love, has repressed her desire for him: 'I had known that he was having bad nights at

Baldry Court [...] But I had not been able to do anything about it' (144). Unable to acknowledge her desire, she displaces it into an identification with *his* desire, and therefore with his choice of love object. Her interest in Kitty is therefore unceremoniously transferred to Margaret. The decisive moment for Jenny, and a surprising moment for the less attentive reader, comes when she succumbs to trauma, the feminine hysteria of repression parallelling that of the male: 'I was near to a bodily collapse: the truth is that I was physically so jealous of Margaret that it was making me ill' (120).

For Jenny, Chris's reversion to the pure love of his youth shows him to be 'so much saner than the rest of us' (134), but resenting his disregard she decides that he must be cured. It is now Chris, 'englobed in peace as in a crystal sphere' with his old lover (143), who must be awoken into the real world, the world of death and of the war he has left behind, even though Jenny knows that Margaret can protect Chris: 'while her spell endured they could not send him back into the hell of war' (147). The analyst who treats him is unable to recognise the nature of the family romance which he has entered – he wants to 'see everybody concerned' (127) but begins with the presupposition that there is only one patient: '"You," he said to Chris, with a naïve adoption of the detective tone, "are the patient."' (151). The analyst fails to recognise that the two women also suffer from repression: Jenny of her love for Chris and Kitty of the loss of her son. So, to an already complex structure is added the ironic vision of a psychoanalysis which no longer recognises the female hysteria on which its discoveries are based, and which has turned its attention from the psychopathology of family life to the normalisation of shell-shocked soldiers.

Chris is to be cured by being shown artefacts which remind him of his son, a kind of shock treatment designed to reverse the earlier trauma which replaces the awakening kiss of the fairy-tale. As she goes out to Chris to show him his son's jersey and ball, Margaret is kissed by Jenny, an astonishing moment in which a female erotic bond is presented as the displaced possession of a man: 'We kissed, not as women, but as lovers do; I think we each embraced that part of Chris the other had absorbed by her love' (184). The awakening kiss has finally arrived, but refracted through such a complex matrix of displacement and ambivalence of motive as to keep open all the cultural and symbolic irresolution which the text has established. When he returns to the house, Chris is, in the final word of the novel, 'cured' (188).

The final section of the novel, in which Jenny is undecided whether it is better to cure Chris or not, opens the question of the novel's ideology. The choice between enchantment and disenchantment revolves around the question of the recognition of reality, the central concern of psychoanalysis. The reality is adulthood and death, now represented by Baldry Court, and by Kitty who finally emerges not as an Ice Queen but as the reality principle, a suffering mother, who, despite being 'the falsest thing on earth', could 'by merely suffering somehow remind us of reality' (181–2). The enchanted state of love is represented by Margaret, but her love is less that of a lover than of a mother protecting a child. Kitty's reality includes the materialism and repression of the bourgeois household, while Margaret embodies the idealised generosity and spontaneity of the poor.[15] Jenny at first idealises this form of love: 'It means that the woman has gathered the soul of the man into her soul and is keeping it warm in love [...]. That is a great thing for a woman to do.' (144). Subsequently she subscribes to the reality principle, deciding that preserved in maternal bliss Chris 'would not be quite a man' (183). The true mother then is Kitty who knows not only what it means to mother a son, but to lose one. In the nursery, Kitty, allowing her repressed emotion to surface, presses the child's picture 'to her bosom as though to staunch a wound' (160–1). This is as she prepares to make Chris 'normal' and so available for military service. Jenny has accepted that a woman must always function as a mother, and must be prepared to sacrifice her son or husband to death. She now believes that the moment of motherhood which Chris seeks from Margaret should not be protracted: it can provide only an illusory protection from the death. Kitty, with the aid of psychoanalysis, can fulfil the ultimate function of motherhood which is to give him up to death. The reader must decide whether the ideas of the narrator embody the ideology of the novel, or whether the reader should know better than this unreliable narrator that Margaret and not Kitty represents the reality of love.

At the close of the novel Jenny's ideas embody the novel's ideology. They have the reality principle on their side: motherhood cannot last forever. *The Return of the Soldier* is a *tour de force* which only reveals its ideology under pressure. The complex fairy-tale variations, the symbolic compression and transformations, and the psychoanalytic subtext, mitigate against any social-documentary reading. It is frankly disappointing to see the war emerge here as a reality principle; shell-shock (what is now called combat fatigue) as traumatic repression; and motherhood in terms of the necessity of sacrifice. Although the vision of the narrator cannot securely be equated with that of the author, the ideology of the text, for all its apparent modernity of method and content, seems finally to have negated questions about the politics of class and war in its fairy-tale structure, while confirming the oldest imperialist ideal of motherhood.

The Magic of Independence: Sylvia Townsend Warner's Lolly Willowes

Buttressed by psychoanalysis, *The Return of the Soldier* asserts the centrality of motherhood. In contrast, Sylvia Townsend Warner's *Lolly Willowes* (1926) is an examination of the figure of the English spinster which also runs strongly counter to the 'new feminist' celebration of marriage and motherhood.[16] While novels such as *Parade's End* and *Death of a Hero* emphasised the social discontinuity between pre- and post-war, *Lolly Willowes* asserts a fundamental continuity with regards to the prospects of women and the structure of expectations which defines their lives. It is an ambivalently comic novel with a pressing social content.

Laura Willowes is brought up in the country with her father and, when he dies, moves to London to live with her brother and his wife. In the household of her father she is 'perfectly contented' (Townsend Warner, 1979: 29) by her light domestic chores, her involvement in the family brewing trade, and her interest in the 'forsaken green byways of the rural pharmacopoeia' (31). She does not marry because of her unusual looks, lack of interest in society outside the home and her vaguely incestuous attachment to her father (26). When she first moves to London she becomes central to her brother's household as the children's 'Aunt Lolly', and after one disastrous attempt no further moves are made to marry her off (58–61). During the war Laura works in a parcel room, efficiently and unnoticed, until the day of the Armistice (69–70). After the war, seeing that her life has become static, she becomes unhappy and dissatisfied (77). The crisis comes when, on a visit to a florist and greengrocer, Laura is overtaken by 'a great longing' (83) for nature. Suddenly inspired by a spray of beech leaves she buys a guide book to the Chilterns which she studies avidly. She is transformed: 'During dinner Laura looked at her relations. She felt as though she had awoken, unchanged, from a twenty years slumber, to find them almost unrecognisable.' (89). To the bewilderment of her relations, she announces her intention to move to the Chilterns, to a village described in the guide book called Great Mop (94). The choice of place seems arbitrary, but the name recalls the 'mop-heads' of the chrysanthemums she has bought (85), and symbolically suggests the witch's broomstick and the housewife's brush. Told by her brother that her scheme is impracticable, she replies: 'Nothing is impracticable for a single, middle-aged woman with an income of her own' (102). For the first time asserting her independence from patriarchy, Laura takes happily to a relatively solitary life in the countryside which is interrupted only when her nephew arrives first to visit and then to take up residence himself:

> In vain she had tried to escape [...]. She had thrown away twenty years of her old life like a handful of old rags, but the wind had blown them back again and dressed her in the old uniform. [...] And she was the same old Aunt Lolly, so useful and obliging and negligible. (162–3)

This unwelcome development is followed by the mysterious arrival of a cat, which Laura recognises as the 'familiar' of a witch, sent by the Devil: 'She, Laura Willowes, in England, in the year 1922, had entered into a compact with the Devil' (169). The reader is unprepared for this development, which is closely followed by passages which anticipate magic realism, including a Witches' Sabbath and conversations with the Devil, who turns out to be pleasant and unpatriarchal. Laura's idea of herself as a witch is to be close to nature, especially the woods, although she believes that she could actually practise magic if she so wished.[17]

As in the more contemporary canon of magic realist works, there is no narrative clue to the reality or otherwise of the magical episodes, but there is at least an explanation of the use of the figure of the witch, given in a speech delivered by Laura to the Devil:

> Women have such vivid imaginations and lead such dull lives. Their pleasure in life is so soon over; they are so dependent on others, and their dependence so soon becomes a nuisance. [...]
>
> When I think of witches, I seem to see all over England, all over Europe, women living and growing old, as common as blackberries, and as unregarded. [...] And all the time being thrust down into dullness when the one thing all women hate is to be thought dull. [...]
>
> [We become witches] to show our scorn of pretending life's a safe business, to satisfy our passion for adventure [...] to have a life of one's own, not an existence doled out to you by others [...]. (234–9)

Laura's realisation of the condition of the spinster is an eloquent one. There is certainly a feminist content which is close to that of *A Room of One's Own*, as when Laura reviews the past tyranny of her relatives:

> There was no question of forgiving them. [...] If she were to start forgiving she must needs forgive Society, the Law, the Church, the History of Europe, the Old Testament, great-great-aunt Salome and her prayer-book, the Bank of England, Prostitution, the Architect of Apsley Terrace, and half a dozen other useful props of civilization. All she could do now was go on forgetting them. (150)

However, while the moment in which patriarchy is rejected is carefully spelled out, this room of one's own is conceived only as a place in which to sit and think. This lack of a positive social mission for women may have been what made the novel palatable to its large readership – the novel was a lucrative success – but the contrast with Woolf, who saw this room as the space of art (if not necessarily of polemic) is marked. There is a marked contrast too with Townsend Warner's later conversion to communism and her examination of the role of the woman as artist – to be more specific, as story-teller – in her partially autobiographic historical novel of the revolutions of 1848, *Summer Will Show* (1936).[18] In an attempt to harness this novel to a particular brand of feminism, one commentator has argued that *Lolly Willowes* counterposes the 'gynocratic green world' of the countryside with the ordered domestic spaces of the 'phallocentric city'.[19] The validity or even the progressive force of identifying women with nature, is one that is scrupulously interdicted by Virginia Woolf, who refuses the equation of the woman's role with nature whether in terms of her role in reproduction or in terms of the assumption that women are or should be confined to what her novels identify as the sheer contingency of nature. Moreover, the narrative method of *Lolly Willowes*, especially as regards style and tone, problematises a straightforward feminist reading. Townsend Warner's method glances back to Jane Austen, across to her friends T. F. Powys (the author of *Mr Weston's Good Wine* [1927]) and David Garnett (author of the fabular *Lady Into Fox* [1922]) and looks forward to Carson McCullers and Flannery O'Connor, with its restricted vocabulary and ironic tone. The narration remains largely external to Laura. The final speech is the most direct representation of her thought and in many ways comes as a violation of the novel's own protocol: it sounds too much like an explanation of the basic idea of the book designed for the reader who would not be happy with a mystery. Embedded in so much fabulation, Laura's *cri de cœur* does not sound as the novel's central tragic utterance.

Better the devil you do not know, than the devil of patriarchy and urban civilisation is the moral of the book, although its equation of patriarchy and the city blurs this analysis. Read for its literal content, the implication remains that the independence of the spinster might culminate merely in isolation and fantasy; but this pessimistic possibility remains in abeyance within the novel itself, and in *Lolly Willowes* the English spinster is given her most memorable and droll representation.

A Question of Life and Death: Aesthetics and History in the Novels of Virginia Woolf

Imperial Education: Jacob's Room

If Sylvia Townsend Warner does not identify art as an issue for women, Virginia Woolf does so consistently. Writing and painting announce themselves on the first two pages of *Jacob's Room*. Betty Flanders writes to Captain Barfoot; the letter blots as she weeps on it, her tears distorting the world she sees and the letter she writes; when she gets up to post the letter she disrupts the painting of a hitherto unannounced artist in a panama hat, whose frustration at this movement within his composition leads him to employ the spontaneous and physical methods of Lily Briscoe in *To The Lighthouse*. 'He struck the canvas a hasty violet-black dab' (Woolf, 1992d: 4).[20] The hasty dab usurps a more patient and considered representation: life moves too quickly to be captured by art. Voice completes the triptych, as Archer calls out for his brother Jacob, splitting his name into syllables ('Ja-cob!'), who does not answer: 'The voice had an extraordinary sadness. Pure from all body, pure from all passion, going out into the world, solitary, unanswered, breaking against the rocks – so it sounded.' (4). 'So it sounded': the phrase announces not simply a crisis of representation and its verifiability, but one of the contingency of the subject and object of perception. 'So it sounded': the words may belong to the narrator or to the painter (presented as a third-person centre of consciousness). 'Sounded' is suspended between two meanings: the voice may have 'sounded' in the sense that it 'made this sound', or, the phrase may mean simply 'so it seemed'. Did the voice sound like this, and does the preceding description belong to the author? If it belongs to the author, then it is a god-like author who redeems each moment by perceiving it in its inner essence, even if its essence is one of forlornness rather than fullness; but the author is not a god, does not rise above time, is herself or himself a prisoner of moments, and art is not a substitute for religion, even if, like the unhappy consciousness of an earlier form of Christianity, it yearns to cross from humanity to divinity. This description may thus be located rather in the mind of the artist; it is he, or she, who as an adult and onlooker finds a cast of forlornness in the child's cry. And not merely in the cry: the forlornness is in the fallen-ness of sound itself, its sheer aesthetic disembodiment, its unrepeatable, irreversible singularity. As it goes out 'into the world' it can never go back: it is said to break on the rocks – rocks which are always a non-human presence in Woolf's work. Where would voice go back to? Does disembodied voice come from the soul, a notion never far away in Woolf's writing? Or is it the disembodied nature of voice which suggests the existence of soul, a suggestion belied by the truths of reason and therefore shot through with pathos – perhaps defining the very nature of the pathetic?

Walter Pater in *Marius the Epicurean*; James Joyce in 'The Dead'; and, later, Vladimir Nabokov in *The Real Life of Sebastian Knight*; each of these works shares with *Jacob's Room* the tradition of an aestheticism which figures the shift from the being-for-itself of subjectivity to a type of being-for-another which proves delusive. Each work repeats a version of the same pathos: it shows that the creation of the sense of another aims at transcendence and falls short; but the work cannot itself renounce and transcend the pathos and closure of a dialectic which remains suspended, unable to move on to the next stage. The type of consciousness concerned in each of the three works named above is conscious of its own inauthenticity; it is not satisfied with its own sensory perceptions which are transient, given over to death. This consciousness seeks solace in the image of another whose consciousness is not given over to death – a young man. However much the consciousness of the other is elusive, the attempt to build up an image of unreflective, unfallen consciousness is itself fallen: it can only work with the externals, with images of things, not with the consciousness or soul of the other which it perpetually seeks to frame. The elusiveness of the other is not then a matter of the simple unknowability of another consciousness: it is involved with the specific problem that the consciousness which seeks knowledge of the other does so from a position of reflective-ness which nostalgically seeks to return to its own unreflective state, a state in which the perception of things – the aesthetic – can matter in and for itself. Joyce's Gabriel Conroy reflects on Michael Furey, the young man who died for love of the woman to whom Gabriel is now married: 'Generous tears filled Gabriel's eyes. He had never felt like that towards any woman but he knew that such a feeling must be love.'[21] Joyce's silent irony – the snow is 'falling' while Gabriel's soul 'swoons' with its vision of universal death – puts a question mark against the generosity of the would-be angel Gabriel, who cannot achieve the God-like transcendence to which he aspires. Pater and Nabokov similarly point to the delusiveness of the willed pathos in the moment in which the reflective consciousness believes itself to have fixed and framed the capacity of the unreflective consciousness for love – whether the love of perception or the love of a woman: a connection familiar to romanticism since Keats.

Jacob's Room certainly belongs to this tradition and the above-named works can be read in dialogue with it. Yet Woolf's engage-ment with the politics and sociology of gender, and of the British state, and her concern with the history of the war as well as with her own biographical trajectory, make *Jacob's Room* and the works which stem from it extraordinary in their combination of aestheticism and socio-historical concern.

As presented in these opening pages, the child Jacob who cannot hear his name being called is discovering the world of life – not human life but the non-human life of the sea. Having heroically scaled a large rock – a notion of heroism which is a constant in these novels – Jacob finds a large crab which fascinates him. This animal is hard on the outside with its soft living part inside, the exact contrary of a living human. When he becomes scared of a couple he has discovered behind the rock who mutely return his stare (the situation is vaguely guilty, a loss of innocence), Jacob runs towards a 'large black woman' on the sand whom he believes to be his nanny. The 'nanny' turns out to be a rock with the sea lapping round it. At the point of panic, Jacob sees an animal skull, which he holds in his arms for comfort. This is a highly charged and often commentated moment. Jacob has learnt of an inhuman and inanimate world which does not reflect his desire for his mother – here, the nanny who is already a substitute. The black rock and the skull will from this point define his sensibility. Jacob will prefer the dead carapace of life to the living, maternal network of relationships, dead culture before living culture, and will enter a process of socialisation – education, family, state – which will confirm him in this preference. Moreover, the orientation towards things and heroic accomplishment will render him object-like, and make him all the more a fascinating object for others, the site of a consciousness which can apparently be for itself. This being-for-itself of consciousness is, however, founded on a denial of death. Moreover, those who seek to capture and frame this hardening male ego will be women, to whom this death-denying male egoism is unavailable. This situation prompts the question of whether Woolf in this novel and the works which follow advances and affirms a notion of the female network and feminine inter-subjectivity as an alternative to the delusions of the blind male ego, or whether in her work the fact of death which springs up in every moment of perception leads to a more blanket pessimism in which male and female worlds are mutually conditioning social facts, and neither can properly be affirmed over the other. This is not only a universal question but has a historical specificity. Jacob's family name is Flanders, the site of many battles in the war, and the death to which Jacob is already given over is not simply a necessary human fact: his actual death will be brought about by the war. The process by which men of certain classes are educated for war by Imperial British society, a process which builds on the ways in which the undeniable fact of death is mediated in the context of the family, is the complex topic of this novel and remains central to the works which follow.

Woolf famously rejected explicit symbolism, and thereby threw many commentators off the scent.[22] In fact, *Jacob's Room* establishes a fairly systematic symbolism which will continue to be developed throughout the following works. The symbolism of Jacob's name is particular to this novel, however, although its use signals Woolf's political purposes with some clarity. The Jacob of Genesis, whose name means 'deceiver', is the inheritor of God's blessing of Abraham who adopts the name Israel and becomes the founder of the nation of Israel. The blessing of God, passed on to him by his father Isaac, promises Jacob abundance and power:

> May God give you of the dew of the heaven,
> and of the fatness of the earth,
> and plenty of grain and wine.
> Let peoples serve you,
> and nations bow down to you.   (Genesis 27: 28–9)

Jacob's elder brother Esau is promised merely:

> By your sword shall you live,
>> and you shall serve your brother.   (Genesis 27: 40)

In the novel Jacob's elder brother is Archer, a rudimentary character, who is subtly associated with Esau. An archer, like Esau, is a hunter: Archer is supposed to remember the meat (Woolf, 1992a: 7), carries a knife – 'What a big knife for a small boy' (17) – and joins the navy while his brother goes to the centre of power, Cambridge. The knife is a consistent emblem of the penis and of militarism in subsequent novels. Jacob is not associated with the military but, towards the end of the novel, with rule itself. He is a sensitive young man, like his namesake, 'a quiet man living in tents' (Genesis 25: 27), and is given to reflection and poetry. The novel is a kind of *Bildungsroman* which asks how a sensitive boy is turned into the type of man who will enter the English ruling class and identify with its project of Empire. Although Jacob's departure for war cuts short his future career, Peter Walsh in *Mrs Dalloway*, James Ramsay in *To The Lighthouse*, and Perceval in *The Waves*, are further attempts by Woolf to analyse the same phenomenon.

Empire and war are Woolf's themes, and the perspective is that of the post-war, although Woolf draws abundantly on her own early experiences. Jacob is modelled in part on Thoby Stephen, who died of typhoid in 1906. By this time her mother, Julia, half-sister Stella, and father Sir Leslie Stephen were already dead, so Woolf's personal experience of loss has more to do with the period up to 1906 than with the war. However, her art is to map the loss of Thoby on to the war in order to examine her own bereavement in the context of that of many others. Jacob is in part based on Thoby, in part on Woolf herself – his favoured reading, interest in the Greeks, and voyage to Greece all reflect this. This signals an ambivalence about upper-class masculinity, and a regret over the mystery of its formation, which is also found in the later novels. There is a sense of nostalgia which accompanies the otherwise unremitting critique of the upper class which arises in part because the war has already begun to put an end to the self-confidence of this class. In fact, the depiction of Jacob and his Cambridge circle reflects Woolf's own initial exposure to Thoby's Cambridge friends, people like Clive Bell and Lytton Strachey who later became central to her life as part of what is now known as the Bloomsbury group.[23] The element of nostalgia in the treatment of ruling-class culture has a tendency in Woolf's work to blunt or suspend the critique. This is apparent in *Jacob's Room* in the treatment of the Cambridge group, where the author deploys a mocking rhetoric but without any sense of offering an alternative vision:

> Detest your own age. Build a better one. And to set that on foot read incredibly dull papers on Marlowe to your friends. For which purpose one must collate editions in the British Museum. One must do the thing oneself. Useless to trust to the Victorians, who disembowel, or to the living, who are mere publicists. The flesh and blood of the future depends entirely upon six young men. And as Jacob was one of them no doubt he looked a little regal and pompous as he turned his page ...(92)

As so much of Woolf's own development depended on her inter-actions with just such a circle of self-confident and able people the satire on Cambridge remains ambivalent.[24]

Jacob's Room is less a biography of Thoby than of his class. At the same time, its narrative method engages with the whole notion of biography as the principal narrative method of history. The narrative throughout juxtaposes the particular – usually as the world of women and of nature – with the universal and eternal, and asks whether life should be understood as a network of impinging momentary real-ities and consciousnesses rather than as a teleological narrative of the biographies of the great and a capitalised History. The parallel of Woolf's Jacob with his namesake in Genesis, and the genealogical narrative of the destiny of the chosen people, which is established in the opening pages, quickly if quietly indicates this theme. An essay called 'Does History consist of the Biographies of Great Men?' lies on the desk in the college room which gives the novel its title (31). The title of Jacob's essay reflects a common Victorian concern. Leslie Stephen edited the *Dictionary of National Biography* (1882–91), was author for Macmillan's English Men of Letters series, and produced the four-volume *Studies of a Biographer* (1898–1902). Woolf was aware too of the tradition of Tennyson's *In Memoriam,* an elegy for another Cambridge alumnus prematurely dead, and her later description of *To The Lighthouse* as an 'elegy' rather than a novel ambivalently aligns her work with this tradition.[25] In reply to the Victorian tradition, Lytton Strachey published *Eminent Victorians* in 1918, a debunking of the Victorians which goes beyond Woolf in its hostility to the past, but which anticipates some of Woolf's method in its introduction:

> It is not by the direct method of a scrupulous narration that the explorer of the past can hope to depict that singular epoch. If he is wise, he will

adopt a subtler strategy. He will attack his subject in unexpected places; he will fall upon the flank or the rear; he will shoot a sudden, revealing searchlight into obscure recesses, hitherto undivined. He will row out over that great ocean of material, and lower down into it, here and there, a little bucket, which will bring up into the light of day some characteristic specimen, from those are depths to be examined with a careful curiosity.[26]

Woolf's method owes little to Strachey, but it reflects these priorities, and Strachey's metaphors of searchlight and sea are frequently echoed in *Jacob's Room* and subsequent works, especially as the lighthouse which makes its first appearance early in *Jacob's Room* (6), casting its intermittent light among the variety of other lamps which illuminate the moments of this text.

The emphasis on the moment of illumination can be connected to other developments in Modernist literature: Pound, Eliot and Proust all suggest suitable analogies. What is striking in the method of *Jacob's Room* is that it does not presume to illuminate its object by way of revealing its entirety in a condensed form, and many of the moments which the narrative features are only obscurely related to Jacob's development. Later novels seek more continuity, but it is important not to regard this book merely as an experimental failure. The narrative is chronological, following Jacob from childhood, through University and travels to his abrupt departure for war. It focuses on his relationship with women, his mother and a series of unrealised love affairs. The emphasis is on the peripheries of his life, that part of his life which he comes to treat as peripheral, as he increasingly rejects the contingent, everyday world of women and orients himself towards eternity. The pattern, which is repeated in the later novels, contrasts teleological ruling-class masculinity to the evanescent lived time of women and organic nature. Some sections of the narrative either neutrally narrate conversations and incidents, requiring the reader to reconstruct their significance at least to the degree that they have a direct narrative or symbolic significance. Elsewhere, the authorial voice is present, but oscillates, as I have outlined above, between mastery and contingency. Those passages which take care to embed the author in the contingency of events ring more true to the intention of denying authorial mastery than other passages in which the author breaks the frame and directly addresses the reader on the subject of the novel's general narrative philosophy in an essayistic style. These passages, of a kind which Woolf never entirely eliminates from her work, seem flawed both because they break the more sophisticated narrative tact of other sections, and because they do not fully account for the strategies of the novel. They are perhaps intended as a half-way house for the nervous reader, and their tone, which depends too much on lyrical plangency and a sentimental 'we', too closely mimics the Victorian tradition which Woolf's fiction in its Modernist elements is keen to challenge. In fact, this ambivalence between the companionable and discursive Victorian author and the detached and unsentimental Modernist author is a recurrent tension in Woolf's work and one which sets her apart from the Modernism of Joyce, Pound and Eliot. As the detachment of masculinity is the central concern of this novel just such an ambivalence might be expected. Jacob's obsession with the monumentality and atemporality of Greek art, especially sculpture, might easily be read as a critique of the masculinist springs of the imagism of Pound and Hulme, although Woolf's own interest in the Greeks, and the involvement of H.D. as a founding figure of Imagism would necessarily complicate such an account. In terms of the reception of the novel, the explicit commentary in the novel on its own methods has led some critics to over-emphasise its abstract Modernist intentions in terms of the undefinability of character, at the expense of noting how and why it is the male character which escapes from the network of knowability. One such passage reads as follows:

> It seems that a profound, impartial, and absolutely just opinion of our fellow-creatures is utterly unknown. Either we are men, or we are women. Either we are cold, or we are sentimental. Either we are young, or growing old. In any case life is but a procession of shadows, and God knows why it is that we embrace them so eagerly, and see them depart with such anguish, being shadows. And why, if this and much more than this is true, why are we yet surprised in the window corner by a sudden vision that the young man in the chair is of all things in the world the most real, the most solid, the best known to us – why indeed? For the moment after we know nothing about him.   (60)

This passage, and others in a similar vein, certainly confirm a reading of Woolf's work in terms of the framing of the moment.[27] There are, however, no comparable passages which make explicit the thematic of the orientation of men towards eternity, and the connection between this and the British ruling class project. This account has to be derived from a reading of what I have already claimed is the consistent symbolism developed in *Jacob's Room* and through the following works.

The main elements in this symbolism are rock, organic nature, the sea and light. Jacob is from the outset associated with rock. His namesake in Genesis goes to sleep with his head on a rock and has a vision of a ladder leading from earth to heaven. This is echoed in the novel not only by the consistent rock imagery but by the repeated image of a person lying on her or his back looking up at the sky, and by the motif of men looking at the stars through a telescope (49). The rock thus signifies permanence in a twofold way: as quasi-eternal in itself and as a vantage point for surveying the universe and hence universality. In *Jacob's Room* there is no dialectic which connects the particular and the universal, a relationship which for women is a matter for fluid speculation but not the object of a choice: 'Sandra, floating from the particular to the universal, lay back in a trance' (134). Jacob instead is depicted as opting out of particularity in a process which is in part social – his institutional education and failed relationships with women – and in part mysterious, something which the novel in its constant allusions to the unknowability of character programmatically leaves outside the frame. Universality is in any case by definition outside the contingency of the frame, and Jacob's escape from contingency will always, on this reading, escape the contingency of representation. His movement to universality is perceived both ironically and as a teasing and fascinating reality – the young man in the chair is after all said to be 'the most real, the most solid' thing known to us. The ironies of course are abundant: when Jacob steps out of the frame of the novel and into the war it is death not transcendence which awaits him; the ladder which connected heaven and earth in Jacob's vision is an impossibility in a secular world and cannot be substituted by culture; the British Empire, which believes itself like Israel to be favoured by God and seeks to monumentalise itself like the Greeks, is itself about to be delivered its death blow by the war (at the time of the novel's publication the independence movement in India and the war of independence in Ireland were stark evidence of the end of the Victorian project).

The tendency to monumentalisation of this decadent culture is a constant topic in Woolf's novels. Jacob's namesake in Genesis is forever erecting pillars, to thank God but also to mark territory. *Jacob's Room* makes much use of gravestones and of the monuments in Whitehall: Nelson's column is given pride of place in a culture based on the monumental memorialisation of space, monuments which, in their psychological effects, their suggestion of an eternity of British domination, are crucial to the maintenance of imperial ideology. It becomes clear in *Mrs Dalloway*, set after the war, that the commemoration of the war and of the war dead by the erection throughout the country of cenotaphs, is at the front of Woolf's mind and would have been very present in the minds of contemporary readers.[28] The process by which young men are turned into a name on a stone is extended by Woolf in the metaphorical economy of this novel into a depiction of the tendency of this class of young men to assimilate themselves to stone, to become statue-like; so Jacob becomes 'statuesque' and 'eyeless' like a statue in the British Museum (149), 'monolithic [...] like a British Admiral' (145), and in a crucial gesture of the novel finds himself, as he sits under the eternity of the Acropolis on a 'drum of marble', spontaneously engaging the question of empire: 'after reading a page he put his thumb in his [guide]-book. Why not rule countries in the way they should be ruled? And he read again.' (131). This moment is seemingly spontaneous, isolated and unmotivated, but the novel shows that it is thoroughly prepared for, the consummation of a process which turns a sensitive boy into an ideologue of Empire who identifies with eternity, and believes that he can rule from the perspective of the universal a world given over to irredeemable contingency.

What Jacob believes to be his subjective values are the product of a system which literally seeks to embody itself as eternity. His becoming statue-like is the final moment of the system's embodiment of itself in him. Jacob the deceiver is deceived.[29] Woolf's novels are famed for their critique of British cultural institutions, and the rock symbolism extends into her examination of these institutions as stone buildings. The description of the British Museum in this novel, which Woolf would pick up again in *A Room of One's Own*, is central in its suggest-iveness about the relationship between official culture and monumentalisation:

> Jacob stood beneath the porch of the British Museum. It was raining. Great Russell Street was glazed and shining – here yellow, here, outside the chemist's, red and pale and blue. [...]
>
> The rain poured down. The British Museum stood in one solid immense mound, very pale, very sleek in the rain [...]. The vast mind was sheeted with stone; and each compartment in the depths of it was safe and dry [...].
>
> Stone lies solid over the British Museum, as bone lies cool over the visions and heat of the brain. (94)

Inside, 'Plato continues his dialogue', while outside there is a woman 'who has come home drunk and cries all night long, "Let me in! Let me in!"' (94). Stone is likened to the skull, the eternal brain contrasted to living perception, the world of masculine privilege contrasted to that of the excluded, underprivileged woman. The rain outside belongs to changing nature, the coloured impressions it creates for the eye are contrasted with the monumental stone which houses the eternal mind.

Rock and stone, then, have an important symbolic role in this novel. The critique which the novel offers is relatively self-evident and decisive. However, the stone mind is not unambiguously rejected, nor is the natural world unequivocally affirmed, even if this is the world of women and the excluded. The problem which Woolf's model generates is apparent in the symbolism which, in its rejection of any dialectical or other connection, displays a contrast which is too net between the eternity of rock/stone and the evanescence of nature, whether as rainwater, cloud, wind, or, as I will explore here, as plants and flowers. The novel frequently deploys flowers as symbols of the transience of nature. Their evanescence is often in evidence. The single leaf does duty in this and other novels as the symbol of the irreducible particular (see, for example, p. 6). Women are associated with the particular realm of nature; Clara Durrant, later to be excluded from Jacob's affections, is seen crushing a verbena leaf and snipping a vine leaf (49, 51). More apparent in *Mrs Dalloway*, the moment of perception of the beauty of flowers represents the moment of aesthetic perception *par excellence.* However, Woolf is not a poet of nature, and nature in this novel has a schematic presence. Although the novel structurally asserts the seasonal shifts of nature against the would-be rock-like perspectives of eternity, the seasons are curiously ill-observed, so lilacs 'droop' in April (11); tulips thrive belatedly in August (146) despite their premature appearance alongside daffodils in January (98); butterflies abound in April (107); cherries are plentiful in May (29); and in a revision of natural history a toad is classified as an insect (25). These are not simply errors (which Woolf acknowledged[30]) but signal that nature as a symbolic presence is more important in this novel than any actual observation of nature – a seeming paradox since the whole point of the organic/inorganic opposition is to assert the primacy of the particularity of the former, what the novel gestures towards in a sentimental flourish as 'the indescribable agitation of life' (143).

The connection of women with evanescent nature and the complex interactions of life does present a problem. Some commentators have identified, and identified with, what they construe as Woolf's celebration of excluded, working-class women in their bodily, working lives, and affirmation of the network of women's communications (conversations and letters) against monolithic, male, logocentric culture.[31] However, there is little sense in these novels of any alternative political and social reality for women. Woolf herself eschewed women's organisations, disliked political meetings and explicitly rejected suffragism.[32] American commentators have at times considered Woolf a socialist feminist and a Marxist,[33] but despite her Labour Party connections, it is difficult to discover in these works a logic of female emancipation. Working-class women appear to be part of nature; they are viewed from the outside; at times it is clear that they are in pain but this pain is never articulated, nor is the potential for its removal hinted at; they are always isolated, never collective; they are present like Eliot's eternal footman, marking the passing vanities of the ruling class. Although Woolf speculates in the pages of *Jacob's Room*, and more famously in her essay 'Mr Bennett and Mrs Brown', about what it would mean to give narrative shape to the lives of such women, she never seeks to do so; nor does she speculate about how the narratives of such women's lives might be altered in their course. Women in *Jacob's Room* of whatever class stand by and suffer; their networks of communication do not communicate very much; their interactions concern not politics and society but a suffering and separation which these very interactions serve only to confirm. Alternatives for women were available and known to Woolf: the older feminism of the pre-war suffragist movement; Trade Unionism; the more muted varieties of post-war feminism; even the sexual reform movement. The neglect of the various collective possibilities must be construed in her novels as determinate rather than accidental, and reflects a pessimism about human possibility in general, as well as about the potential of women's lives. If everything is already given over to death in a world unredeemed by God then the blessed are not those who are locked helplessly in contingency but those who strive towards an illusory transcendence, with the blind assurance of youth which Jacob possesses in abundance, and which so irritates others (such as 'Miss Julia Hedge, the feminist' [91]).

Woolf's most famous symbol, the lighthouse, symbolises and eternalises the opposition of contingent particularity and the universal. The sea is contingent, the tower a stone erection, the intermittent light is the subjective consciousness which enters into temporary relationships of mutual illumination with the objects of reality.

However, the contingency of the sea is qualified by the fact that while the waves may vary, and the works of Shakespeare, for example (39), may disappear into them, the underlying continuity of life remains a fixity. It is this prehistoric continuity which the novel, in almost Jungian fashion, is concerned to assert. We must grasp not history but 'life'. The repeated association of working women with the sea in this symbolic economy returns them to a substratum of existence where, it seems likely, they are expected and desired to remain, albeit shrouded in a mist of eternal wisdom: 'The wise old woman, having fixed her eyes upon the sea, once more withdrew' (44). The woman in question is Mrs Pascoe: 'her face was not soft, sensual, or lecherous, but hard, wise, wholesome rather, signifying in a room full of sophisticated people the flesh and blood of life' (44). Clearly, although its critique of ruling class masculinity is strikingly articulated, informed as it is by its proximity and the author's sympathy, the symbolic schema which Woolf begins to employ in *Jacob's Room* tends to freeze and aestheticise its own social situation, and the particular history with which it is otherwise so passionately engaged.

Beneficiary of Empire: Mrs Dalloway

Jacob's Room thus shapes a symbolic schema in which broader questions of culture and society are framed as aspects of the problematic of the aesthetic in a universe of transience. *Mrs Dalloway* (1925) advances in time to the post-war. Its focus remains principally the condition of the upper class and its institutions, although an attempt is made to extend the social range further. The narrative method is more tightly focussed (even in its deviations) than that of *Jacob's Room,* and the action is restricted to one day, following the pattern of *Ulysses* which is frequently echoed. Influenced by Proust,[34] Woolf uses memory flashbacks, what she calls her 'tunnelling process', to extend the sense of psychological depth, a change not only to the method of *Jacob's Room* but also to its perspective, which was radically anti-Bergsonian, contrasting the vividness of the present with the abstraction of male teleology, bypassing altogether Bergson's notion of the experience of time not as immediate sensation but as duration. Duration, the sedimentation of lived experiences through-out time, becomes the controlling notion of how human existence is shaped and must understand itself in this novel, as well as its principal narrative assumption. Although *Mrs Dalloway* will repeat those gestures of *Jacob's Room* which showed human reality as a network of interconnected and overlapping perceptions (although not as a transparent, discursive intersubjectivity), the narrative shifts are more controlled, more easily grasped as parts of the whole, while the memory flashbacks are rigorously harnessed to the novel's psychological portrayal.

Mrs Dalloway therefore on the face of it looks more like a novel. That is, it reins in the Modernist discontinuity and narrative scepticism of its predecessor, and addresses the tasks of the realist novel as understood by Lukács.[35] However, for all its emphasis on modern London, the project of this novel is not documentary. Although the social status of the leading figures is important, the narrative avoids those material descriptions – of houses, furniture, clothes – which Woolf claimed dogged the work of the superseded Edwardian novelists. What it does have is a theory of character, or rather, *at least one* theory of character. It is usually argued that Woolf read Freud late, but that she acquired a general knowledge of some of his precepts from conversation.[36] (It is even claimed that she evolved a version of Freudian and Kleinian ideas virtually independently.) However it might have got there, it is certain that *Mrs Dalloway* utilises a notion of character which is generally in line with the emphasis in psychoanalysis on formative scenes and early sexual experience. The Kleinian element is very apparent in the flashback which concerns the intrusion of the masculine principle into the bond between daughter and (symbolic) mother.[37] Thus, the famous chaste kiss between the young Clarissa and her friend Sally Seton, spoilt by the arrival of her suitor Peter Walsh, all narrated as a flashback from many years ago, now compellingly reads as a daydream in which the scene of the daughter's severance from the mother (here mother-substitute) is revisited. The social necessity of heterosexual marriage displaces the lesbian potential of Clarissa and of the average female subject in general, and we can understand from this loss of the maternal body Clarissa's unfulfillment, her physical coldness and her choice of the distant Richard Dalloway, now a Conservative MP, as husband, as against the progressive Peter Walsh, whose desire for intimacy with her threatened the image of lost intimacy with the mother. Richard Dalloway poses no such threat and leaves Clarissa to her own sphere, the house (while his is the House), the party (he has his Party), and to her own bed, where she can still feel the after-image of her lost chastity.

One notion of character central to the novel, therefore, depends on a version of psychoanalysis, and on a narrative method which uses the flashback of recollection as a type of daydream in which formative or highly symbolic scenes are recalled. On this account character would not be an orderly succession of events, the series of accomplishments which comprise the 'great man', but a series of decisive and mostly early events which determine the trajectory of character. This character, however, is internally both discontinuous and repetitive: it does not possess itself as self-unfolding narrative development, but compulsively repeats, and consequently mires itself in, its own unpleasure. Alongside this notion of character psychology, *Mrs Dalloway* continues the critical account of British ruling-class institutions begun in *Jacob's Room*, an analysis which, as we have seen, projects a quite different notion, understood in largely symbolic terms, of the relationship between individual and society. The effect is of a complexity in which neither model can be reduced to the other. The resulting account of a woman shaped by norms which she has lacked the imagination to challenge or deflect is painful and almost unredeemed. Woolf persistently aligned herself with the tradition of Jane Austen, and a third notion of character is present here which is absent from *Jacob's Room*: the character of the novelist who must provide a point of identification and enjoyment for the reader. In *Emma*, Austen famously depicted a heroine 'whom no one but myself will much like', and Woolf follows and indeed exceeds this example with a vain, snobbish, uncreative and self-pitying heroine, the internal product of an Imperial system which she endorses and of which she is the beneficiary, but whom the reader is nevertheless asked to find *not all bad*. An earlier generation of American critics considered Clarissa a 'queen' and source of regeneration in the post-war world.[38] Not only does the metaphor ignore Woolf's clearly signposted critique of the Royal Family, but these attempts to construct an affirmative version of Clarissa ignore that the reader is quite deliberately challenged to find anything to affirm given full knowledge of the facts.

As in *Jacob's Room*, the pessimism of this novel is rooted in its unblinking recognition of death, and its assertion, as in the previous work, that death is central to the whole edifice of Imperial culture. The symbolism of the work is revived here from the first lines: 'Mrs. Dalloway said she would buy the flowers herself'. The servants are busy, Clarissa will help them, and the day is inspiring: 'what a morning – fresh as if issued to children on a beach' (Woolf, 1992b: 3). Clarissa is thus connected with flowers and the immediacy of day – early holidays in Cornwall as well as the Jungian symbolism of the sea as the origin of life and a general perspective derived from the English romantic poets inform this choice – but there is an added element: economics. For just as her husband as a member of government is in charge of the national economy, Clarissa is in charge of the domestic economy (that is, the original meaning of the word). Beauty is the principal commodity of this economy, whether as flowers and gardens or as the hats and gloves with which she is continually associated. Economy means not just the organisation of money but of labour, and Clarissa's goodwill in wishing to help her overworked servants is mitigated by the inevitable fact that it is she who overworks them. Her willingness to help those who provide her with services may be read as the utopian expression of a desire for co-operation which might be realised in a classless society. This is a class society, however, and the novel shows how even those who provide the services assent to their role, and so the servant Lucy admires in Clarissa that which she admires in herself, her ability to organise an event, give a centre to dispersal. The party, in Lucy's view, gives a sense 'of something achieved', an achievement in Clarissa's mind not of material organisation but of giving a focus to a collective life surrounded by death. To Lucy's self-oppressive way of thinking, Clarissa is 'the mistress of silver, of linen, of china', a definition which on the one hand stops at the material fact and misses the more intangible goals of the party, but on the other signals the immersion of this life in the deadness of things, as well as Clarissa's own immersion in commodification.

There is an important schematic tension in the person of Clarissa, between the moment of beauty and connection in all its transience, and the thing-like nature of the culture to which she belongs and propagates. *Jacob's Room* divided these functions between thing-like Jacob and the women associated with flowers and sea. The result was to make Jacob ever more mysterious and statuesquely impenetrable. *Mrs Dalloway* combines these features in one figure, and in so doing the life-affirming and the death-oriented confront each other not across class/gender divides but within one person. The novel sets itself the task of giving a psychology to a ruling-class woman and eschews the easy polarisation of the earlier novel which had simply equated masculinity and class-rule on the one hand, and femininity and subordination on the other. The figure of Clarissa is therefore more than an attempt to map a 'real' person or psychology, and more too than an attempt to create a self-deceiving successor to Austen's Emma (although this aspiration is clearly signalled: 'her

only gift was knowing people almost by instinct, she thought...' [9]).
Rather, continuing to privilege a Wordsworthian notion of the loss of
childhood sensibility in the process of acculturation (alongside a
psychoanalytic model!), the novel examines what it means for
sensitivity to the moment – which continues in this text to occupy the
position of the greatest human good – to exist inside a life which is
formed from the outside by the demands of a dead culture. So, while
Jacob embodied an externality without internality, this novel adopts
a model in which internal demands, formed in childhood and
possibly archaic in nature, coexist uneasily with external demands
which are internalised in a thing-like way.

It is Clarissa's former suitor, Peter Walsh, who notes her thing-like
nature; she is cold, wooden, impenetrable, 'like iron, like flint, rigid
up the backbone' (70). Those passages which identify her passion
for the moment tend to be a combination of authorial comment and
third-person centre of consciousness narrative. As in *Jacob's Room*
there is a tendency to essayistic lyrical affirmation: 'Heaven knows
why one loves it so, how one sees it so, making it up, building it
round one, tumbling it, creating it every moment afresh [...]' (4).
This is given as Clarissa's thought. At other times her voice is
seamlessly overtaken by a rhapsodic authorial voice which invites the
reader to share a perceived truth:

> So on a summer's day waves collect, overbalance, and fall; and the whole
> world seems to be saying 'that is all' more and more ponderously, until
> even the heart in the body which lies in the sun on the beach says too,
> That is all. Fear no more, says the heart, committing its burden to some
> sea, which sighs collectively for all sorrows, and renews, begins, collects,
> lets fall. And the body alone listens to the passing bee; the wave breaking;
> the dog barking, far away barking and barking.   (43)

By contrast, Clarissa's affirmation of her own capacity to feel the
moment is shown to be already locked into a class economy, viewed
as a currency with which she can pay back the debt of her social
dependence: 'one must pay back from this secret deposit of exquisite
moments, she thought', pay back alike to servants, husband, and
'dogs and canaries', although what it is that must be paid back
Clarissa does not at this point articulate to herself (31–2).

It is often affirmed that Clarissa's limited triumph in the novel is
over her own being 'half in love with easeful death', the urge, as
expressed in the passage above, to return her identity to the primal,
maternal element. Unlike the shell-shocked soldier, Septimus
Warren Smith, whose narrative parallels hers in this novel although

they never meet, Clarissa does not commit suicide. At one level, the novel is committed to a particular form of social critique of the ruling class and, unlike *Jacob's Room* which was entirely retrospective, it gestures towards the portrayal of a specifically post-war history (a bankrupt ruling class blindly dedicated to business as usual in the face of national and international changes) and of a post-war London characterised by motor cars, omnibuses, the recent fad for sky-writing, and a new *joie de vivre*. In another aspect, and in contradiction to this, the novel is pessimistic, representing human life in terms of the eternal vocabulary of the elements and the universal fact of death. This combination of contradictory structures may be thought of as a facet of the novel (hence a representation or construct which could just as easily be replaced by another) or as the manifestation of an unmasterable and irreducible truth for which the novel provides a structural analogue. However it is seen, it appears to offer the reader interpretative options, and leads to the creation of contrasting models of the author as an aesthete or a socialist feminist. I think that the socialist element in Woolf's work is very much in abeyance in *Mrs Dalloway*, which continues to see social questions in terms of an existential model which remains rudimentary precisely because it over-valorises the moment of authentic sense-perception, and I think that view can be evidenced with reference to the treatment of the contemporary in the novel: in the depiction of the shell-shock or neurasthenia of Septimus Warren Smith as a false redeemer, in the portrayal of lower-class women as archaic and eternal, and in the analysis of the class envy or what Nietzsche calls *ressentiment* of socialism and philanthropy in the figures of Peter Walsh and Miss Kilman. The construction of the novel, the elusiveness of its point of view which is not identical with that of any one protagonist, allows for a different reading but not, I think, for the contrary claims: that Septimus is a redemptive figure, that working class women are viewed as the source and site of social change, or that the *déclassé* socialism and feminism of Walsh and Kilman is motivated by a commitment to justice with its sources in genuine fellow-feeling combined with pure intellectual endeavour.

The reviewer of *Mrs Dalloway* for *The Calendar of Modern Letters* seems not to have noticed its protagonist at all for he does not mention her. The review is more concerned to set the record straight on the author's ability to portray male characters. It criticises the figure of Peter Walsh, a man in a mid-life crisis who fears that he is a 'failure', has fallen in love with a married woman, and is seen on the day of the novel following an unknown young woman in the street in an attempt to capture the sexual adventurousness of youth, and fiddling agitatedly with a penknife which he keeps in his trouser pocket. This mildly masturbatory middle-aged man, a literary relation of Joyce's Leopold Bloom, triggers an anxious response in the reviewer. However, the portrait of Septimus Warren Smith is found to be a plausible and sympathetic account of a shell-shock victim. In retrospect, this anxious reviewer seems to have got it the wrong way round, for while Walsh's conflicts and self-deception have become the stuff of the characteristically modern novel, the neurasthenia or madness of Septimus seems like an elaborate confection, on the one hand drawing on Woolf's own experience of manic depressive illness,[39] on the other reviving the opposition established in *Jacob's Room* between female existence in the moment and the male desire for teleological transcendence. If the novel can be thought of in terms of a key ideological model, it could be seen as rejecting the impulse to an absolute transcendence of Septimus in favour of the desire to create central points or events in disparity of Clarissa. *Jacob's Room* did not allow for this middle way, although it did advance the sea as a metaphor for the underlying connection of the collective life of humanity in particular and of organic existence in general. So it is that the topic of connection occupies the mind and mentalities of both Clarissa and Septimus. While the former takes a worldly and realistic view, the latter, tormented by the vision of a nature which appears to speak to him in incomprehensible tongues, has a vision of universal love and believes himself to be the founder of a new religion, indeed, the redeemer of a world which cannot share his vision of interconnectedness:

> Look the unseen bade him, the voice which now communicated with him who was the greatest of mankind, Septimus, lately taken from life to death, the Lord who had come to renew society, who lay like a coverlet, a snow blanket smitten only by the sun, for ever unwasted, suffering for ever, the scapegoat, the eternal sufferer, but he did not want it [...].(27)

In his vision, human contingency, the isolation of the moment, is the origin of an evil which must be transcended: 'For the truth is (let her ignore it) that human beings have neither kindness, nor faith, nor charity beyond what serves to increase the pleasure of the moment' (98). The 'her' bracketed from Septimus's consideration is his Italian wife Lucrezia, of whose suffering on his account he is unaware, the novel's point being to contrast his inability to identify with the particular moment or person in his vision of redemptive transcendence with the female immersion in contingency: two contrasting versions of 'love' are offered, of which the latter is preferred. As with the flowers of *Jacob's Room*, which are offered as symbols of the particular rather than examples of it, the figure of Septimus is more symbolic than realistic, although the portrayal of his treatment by doctors owes something to historical fact as well as to the author's own experiences with the profession. However, the symbolism associated with Septimus is itself a matter of historical fact. As well as fitting the map of the teleological male death-drive which Septimus shares with Jacob, Septimus's Christ identification also recalls a *locus classicus* of the poetry of the war which saw the young dead soldier as a Christ figure and implicitly called the women of the race to fulfil the role of the Virgin in the *pietà*.[40] This is the role which Lucrezia must fill for Septimus, mourning the living death of post-war man; it is the role which Clarissa, also identified with the Virgin, will not fulfil. In a much-commented scene, Clarissa retreats from her party to a back room to consider the death of Septimus, whom she does not know. She decides not to mourn him, but to return to the party and to the network of life:

> The clock began striking. The young man had killed himself; but she did not pity him; with the clock striking the hour, one, two, three, she did not pity him, with all this going on. [...S]he repeated, and the words came to her, Fear no more the heat of the sun. She must go back to them. But what an extraordinary night! She felt somehow very like him – the young man who had killed himself. She felt glad that he had done it; thrown it away while they went on living. (204)

Clarissa feels no pity, will not be the Virgin in the *pietà*. The refusal concerns not only Septimus, but all the war dead who were seen in the Victorian optic of the culture of war poetry as Christ figures, sacrificed for the good of the nation. The refusal to mourn, however, does not take the form of an assertion of the death-denying hedonism of the 1920s. The mournful words from *Cymbeline* are an acceptance of death but become the motto of Clarissa's determination to live, and her feeling of being in some way like Septimus makes this refusal to mourn an act not of betrayal but of solidarity, a perception, in her own opinion at least, of an underlying unity beneath the divisions of class, gender and historical experience.

In her *Diary* Woolf described the intention for her work in progress 'to criticise the social system, & to show it at work, at its most intense'. The criticism is not restricted to the ruling class and its party. The pessimistic image which Woolf conjures is of a society which has a need for an unavailable centre: 'Death was an attempt to communicate, people feeling the impossibility of reaching the centre which mystically evaded them' (Woolf, 1975–80: 202). Septimus commits suicide in defiance of the contingency of his own life. Others, as if unaware of their radical contingency, invest with mystery the dominant institutions, thereby reinforcing them: capitalism thus titillates with the sky-writing advertisement which all interpret differently, and an important-looking car with an invisible occupant inspires differing varieties of reverence among bystanders, who variously imagine that it contains the King, the Queen, or the newly fashionable figure of the Prince of Wales. These uninterpretable signs (writing and car) are interpreted differently by each viewer, and are therefore revealed not to have a fixed, transcendent meaning. However, these episodes do not merely exemplify a Modernist point about multiple perspectives and the unavailability of a single, truth-bearing point of view. Rather, they portray a general deference within English culture as a desire in consciousness itself for a central and collective image, a role which, in a sceptical age, God can no longer fulfil. On the one hand, the novel satirically exposes royalism as false consciousness, and mocks its quasi-religious role in the ideology of Empire and war. On the other hand, it deploys a reified notion of consciousness, as always tending to seek such a false centre, and disallows a more fundamental questioning as to what produces consciousness and how it might be produced differently. Opponents of ruling ideology are therefore not seen in terms of their possession of insights which can unmask ideology or change the system, rather, their desire to unmask and overthrow the ruling class is seen in terms of the resentment of privilege in the context of a hypocritical dependence on or fascination with the dominant class. The socialist and would-be writer Peter Walsh is described in terms of his complicity as he admires a parade up Whitehall:

> on they marched, past him, past every one, in their steady way, as if one will worked legs and arms uniformly, and life, with its varieties, its irreticences, had been laid under a pavement of monuments and wreaths and drugged into a stiff yet staring corpse by discipline. One had to respect it; one might laugh; but one had to respect it, he thought. There they go, thought Peter Walsh, pausing at the edge of the pavement; and all the exalted statues, Nelson, Gordon, Havelock, the black, the spectacular images of great soldiers looking ahead of them, as if they too

had made the same renunciation (Peter Walsh felt he, too, had made it, the great renunciation), trampled under the same temptations, and achieved at length a marble stare. But the stare Peter Walsh did not want for himself in the least; though he could respect it in others. He could respect it in boys. They don't know the troubles of the flesh yet, he thought [...].   (Woolf, 1992b: 56)

This passage is shortly followed by one which displays his acceptance of the panorama of class society as he admires the bustle in Regents Park:

> Coming as he did from a resectable Anglo-Indian family which for at least three generations had administered the affairs of a continent (it's strange, he thought, what a sentiment I have about that, disliking India, and empire, and army as he did), there were moments when civilisation, even of this sort, seemed dear to him as a personal possession; moments of pride in England [...]. What with one thing and another, the show was really very tolerable; and he would sit down in the shade and smoke. (60)

The first passage harks back to the symbolic analysis of the formation of military character in *Jacob's Room*. The second confirms the first in its depiction of the shallowness and hypocrisy of upper-middle-class progressive thought.

The analysis of the relationship between class and politics in the figure of Peter Walsh is in itself observant and convincing. That of Miss Kilman, the philanthropist and recent Christian convert who, to Clarissa's dismay, has befriended her daughter Elisabeth, is less persuasive. In a series of descriptions echoing Dickens's depiction of 'telescopic philanthropy' in *Bleak House*, Woolf creates an implausible figure whose hatred of the ruling class and concern for distant nations is motivated by sheer resentment of the good fortune of others and a repressed identification with the rich, combining to form a character unable to enjoy her own life or enhance that of those around her. Clarissa is the focus of Miss Kilman's resentment:

> But Miss Kilman did not hate Mrs Dalloway. Turning her large gooseberry-coloured eyes upon Clarissa, observing her small pink face, her delicate body, her air of freshness and fashion, Miss Kilman felt, Fool! Simpleton! You who have known neither sorrow nor pleasure; who have trifled your life away! And there arose in her an overmastering desire to overcome her; to unmask her. If she could have felled her it would have eased her. (137)

This satirical figure, the least lifelike and least sympathetically treated in the whole novel, is present as the representative of the whole self-educated lower-middle class. Her relationship with Clarissa mirrors some of Woolf's own difficulties in dealing with politically articulate and socially active working women.[41]

In Peter Walsh and Doris Kilman the roots of any articulate alternative to the ruling class are put into question. These figure are in any case carefully segregated from the working-class itself, and working-class women are brought on stage only to be identified with archaic life and its symbolic element the sea:

> Hadn't Mrs Dempster always longed to see foreign parts? She had a nephew, a missionary. It [the sky-writing plane] soared and shot. She always went on the sea at Margate, not out o' sight of land, but she had no patience with women who were afraid of water.   (30)

The centre point of this symbolic schema is reached in the figure of the old woman singing outside the Tube station: 'A sound interrupted him; a frail quivering sound, a voice bubbling up without direction, vigour, beginning or end, [...] the voice of no age or sex, the voice of an ancient spring spouting from the earth[...]' (88). She has sung here through the ages, since London was a swamp, a song of 'love which has lasted a million years' (89). She is a pump, fertilising the land, an 'eternal spring'; she once walked 'where the sea flows now' (90). The song itself consists of uninterpretable sounds. The novel seems content to locate the poor in this clumsy, sentimental and politically regressive symbolic framework.

Imperial Family Values and the Quasi-Transcendence of Art: To The Lighthouse

The symbolic framework, adapted and developed from *Jacob's Room*, within which *Mrs Dalloway* articulates its critique of contemporary political institutions arrives at an uncritical impasse, and it seems logical that *To The Lighthouse* should revert in substance to the pre-war era, mirroring contemporary events at a greater remove.

The plot and structure of this novel are well known to many readers but I offer a brief outline for those who are less familiar. The narrative concerns the Ramsay family and their house guests and is set at their holiday home in the Hebrides. Mr and Mrs Ramsay are modelled on Woolf's parents, Leslie and Julia, and the house is modelled on the Stephens' holiday home in St Ives, Cornwall, where the family holidayed regularly until 1895. In 1905 Virginia revisited the house during a holiday at nearby Carbis Bay,[42] and the structure of the novel, which focuses on two days ten years apart, reflects this pattern. The autobiographical content is heavily reworked in the novel, as is apparent from the shift in time scale from 1895–1905 to something like 1910–20 (no actual dates are given). The ten years between the two occasions is treated in the much celebrated central section of the novel, 'Time Passes', which describes the house and environs during the absence of the central characters, documenting their activities only in brief parentheses. The shift in time makes the war, and more recent political changes, form the new backdrop to the novel and enables Woolf to connect her own 'elegy' for her family with the social and political topics of the earlier novel. The novel is an elegy, because it deals with loss, principally the death of Mrs Ramsay, along with a daughter, Prue, who dies in childbirth, and a son, Andrew, who is killed in the war. Mrs Ramsay is centrally present in the first section and centrally absent in the third and final section, while Mr Ramsay, their son James and daughter Cam are the main family figures present in both sections. Woolf does not position herself in the novel as one of the children. The narrative utilises the third-person centre of consciousness method of *Mrs Dalloway*, with more rapid changes of perspective, and the identification of an authorial position is a matter of deduction for the reader. However, Woolf does go some way to providing a focus in the person of Lily Briscoe, a guest centrally present in each section, whose amateur interest in painting and advanced aesthetic ideas connect her to both Virginia and her sister Vanessa. In the depiction of Mrs Ramsay the novel continues to explore the idea of woman as social and symbolic centre begun in *Mrs Dalloway*, and like Clarissa, Mrs Ramsay is an ambiguous figure, not least because of her complicity with the patriarchal family structure and hence with the whole Imperial project. Patriarchal culture is examined through Mr Ramsay and his male guests, whose arrogance has much in common with Thoby's Cambridge set as realised in *Jacob's Room*. James follows Jacob in the examination of masculine cultural formation, moving from the continuous sensibility of childhood to the goal-orientation of the young man. Jacob's trajectory was depicted as in some way mysterious; here, Freud's Oedipus complex is grafted on to the symbolic understanding of *Jacob's Room* to make the process less mysterious. Mr Tansley takes over from Miss Kilman as an example of violent lower-middle-class *ressentiment*, while Lily Briscoe is the occasion of an examination of the meaning of art in general, and of women's art in particular, in a post-theological world which can no longer look to art for transcendent value or authentic representation. Finally, the symbolic ramifications of the lighthouse, which made an earlier appearance in *Jacob's Room*, are further developed.

The opening of the novel thus establishes a tension between the unformed male child's consciousness and the culture's need that the young man be incisive and goal-oriented. Mrs Ramsay is shown as participating in the purposes of society, fantasising about her son's future as a judge or politician, and encouraging James to cherish an unrealistic goal by encouraging him to believe that he will be able to make a trip to the lighthouse, despite the adverse weather. Mrs Ramsay says 'yes' to James, the first word of the novel, followed by a qualifying 'if' which her son manages not to hear. Mr Ramsay's first word is a cautionary 'but', as he discourages his wife from giving their son false hope. Many accounts of this novel treat Mr Ramsay as the patriarchal nay-sayer, and the approximately Oedipal relationship between father and son which the novel describes seems at first sight to support this view. His first word, the word of the reality principle, is not 'no' but 'but'. Many accounts of this novel have found Mrs Ramsay's role in this conflict to be a positive one, while the father's is negative. So for Maria DiBattista, Mrs Ramsay is the 'archetypal mother', and 'Woolf's narrative honors the life-sustaining role of the mother as the foundation of social life; yet it also acknowledges that dependence on the mother is a real threat to the growth and transformation of unreflecting life into autonomous consciousness.'[43] Makiko Minow-Pinkney describes the polarity of Mr and Mrs Ramsay as 'an opposition between literal meaning and metaphoricity', so 'Mrs Ramsay [...], as an artist whose raw materials are emotions, distorts and exaggerates as necessary according to the human context of her discourse'.[44] For Elizabeth Abel, James's development and ultimate reconciliation with his father, in the final section when the journey to the lighthouse is made, is a 'knowledge' gained only at the cost of the repression of his mother's memory and the 'internalisation of paternal censorship'.[45] Whether indebted to myth-criticism, as in DiBattista's case, or to Freud, Klein and in recent accounts Lacan and Kristeva, there is a tendency to valorise the mother's world as good and to see the father as a destroyer, the enemy of maternity, art and the maternal body and the language of the semiotic *chora*. Yet on her first page, Woolf is careful to show how Mrs Ramsay fosters in James that very feeling of invulnerability which, as argued above, is so central to *Jacob's Room*. Certainly, the mother is, in DiBattista's words, 'the foundation of social life', but precisely of that very social life which it is the object of these novels to subject to critical scrutiny. 'Dependence' on her is not a 'threat to growth' but is a crucial stage in the developmental process which Woolf questions. That art is about distortion and exaggeration is a moot point, but certainly, Mrs Ramsay does what is necessary in a 'human context' which is not some pre-social given, but is the context of the upper-middle-class family developing its children for the work of Empire. The reference to 'life', or more coyly to 'the human context' in these accounts, is indicative of a critical gap: as I have argued, the term 'life' is so ideologically loaded in Woolf's writing that its uncritical reappearance in the critical discourse about Woolf represents a serious blind spot, and curiously recalls Leavis's criticism of Lawrence, which forever repeated this key term in Lawrence's work without problematising it.[46] Finally, it may be that James forgets his mother and learns to live in her absence, but he does so by fulfilling the programme of separation which she herself has outlined for him and which she has used her maternal presence, and the illusion of invulnerability which it bestows, to foster.

Woolf's use of the classic Oedipus complex[47] in this novel can divert attention away from the critical and symbolic schemata which are in use alongside it. As James plays, his consciousness is that of a child who 'cannot keep this feeling separate from that' (Woolf, 1992d: 7). As a child, he has privileged access to the complex phenomena of the present, the unarticulated and profoundly impressive nexus of impressions of 'life' found in the moment: 'even in earliest childhood any turn in the wheel of sensation has the power to transfix the moment upon which its gloom or radiance rests' (7). However, the play which Mrs Ramsay supervises has already embarked James on the course of separation from the moment and from the mother, as he cuts out images from an Army and Navy catalogue. The scissors are linked to Archer's knife and Peter Walsh's pen-knife: they are the tool of independence which might not only snip the umbilical cord connecting James to the archaic maternal reality and ultimately to the sea (which, as a sailor, he must go on to conquer), but which will also cut apart the fabric of lived existence. As his mother speaks, investing the moment with 'bliss', James is cutting out the image of a refrigerator. Unaware of the author's irony, Mrs Ramsay looks on benignly and imagines the future to which her nurture will lead him: 'his mother, watching him guide his scissors neatly round the refrigerator, imagined him all red and ermine on the Bench or directing a stern and momentous enterprise in some crisis of public affairs' (7). Mrs Ramsay, as she contemplates her role in the house with regard to the young men whom her husband has invited, reveals herself to be quite aware of her role as protector:

> Indeed, she had the whole of the other sex under her protection; for reasons she could not quite explain, for their chivalry and valour, for the fact that they negotiated treaties, ruled India, controlled finance; finally for an attitude towards herself which no woman could fail to feel or to find agreeable, something trustful, childlike, reverential [...].   (10)

It is possible to go on from here to demonstrate the extent of this novel's continuity with its predecessors in terms of its critical account of the ruling class and its institutions from the perspective of the process of psychological formation in the family. It is also possible to show in some detail how the symbolic system which I have identified in the earlier novels is present here to support a questionable and static notion of 'life' where a more optimistic and nuanced account of human possibility might be looked for. Space dictates that a selection be made, however, and it is the figure of Lily Briscoe, the novel's most decisive innovation, which requires attention.

Because *To The Lighthouse* makes art itself a more explicit topic than earlier works do, its formulation of the subject is more elaborate. Specifically, an opportunity is created to confront the transcendent claims of knowledge and the more limited claims of art, and to ask whether art is flawed in its project, divided as it is between the transcendent claims of philosophical knowledge and the evanescence of the moment. The figure of Mr Ramsay, modelled with humour and affection on Leslie Stephen, links the teleological aims of adventurers and soldiers to what is loosely depicted as the masculine project of knowledge. The engagement with philosophy is left deliberately superficial in the novel: it is characterised either in terms of a debate, proper to scepticism, about the actuality of reality ('Think of a kitchen table [...] when you're not there' [28]), or in terms of Mr Ramsay's attempt to develop a system of thought starting from A and proceeding to Z, although he is stuck and cannot reach R. The second version, a loose parody of the claims of systematic philosophy, is represented as the intellectual equivalent of military and sporting adventure and the rhetoric of pathos and self-pity that accompanied the idea of the hero in pre-war culture and fed the public taste for war. The reference here is to Robert Falcon Scott, whose expedition to the South Pole of 1910–12 failed to return. The account of the expedition given in Scott's recovered diary portrays a sense of calm in the closing stages of the expedition, with an under-current of despair but no hysteria, which became an ideal of heroism and sacrifice and is central to Mr Ramsay's self image:

> Qualities that in a desolate expedition across the icy solitudes of the Polar region would have made him the leader, the guide, the counsellor, whose temper, neither sanguine nor despondent, surveys what is to be and faces it, came to his help again. R – [...]
>
> Feelings that would not have disgraced a leader who, now that the snow has begun to fall and the mountain-top is covered in mist, knows that he must lay himself down and die before morning comes.   (40)

Lily Briscoe has no such illusions about the scope of her art, and this is not only because she is discouraged by Charles Tansley's misogynist response to her efforts. Her principal effort is to capture her impression of Mrs Ramsay in her art, in an image from which she is absent, and thereby to exorcise her and the old social order which she represented and sought to reproduce. The journey to the light-house is, of course, the emblem of the teleological quest. There is no notion that any real centre can actually be arrived at, and it is on the way to the lighthouse, not at the moment of arrival, that the important shift in Mr Ramsay's relationship with his children occurs.

The final section of the novel juxtaposes the final moment of arrival with the completion of Lily's painting. It is important in this final section that Lily does not witness the landing at the lighthouse, which is out of sight. The novel cannot permit such an unam-biguously totalising resolution. Lily projects the completion of the journey in her imagination, and her words borrow a Christian resonance; ' "He has landed," she said aloud. "It is finished." ' (225). The Christian motif is reinforced by Lily's ally, the pagan Mr Carmichael: 'He stood there spreading his hands over all the weak-ness and suffering of mankind; she thought he was surveying, tolerantly, compassionately, their final destiny' (225). The story of Scott is merely an echo of the pathos of the crucified Christ, the official role model of Victorian culture, whose cross is his monument and his destiny, the ultimate image of a teleological journey, of sacrifice and a transcendent end. The inscription over Christ's head labels him the 'King of the Jews', mocking him that has not inherited the Kingdom of Israel – that is, the kingdom founded by Jacob from whom Christ is said to descend. According to Matthew, Christ calls to God to ask why he has been forsaken, as if in this final moment caught between contingency and transcendence. His final words, 'It is finished', are echoed by Lily when she completes her painting in a famous final flurry: 'With sudden intensity, as if she saw it clear for a second, she drew a line there, in the centre. It was done; it was finished. Yes, she thought, laying down her brush in extreme fatigue, I have had my vision.' (226). What occurs here is far from being a straightforward affirmation of art. Lily's 'vision' might simply be the physical fact of seeing, or it might imply a mystical insight. This ambivalence is confirmed by the connection of art to the Christian pathos and links it to the teleology which is elsewhere rejected. Already, any artistic representation tends towards the symbolic; that is, the particular, once represented, already belongs to the illusory transcendence of meaning. So, art like the doubting Christ is painfully divided between contingency and transcendence, operating on a brink of quasi-transcendence. A rejected phrase from an earlier section of the novel defines the 'symbolical' as 'Crucified, & transcendent' (80, 240n). Woolf was surely right to eliminate this clumsily explicit phrase, but the connection of symbol, crucifixion and transcendence does helpfully look forward to the concluding section, which features all three of these motifs. For Lily, at least for one moment, the curse of contingency is lifted. However, the pathos-laden sense of weariness which accompanies this moment of limited transcendence echoes the self-pitying world-weariness of Mr Ramsay. The configuration of the concluding section indicates that art, although it begins by seeking to affirm the moment against the transcendent goals of the official Imperialist culture, hence acknowledging the contingency of life which that culture denies, nevertheless ambiguously shares with that culture the same transcendent impulse. This final moment preserves the dichotomy which, from *Jacob's Room* onwards, has informed Woolf's analysis of British culture in an emblematic form which, as if to acknowledge the limitations of its initial dualistic model, finally admits the androgynous nature of art – androgynous in its uneasy accommodation of the male teleological impulse and the female affinity for life.

There are important differences between the notion of androgynous art and the version of androgyny which emerges in *A Room of One's Own*. There, the emphasis is on the desideratum that art be created by an androgynous *mind*, such as the 'man-womanly mind' of Shakespeare, the notion that Woolf arrives at, curiously, by analogy with marriage, of a mind which can eschew the partisanship of sexual politics. 'It is fatal for anyone who writes to think of their sex', claims Woolf: 'Some collaboration has to take place in the mind between the woman and the man before the art of creation can be accomplished. Some marriage of opposites has to be consummated. [...] There must be freedom and there must be peace.'[48] This account of androgyny is formulated by Woolf with the specific purpose of warning women to produce an art which is not driven by anger. It is best regarded, therefore, as a strategic and local formulation, and does not overdetermine the different account which I have dislocated from the novels, where art's androgyny is not framed in terms of the loose analogy with marriage and the casual psychologising which these claims employ. Instead, art is located in the art object rather than simply in the mind, for it is this object which is situated between the masculine monument, which promises unrealisable transcendence, and the feminine affinity with nature and the present, which promises only irredeemable contingency. On the terms of Woolf's novels, the art object partakes of both moment and monument but is equivalent to neither; it is a vision which is beyond the contingent subjectivity of physical sight or other subjective affect, but a vision which is free from the transcendent illusion of the visionary. If in *A Room of One's Own* Woolf asks for an austerity from the female writer, who might well, she fears, choose to respond to centuries of misogyny with a symmetrical and equally fruitless endeavour, then it is because her own notion of art is austere. On the terms of the novels, art can or should be the space where the specific and historically given modes of masculinity and femininity, in culture and not merely in consciousness, are overcome and negated by something which partakes of each.

Notes

1. Irene Clephane, *Ourselves: 1900–1930*, p. 170.
2. See Gail Brabon, *Women Workers of the First World War*, p. 182, and Deirdre Beddoe, *Back to Home and Duty*, pp. 61–3.
3. Brabon, *Women Workers*, p. 179.
4. Clephane, *Ourselves*, p. 173.
5. For a further account of suffragist response to the war see Johanna Alberti, *Beyond Suffrage*, pp. 38–70.
6. Noreen Branson, *Britain in the Nineteen Twenties*, p. 203.
7. Branson, Britain *in the Nineteen Twenties*, p. 203.
8. See Billie Melman, *Women and the Popular Imagination in the Twenties*, pp. 17–18.
9. See Robert Graves and Alan Hodge, *The Long Week-End*, pp. 36–9; John

Collier and Iain Lang, *Just The Other Day*, pp. 145–75; Clephane, *Ourselves*, pp. 178–80.

10. See Beddoe, *Back to Home and Duty*, pp. 12–13.

11. See Sheila Jeffreys, *The Spinster and Her Enemies*, pp. 148–51, and Beddoe, *Back to Home and Duty*, pp. 138–9.

12. Jeffreys, *The Spinster*, pp. 151–5.

13. Dora Russell, *Hypatia*, pp. 37–9.

14. The narrator's 'This was the saddest spring' (p. 132) echoes *The Good Soldier*'s 'This is the saddest story'.

15. This point is made in an excellent discussion by Claire M. Tylee, *The Great War and Women's Consciousness*, pp. 142–50, which emphasises the class content of the novel and its equation of civilised modernity and war.

16. For a general account of 'Literary Spinsterhood in the 1920s' see Maroula Joannou, *'Ladies, Please Don't Smash These Windows'*, pp. 77–101, which deals principally with F. M. Mayor's *The Rector's Daughter* (1924), and makes additional reference to May Sinclair, *Mary Oliver: A Life* (1919) and *The Life and Death of Harriet Frean* (1922); Radclyffe Hall, *The Unlit Lamp* (1924); Winifred Holtby, *The Crowded Street* (1924); Katherine Mansfield's 'Miss Brill' and 'The Daughters of the Late Colonel' in *The Garden Party* (1922); Sylvia Stephenson, *Surplus* (1924); as well as *Lolly Willowes*.

17. Warner had been influenced by reading Margaret Murray's *The Witch-Cult in Western Europe* (1921). She had concluded that 'these witches were witches for love; that witchcraft was more than Miss Murray's Dianic cult; it was the romance of their hard lives, their release from dull futures'. Quoted in Claire Harman, *Sylvia Townsend Warner*, p. 59.

18. For an account of this novel, see Janet Montefiore, *Men and Women Writers of the 1930s*, pp. 168–77.

19. Jane Marcus, 'A Wilderness of One's Own', in Susan Merrill Squier (ed.), *Women Writers and The City*, pp. 134–60; see p. 136.

20. One account of the meaning of this dabbing, as the origin of art in pre-verbal process, in *To The Lighthouse*, is to be found in Mark Hussey, *The Singing of the Real World*, p. 76.

21. James Joyce, *Dubliners*, p. 224.

22. See *Letters, III*, p. 385: 'I meant *nothing* by The Lighthouse. [...] I can't manage Symbolism except in this vague, generalized way.'

23. See, for example, *Letters, I*, p. 208, where Woolf describes the 'great trial' presented by the presence of two 'silent' and difficult 'Cambridge youths' who visit her at Carbis Bay in Cornwall, and remarks: 'Oh women are my line and not these inanimate creatures.' This 'silence' becomes an attribute of Jacob, and the whole holiday is central to *To The Lighthouse* ('It is a strange dream to come back again': *Letters, I*, p. 203), with its parade of unwanted guests.

24. Sue Roe guesses that the 'six young men' refers to Thoby's inner circle:

Clive Bell, Lytton Strachey, Saxon Sydney-Turner, Desmond MacCarthy and Maynard Keynes (*Jacob's Room*: p. 176n).

25. Woolf, *Diary, III*, p. 34.
26. Lytton Strachey, *Eminent Victorians*, p. 6.
27. A theme explored at length in C. Ruth Miller, *Virginia Woolf: The Frames of Art and Life*.
28. On this topic see, for example, Graves and Hodge, *The Long Weekend*, pp. 29–30.
29. I differ here from Makiko Minow-Pinkney, *Virginia Woolf and the Problem of the Subject*, p. 41, which sees a contradiction between Jacob as 'idealist rebel', on the one hand, and 'adherent of the masculinity' on which Imperial patriarchy is founded, on the other. Woolf seems to me precisely to be concerned with the apparent contradiction in reality which allows the former to be assimilated to the latter.
30. See *Letters, II*, pp. 577–8.
31. See, variously, Minow-Pinkney, *Problem of the Subject*, p. 49; Clare Hanson, *Virginia Woolf*, pp. 48–50; Jane Marcus, *Virginia Woolf and the Languages of Patriarchy*, p. 13; according to William Handley, Woolf seeks 'to free culture from its stony, objectified entrapment in order to include and emancipate the marginalised within a more democratic cultural discourse': see 'War and the Politics of Narration in *Jacob's Room*', in Mark Hussey (ed.), *Virginia Woolf and War*, p. 117. This volume also includes an important essay by James M. Haule which examines the significance (and progressively decreasing importance) of the charwomen in successive revisions of the 'Time Passes' section of *To the Lighthouse*. '*To the Lighthouse* and the Great War; the Evidence of Virginia Woolf's Revisions of 'Time Passes', in Hussey (ed.), pp. 164–79.
32. On the last point see Woolf, *Diary, I*, p. 104.
33. See Marcus, *Languages of Patriarchy*, p. 9, and more recently Kathy J. Phillips, *Virginia Woolf Against Empire*, p. xxvii.
34. See Hermione Lee, *Virginia Woolf*, pp. 410, 468, 510, on Woolf's reading of Proust.
35. I have in mind the argument of Georg Lukács, *The Meaning of Contemporary Realism*, which attacks the 'pathology' of Modernism, especially in its 'formalist' and Freudian aspects, and defends the proto-socialist dimension of 'critical realism' (that is, the high bourgeois novels of Dickens and Thomas Mann) as being capable of describing if not necessarily addressing 'the social and ideological crisis of bourgeois society' (p. 60). As I am arguing here, Woolf's novels certainly have this 'critical realist' function, amongst others.
36. Lee, *Virginia Woolf*, pp. 722–6, details Woolf's reading of Freud in 1939.
37. See Elizabeth Abel, *Virginia Woolf and the Fictions of Psychoanalysis*, p. xvi, which argues generally for a shift from Freudian to Kleinian positions throughout Woolf's work.

38. Sandra M. Gilbert and Susan Gubar, *No Man's Land. Volume II: Sexchanges*, p. 317.
39. In preferring this term to the term 'madness' I am following the account of *Mrs Dalloway* in Thomas Caramagno, *The Flight of the Mind*, pp. 210–43. This psychobiographical study emphasises the expressive and therapeutic aspects of Woolf's writing: 'in *Mrs Dalloway* Woolf extends Jinny Carslakes's brief vision [in *Jacob's Room*] of a profound unity and expands her own sense of and control over herself in ways that anticipate effective treatments of depression by contemporary cognitive psychologists.' (p. 210). This approach is interesting but, as in the series of Freudian studies which Caramagno rejects, it tends to ignore the systematic structuration of philosophical and cultural context and content, so characteristic of all of Woolf's works, which I have emphasised here.
40. On this topic see Claire M. Tylee, *The Great War and Women's Consciousness*, p. 67.
41. See Lee, *Virginia Woolf*, pp. 328–9, 347–8, 354–6, 360–1.
42. See *Letters, I*, pp. 203–9: 'It is a strange dream to come back here again.' These letters also document Woolf's discomfort with the house guests on the second occasion and refer to her sister Vanessa's painting – two topics central to the novel.
43. Maria DiBattista, *Virginia Woolf's Major Novels*, pp. 75–6.
44. Minow-Pinkney, *Problem of the Subject*, pp. 85–6.
45. Abel, *Fictions of Psychoanalysis*, pp. 51–2.
46. In *D. H. Lawrence: Novelist*, Leavis contrasts Eliot's '"standing off" from life' to Lawrence's 'affirmation of life' (pp. 28, 32). Linking his claim for Lawrence's genius to his intuitive grasp of 'life' in his account of *The Rainbow*, Leavis writes: 'The oneness of life; the separateness and irreducible otherness of lives; the supreme importance of "fulfilment" in the individual, because here [...] is life – the peculiar Laurentian genius manifests itself in the intensity, constancy and fulness of the intuition' (pp. 120–1).
47. For a classic account of the Oedipus complex, see Freud, *On Metapsychology*, p. 371.
48. Woolf, *A Room of One's Own*, pp. 89, 94.

3

Mass Civilisation and Minority Culture

Rᴇғᴇʀᴇɴᴄᴇꜱ ᴛᴏ ᴄʀᴏᴡᴅꜱ, ʜᴇʀᴅꜱ, masses, or the 'man in the street' are commonplace in pessimistic cultural commentary of the 1920s.[1] The social and technological developments during the war and the subsequent decade confirmed a pessimism, generally in middle-class quarters, about the emergence of contemporary 'mass society'. This pessimism had its intellectual roots in the reading of a range of pre-war thinkers including Burke, Arnold, Marx, Nietzsche, Sorel and Le Bon. The 'mass society' analysis had a variety of determinants. It was related to developments in communications technology throughout the period, with the propaganda role of the press during the war now being supplemented by film, radio and the gramophone. It was feared that these technologies would erode individuality, homogenise experience and ideas, and be used to cultivate hysterical and unreflecting crowd behaviour. The art and culture of the minority could no longer intervene effectively between the government and capitalist manipulators on one side of the radio apparatus and the 'man in the street' on the other. The mass society hypothesis was reinforced by a huge increase in sport and leisure activities which became much more widely available and widely practised.[2] The construction of suburbs around London in particular and the emergence of the office commuter also triggered an élitist backlash. The novelist Douglas Goldring described the new 'mass' type in these terms: 'During the 'twenties a horrifying sub-human suburban type came into existence which was genially depicted as the "little man", by the cartoonist Strube. This odious homunculus and his revolting wife – ignorant, stupid, a moral craven but easily capable of being infected with mob-hysteria – exemplified one of the worst outcomes of the so-called "Peace".[3] However, despite the impact and importance of these often-emphasised cultural factors, the middle-class sense of threat from mass society owed more to changes in class structure than to new media technologies, sport, or the creation of suburbia. From the point of view of the working class, who did not share the panic about 'mass society', the decade was dominated by unemployment, and witnessed the near-complete erosion of the advantages which had been won in the war, with the effective defeat of the Trade Union movement only marginally offset by the growing role of the Labour Party in Parliament.

The war brought about an acceleration of the rate of automation in factories and widespread application of the new strategies of scientific management. These changes in work practice already suggested the emergence in England of the type of administrative society outlined in Germany by Max Weber (whose work was influential on Adorno, Horkheimer and the Frankfurt School).[4] More than this, workers' organisations assumed new political importance, as trade unions engaged in frequent rounds of collective pay bargaining with employers, and trade union representatives were taken on to government committees for the first time.

However, the notion of massification involves more than centralisation and collectivisation. It implies the erosion of previous social distinctions, a process in which the differentials of a highly nuanced class society are eroded. The war effected or accelerated important changes in the social structure, especially in terms of the inner structure of the working class and its position in relation to the middle class.[5] The need for certain forms of labour meant that large sections of the working class became visibly central to the patriotic war effort. Inflation during the war resulted in large pay awards to skilled and non-skilled workers alike. The consequences of this were twofold. Flat-rate pay awards made to all sections of the working class tended to erode the distinction between the skilled and the semi- or unskilled which had been widely recognised at the start of the war. While these pay awards enabled the working class as a whole to keep pace with inflation, at least to some degree, the middle class had little collective bargaining power and, as inflation undermined the value of savings, began to lose its class prerogatives, symbolised chiefly by access to private education and the employment of a single domestic servant in the middle-class household.[6] Middle-class anxieties were evidenced by the formation during the war of a

Professional Classes War Relief Council (linked to the Eugenics Society) which offered to help with school fees, and the creation in 1919 of a nebulous, proto-Fascist Middle Classes Union which aimed to restore the pre-war balance of class power.[7]

Official unemployment reached 1.5 million in June 1922, dipping during the middle of the decade and rising again to 2.5 million in December 1930. Real levels were certainly much higher.[8] It added to the climate of middle-class unease and fuelled the right-wing propaganda against Bolshevism. As Irene Clephane noted in 1933: 'the heroic status of the fighters was of bitterly short duration. Within two years of the cessation of fighting the men who had fought – for whom nothing was to be too good – underwent transformation in the popular middle class imagination into lazy good-for-nothings of revolutionary tendencies whose sole idea was to avoid work and live on the "dole".'[9]

Criticism of profiteering from 1915 onwards created a climate in which trade unions would pursue their share of industry profits more aggressively: in the context of the war, capitalist profit-taking lost a good deal of its legitimacy. The middle class resented these developments, and this became apparent during the General Strike of 1926 when they enthusiastically participated in strike-breaking activities. The apparent decline of the traditional landed aristocracy, many of whom sold their land to tenants (and invested the proceeds lucratively in securities), reinforced the impression of the advance of the working class. It seemed to some commentators that the Marxist vision of a society divided into two great camps was a reality, and that the middle class must become 'declassed', politically and economically disenfranchised. Middle-class panic in the period resulted from the impression that class war was imminent, or that the formation of a new bipartisan state was being engineered, based on an accommodation of capital and labour and which would exclude the middle class.

Demobilisation and the adjustments of industry to new conditions led to a series of strikes in 1919, most notably on Clydeside, where strikers were confronted first by police with batons – a course of action which led to riots – then by the army, equipped with trench mortars and Lewis guns. The Government's ability to keep order – that is, suppress strikes – throughout the country was dependent primarily on the police and ultimately on the army. The army was no longer a professional force with its own monarchist ethos – the situation which is carefully maintained today – and was therefore unreliable, while the police seemed to be concentrating on advancing their own demands through the Police Union, which voted in May ten to one to strike over pay; a strike which, in the event, was only partially successful when it began in August (although it led to looting in Liverpool where the army was called in to restore order), but which confirmed the image of a nation on the brink of revolution or anarchy. It was this impression which enabled the Government and its allies in the press to switch attention away from the ethical basis of the strikers' claims. Contemporary historians John Collier and Iain Lang made the following observation about the strikes of 1919:

> Where the Cabinet Ministers exaggerated and distorted was in alleging a Bolshevist purpose in direct action. Partly strikes expressed the vanity of the skilled workman [...], a vanity pathetically unaware that the superiority of skilled workmanship was challenged by new methods of production; partly they expressed mere anger and hysterical violence; partly a simple eagerness to get as much for as little as possible. But there was hardly an iota of hard, cold Leninism.[10]

Nevertheless, the effect of class polarisation was marked, especially in the aftermath of the 1919 Railway strike, which Collier and Lang describe in these terms:

> All the solemnities appropriate to an outbreak of war were observed. Field-Marshal Haig, Commander-in-Chief of the Home forces, and Major-General Feilding [sic], in command of the London District, were summoned to conference with the Cabinet. There was a call for volunteers – and it was this that gave the strike its distinctive post-War note. A volunteer force answered more than practical necessities; it was the mobilization of middle-class-consciousness, a consolidation of ex-officer sentiment. [...] The volunteers lined up. Mr. and Mrs. Everyman suffered a great deal of material inconvenience, and enjoyed a spiritual salvation.   (Collier and Lang, 1932: 67–8)

While the middle class relished any opportunity to side with the Government against the workers, the working class itself was divided. Skilled workers had lost their prerogatives as a consequence of the narrowing of wage differentials – a Government policy aimed at tackling poverty – and the process of wartime 'dilution', by means of which less skilled men were accepted into skilled jobs to ease labour shortages. Further, despite a high degree of social idealism amongst organised labour, the working class itself was not in a revolutionary mood. Retrospectively it seems that, although the war had brought the conflict of interest between capital and labour into the open, workers were much more willing to fight for a share of capitalist profits than to fight against capitalism itself, and despite the advances of the Trades Union Congress and the Labour Party, patriotism and royalism remained stronger factors in the English working class than a socialism which was still perceived by many as the province of intellectuals and the upper classes.

In 1920–1 and again in 1925–6 the coal industry was at the centre of disputes between labour and capital. In the wake of the Russian Revolution, the strike of 1921 was seriously considered to be a potential trigger for social revolution. During the war the Government had taken direct control of the mines, and the centrality of coal to the war effort had given the miners' union considerable leverage. After the war the miners, with majority support from a Government-commissioned committee, sought nationalisation of the industry. However, in 1921 the mines were returned to private hands, and the owners sought to dismantle the national wage structure which had been established during the war. This provoked a three-month conflict in which the miners were promised and expected the support of the rail and transport unions – the 'Triple Alliance' which, it was hoped, could force employers and the Government to back down. In her 1933 survey of recent history, Irene Clephane concluded bluntly: 'In 1921 it is conceivable that well-planned, unanimous, well-informed, and well-concerted action on the part of the whole body of trade unionists might have effected, bloodlessly, a revolutionary change in the social organisation of Great Britain.'[11] However, revolution was not the goal of the trade union leadership, and in 1921, when the support of the other unions in the Triple Alliance failed to materialise – on 15 April, a date which became known as 'Black Friday' – the miners were doomed to defeat.

The General Strike of 1926 was not seen as a revolutionary threat by the Government. After the experiences of 1919–21 legislation and emergency measures had already been put into place which meant that it was very prepared to meet the strike. The 1921 strike had culminated in a four-year agreement whereby a Government subsidy was agreed to supplement the new wage structures in the mining industry. Demand for coal continued to decline, and when the agreement ended in 1925, employers sought to increase hours and reduce wages. The Government attempted to intervene to avert another conflict, but the miners went on strike in April 1926, with the slogan: 'Not a minute on the day, not a penny off the pay'. On 1 May, a resolution for a general strike in support of the miners was passed in the General Council of the Trades Union Congress by 3,653,529 votes to 49,911. Although only about one-third of workers belonged to organised trade unions, working-class support for the strike was overwhelming, and there was widespread international solidarity. Douglas Goldring notes that the strike was seen globally as a revolutionary outbreak, even although the TUC leadership only entered the strike unwillingly and under pressure from the rank and file. Influenced by the aggressive anti-Bolshevism of Churchill, the Baldwin Government treated the strikers as revolutionaries – which they were not – 'secure in the certainty that the whole of the middle and upper classes would rally to the defence of "King and Country"' (Goldring, 221). When the TUC called newspaper operatives out one day early to prevent publication of its lead article dealing with the strike, the *Daily Mail* was printed in Paris and flown over to Britain. 'A general strike is not an industrial dispute', claimed the *Daily Mail* leader on 3 May, the first day of the strike: 'It is a revolutionary movement intended to inflict suffering upon the great masses of innocent persons.' When the strike ended on 12 May the *Mail* proclaimed 'Surrender of the Revolutionaries' and 'A Triumph for the People'.[12] The strike had not been revolutionary, and the TUC had been only too keen to take the opportunity to end it when the possibility of a settlement was aired. While some miners drifted back to work over the subsequent weeks, others remained on strike until the winter. The Government had scored an immense victory over the labour movement and for a while rode high on its perceived defeat of a revolutionary threat. In the eyes of the middle classes, who had rallied to break the strike by acting as 'volunteers' in middle-class parlance, or as 'blacklegs' in the vocabulary of the working class, the shift from heroes to failed revolutionaries was completed.

The effect of the strike on the working class is vividly registered by D. H. Lawrence in his posthumously published essay, 'Return To Bestwood',[13] which relates a visit to his native village of Eastwood in Nottinghamshire, in September 1926, where the miners remained on strike. It was this experience which accounted for the revised political orientation of *The First Lady Chatterley* (see Chapter Five). Lawrence describes the silent routine in which a small number of blackleg workers (the 'dirty ones') are escorted by police (the 'blue-bottles') to work the mines, past the silent figures of the striking miners (the 'clean ones'), and is led to re-evaluate his own connection with the people of the district, noting the difference bestowed on him by his vastly different life experiences, and the underlying sympathy and solidarity based both on common origins and on a fundamental similarity of outlook and aspiration:

> I feel I hardly know any more the people I come from, the colliers of the Erewash Valley district. They are changed, and I suppose I am changed. [...] At the same time, they have I think, an underneath ache and heaviness very much like my own. [...]
>
> They are the only people who move me strongly, and with whom I feel myself connected in deeper destiny. It is they who are, in some peculiar way, 'home' to me. [...]
>
> And now, this last time, I feel a doom over the country, and a shadow of despair over the hearts of the men, which leaves me no rest. Because the same doom is over me, wherever I go, and the same despair touches my heart.   (Lawrence, 1967: 204)

Lawrence concludes that 'the ownership of property has become, now, a problem, a religious problem. But it is one we can solve.'

> I know that we could, if we would, establish little by little a true democracy in England: we could nationalise the land and industries and means of transport, and make the whole thing work infinitely better than at present, *if we would*. It all depends on the spirit in which the thing is done.
>
> I know we are on the brink of a class war.   (265)

Lawrence was moved by his vision of the state of the working class to accommodate his own desire for 'a new conception of what it means, *to live*' to the socialist demands of the striking miners, although his sense of the imminence of class war is contradicted by his own evaluation of the hopelessness which has descended on people whose former vitality he now perceives to have been the spur to his own celebration of human vitality in general:

> After the war, the colliers went silent: after 1920. Till 1920 there was a strange power of life in them, something wild and urgent [...]. But now, the miners go to the foot-ball match in silence like ghosts [...]. They go to the welfare clubs, and drink with a sort of hopelessness.   (264)

The hopelessness Lawrence saw was not merely the product of the miners' own strike, but the symptom of the defeat of the whole Labour movement which had begun in 1921 and was resoundingly confirmed in 1926.

Against this background, a reorganisation of publishing took place, with new companies emerging and older ones seeking a new role.[14] With the advent of the newly so-named 'bestseller', commercial publishers increasingly emphasised fiction in their lists and aimed ideally to create lists which combined novelists with a serious cachet and mass market bestsellers. The role of poetry in the public sphere became very limited, and despite the stimulation to the writing of poetry created by one work – Eliot's *The Waste Land* (1922) – confidence in the potential role of a serious literary culture centred around poetry became eroded. Ezra Pound, whose ambivalence about his role on the London literary scene caused him to decamp to Paris in 1920, expressed his disillusion with London literary culture in *Hugh Selwyn Mauberley* (1920), where in one section the powerful newspaper reviewer 'Mr Nixon' (usually identified with Arnold Bennett) patronisingly tells the poet: 'give up verse, my boy,/ There's nothing in it', and in another, the serious writer described only as the 'stylist' is found living a marginal existence, 'unpaid, uncelebrated'.

The question of the relationship between literature and the market had assumed an acute if not entirely new form, a background against which new claims for the role and purpose of literature and 'English' were to be formulated. This chapter proceeds with an account of the attempts of three important literary journals of the 1920s to create a new public sphere for art and literature and to give a sense of the ways in which the social and intellectual climate of the decade gave shape to the project of 'English'. This is complemented by a description of Q. D. Leavis's *Fiction and the Reading Public* which shows how the construction of English literature as a modern University subject depended on an interpretation of the nature of the new mass society in which middle-class intellectuals had lost all leverage. The chapter continues with an examination of *Clash*, the most important contemporary novel to deal with the General Strike and a salient example of the propagandistic use of the popular novel form, written by a sitting Labour MP, Ellen Wilkinson. While *Clash* deals with the local situation of the strike, D. H. Lawrence's much earlier novel, *Kangaroo*, is shown to take a far-sighted view of the emergence of a new global alignment, in which the confrontation between the mass politics of Communism and Fascism replaces the old order of national conflict.

Reaction and Revolution in The Calendar of Modern Letters, The Criterion *and* The Adelphi

The social reconstruction brought about by the war seemed to have dealt a death blow to the idea of a 'public sphere'. The eighteenth-century public sphere had depended on education and exclusion.[15] The more people were include in the democratic process, and the lower the general level of education, the less well could the public sphere function, until it seemed that the radio loudspeaker had replaced the process of dialogue. If the middle class in general felt that it was being squeezed out in the post-war state, artists and intellectuals had similar reasons to fear exclusion. Writers now had no natural class allegiance since the governing and owning classes no longer depended on culture but on communications. Literature and the arts urgently needed to theorise their new role and define their audience. Bracketed by the facetious contemporary label 'highbrow', a number of journals sprang up which did not pretend to the culture-consumer readership of the pre-war journals, but were platforms from which the arts could test their purpose and very possibility. T. S. Eliot's *The Criterion,* John Middleton Murry's *The Adelphi,* and Edgell Rickword's short-lived *The Calendar of Modern Letters,* are nominated by Q. D. Leavis in *Fiction and The Reading Public* as the pre-eminent highbrow journals (Leavis, 1965: 20). Each of these journals had low sales compared to the mass market and they were in no sense conceived to meet a market need. *The Calendar* was so unstable that it lasted only two years, but *The Criterion* and *The Adelphi* survived throughout the 1920s and for much of the 1930s as journals with a highly specific tone and niche. All three journals recognised that the role of literature, and of the arts in general, had been fundamentally altered and set out to confront changed social circumstance in different ways.

The Calendar of Modern Letters featured work by the ubiquitous D. H. Lawrence, as well as essays and creative work by Wyndham Lewis, Iris Barry, Robert Graves, Siegfried Sassoon and Edwin Muir amongst others. Its agenda was quality in literature independent of politics, although its editor Edgell Rickword leaned towards the Nietzschean pessimism of regular contributor Wyndham Lewis, whose essay 'The Dithyrambic Spectator' *The Calendar* published, as well as a positive review of *The Art of Being Ruled* which Rickword said 'should stand towards our generation in the same relation that

Culture and Anarchy did to the generation of the 'seventies'.[16] In common with Eliot and Murry, Rickword and his co-editor Douglas Garman were interested in establishing more rigorous literary-critical standards, and opposed the loose essayism of the previous generation. Arnold Bennett, so frequently the target of 1920s writers, receives short shrift from the pen of Edwin Muir in one of the regular re-evaluative 'Scrutinies' which defined the stance of *The Calendar*. Bennett is defined as a spiritual Victorian, so naïvely fascinated with the machinery of modern life and oblivious to its human meaning that he writes like a man giving street directions.[17] However, *The Calendar* did not stand for the modern against the old, and was equally prepared to condemn the latest volume of the systematically modern Dorothy Richardson:

> The bleak truth is that Miss Richardson perfected a way of saying things without having anything to say. [...] To the associations of her early youth she attaches so much importance that she vomits them on her public. It is so crude and it is so dull.[18]

It was easier to find writing to condemn than to praise, however, and *The Calendar* frankly acknowledged the decline of the serious literary public sphere to the point that 'verse [now] offers less nourishment to the sophisticated adult than it has done at any time in the last three hundred and thirty years'.[19] Wyndham Lewis, in an account of the visual arts which might equally be applied to literature, put a further gloss on this:

> But today none of the pictorial and plastic arts, at least, are any more than an adjunct to the critical and historic faculty. The contemporary audience is essentially an audience of critics, that is to say, they are as active as the performer, who, indeed, exists chiefly in order that the critic may *act* – as a Critic. The only *rationale* of the professional artist to-day is to provide the critic with material for criticism; it is no longer to give delight or serve any useful end. And were it not for this the whole elaborate pretence that the fine arts are still an effective part of our life would be immediately abandoned.[20]

Hegel had described the decline of the importance of art in modernity in terms of the ascendancy of philosophy and science. Unlike ancient art, modern art is the ironic product of an artist who is reflective and detached. Ancient art was the principal mode of understanding in ancient society, whereas, in Hegel's view, modern art is exhausted and superseded, no longer the site of a primary knowledge.[21] It was common in the 1920s to perceive science as a form of knowledge superior to the arts. Popular science books were common and, in a new departure for a literary magazine, *The Adelphi* ran a series of articles attempting to explain the salient features of modern science in an accessible manner, and this in its turn contributed to that journal's anti-materialist emphasis on subjectivity and spiritual values. However, what Lewis notes in his article is not the historical eclipse of art as a form of knowledge, nor its consequent eclipse from public life, but the specific restructuring of the social role of art in industrial society and the emergence of a segregated public sphere of art which is no longer a general public at all. This argument coincides with *Fiction and the Reading Public* in identifying business and the apparent democratisation of leisure as the cause of this eclipse, but exceeds Leavis's pessimism in its description of the corrosive effects of this shrinking of the artistic public sphere on the nature of artistic practice itself.

The Calendar could wring its hands about the state of culture and publish the few authors it regarded as presentable, but it lacked a political strategy. The same cannot be said of *The Criterion* which began publication in 1922 and presented itself as the organ of literary classicism with connections to French Catholic intellectuals and the right-wing Action Française. Early issues were impressive in terms of their literary content alone, especially the first issue which features *The Waste Land*. Eliot would continue to publish some of his most significant critical essays in *The Criterion*, and was able to depend on contributions from May Sinclair, Ezra Pound, Roger Fry, Virginia Woolf, Herbert Read, William Butler Yeats, Richard Aldington, Ford Madox Ford and Wyndham Lewis – amongst others – in the first six months. Eliot was also keen to feature translations of work in French, German, Italian, and Russian (via French) by authors who had impressed him: early numbers include Hermann Hesse, Stéphane Mallarmé, Paul Valéry, Marcel Proust, and several instalments of previously unpublished material by Dostoevsky.

In the editorial 'Commentary' of the seventh issue Eliot sets out his aesthetic and political stall. The occasion is the publication of *Speculations* (1924), a posthumous collection of the essays of T. E. Hulme. Hulme, who had been killed in action in 1917, was a substantially self-taught philosopher and aesthetic thinker who had been an influence on the Imagist circle before the war. His profound anti-humanism and anti-romanticism, although perhaps not his pro-military and anti-pacifist stance, made him a cornerstone for the thought of intellectuals who, like Eliot and Lewis, rejected the secular faith in a benevolent human progress which had been the hallmark of the pre-war generation, and most typically of Bernard Shaw. In his 'Commentary' on Hulme, Eliot regretted that *Speculations* had been neglected since its publication and advertised the book's importance in stark terms:

> In this volume he appears as the forerunner of a new attitude of mind which should be the twentieth-century mind [...] Hulme is classical, reactionary, and revolutionary; he is the antipodes of the eclectic, tolerant and democratic mind of the end of the last century. [...] Classicism is in some sense reactionary, but it must be in a profounder sense revolutionary.[22]

The revolution which Eliot intends is certainly not social revolution – he consistently supported existing social authority in the form of the constitutional monarchy – but rather a revolution of attitude. At the core of Hulme's philosophy is a distinction, made in the first essay of the collection, between 'Humanism and the Religious Attitude'. From the religious perspective, 'man himself is judged to be essentially limited and imperfect. He is endowed with Original Sin.' By contrast, humanism rejects the religious conception of 'absolute value', declares that all values are relative to human desires, and consequently

> you get a refusal to believe any longer in the radical imperfection of either Man or Nature. [...] This leads to a complete change in values. The problem of evil disappears, the conception of sin loses all meaning. [...] Progress is thus possible and order is a merely negative conception.
> (Hulme, 1977: 37–8)

This notion of human imperfection also opens out on to a new approach to aesthetics, as Hulme argued in his profoundly influential essay 'Romanticism and Classicism'. 'I want to maintain that after a hundred years of romanticism, we are in for a classical revival, and that the particular weapon of this new classical spirit, when it works in verse, will be fancy' (113). Hulme polemically privileges fancy over imagination, in contrast to the romantics who, immersed in Rousseau, had backed the chaos of the French Revolution in the hope of human progress.

> Here is the root of all romanticism: that man, the individual, is an infinite reservoir of possibilities; and if you can so rearrange society by the destruction of oppressive order then these possibilities will have a chance and you will get Progress.
> One can define the classical quite clearly as the opposite to this. Man is

an extraordinarily fixed and limited animal whose nature is absolutely constant. It is only by tradition and organisation that anything can be got out of him.   (116)

Hulme declares his affinity with Charles Maurras and the Action Française, and claims that while the Church is classical, romanticism is 'spilt religion'.

Eliot would never identify himself completely with any other point of view, but in Hulme's 'revolutionary' grouping of religious, social and artistic matters under the head of classicism, *The Criterion* found the alternative to social revolution and rambling, subjective art. In 'The Idea of a Literary Review' Eliot declared that *The Criterion* would remain open to all political perspectives. However, the mainly right-wing French intellectuals who had influenced Hulme were given a significant role. Eliot's article recommends to his readers the work of Georges Sorel (whose work had been translated by Hulme), Charles Maurras, Julien Benda and Jacques Maritain, and criticises the Holy Trinity of British liberalism, H. G. Wells, George Bernard Shaw and Bertrand Russell.[23] *The Criterion* preferred the authoritarian élitism of Maurras to the authoritarian populism of Fascism. In a review of works on Fascist political theory, Eliot remarked that 'most of the concepts which might have attracted me in fascism I seem already to have found, in a more digestible form, in the work of Charles Maurras'.[24]

The most pessimistic account of the state of European culture to be published by *The Criterion* appeared in two extracts from Henri Massis's *Defence of the West*. Massis was a chauvinist whose particularly French approach to Europe would have limited resonance in the English context. Yet his account of a post-colonial Europe being undermined by the alien beliefs of the very cultures over which it was now losing domination would find substantial echo in the work of Eliot and Lewis.[25] The two excerpts from Massis which appear in *The Criterion* are core documents worth examining in some detail. Massis contextualises his discussion by referring to 'the crisis of Western civilisation and the danger of asiaticism' and 'the formidable problems raised by the awakening of the nations of Asia and Africa, united by Bolshevism against Western civilisation'.[26]

With the first signs that telecommunications were set to create a world-wide cultural hegemony, Massis wrote: 'the ease of material communications, which was, according to democratic doctrines, to bring about a union of minds, has succeeded in making the world uniform, not in uniting it.'[27] Massis argues that European weakness caused by internecine war and cultural decline will bring about the eclipse of Europe by an Asia which it has previously dominated both militarily and culturally. He is critical of the recent and contemporary reception of Oriental culture in Europe, especially in Germany, seeing an interest in Buddhism and Hinduism as a form of intellectual surrender:

> On the pretext of bringing us what we need, a certain kind of Asiaticism is disposing us to the final dispersal of the heritage of our culture and of all that which enables the man of the West still to keep himself upright on his feet. Personality, unity, stability, authority, continuity – these are the root-ideas of the West. We are asked to break these to pieces for the sake of a doubtful Asiaticism in which all the forms of human personality dissolve and return to nothingness.[28]

Massis's targets include a new fatalism (especially that of Spengler), a new obsession with novelty and change, 'Rousseauism', and the French literary moderns, Proust and Gide, in whose work he finds the 'dissolution of the human personality' and warns, 'it is here that Asiaticism lies in wait for us'.[29] The defence of the West against the annihilation of the personality by high and low cultural institutions alike is a perpetual theme of the work of Wyndham Lewis, notably in *Time and Western Man* (1927: it was originally entitled *The Politics of the Personality*), and Eliot's own work makes a more guarded use of it. In one of his 'Commentaries' for *The Criterion*, Eliot wrote:

> For the Russian Revolution has made men conscious of the position of Western Europe as (in Valéry's words) a small and isolated cape on the western side of the Asiatic Continent. And this awareness seems to be giving rise to a new European consciousness. It is a hopeful sign.[30]

The combination of fact and fantasy involved in this militant Eurocentrism in many ways mirrors the Orientalism which it criticises; the focus on personality as the last line of defence of Europe against its Asiatic other is a striking one, and begs questions about the internal other which Europe must also resist (workers, women and Jews are all potentially the internal representatives of Oriental otherness); finally, although few readers of *The Criterion* would have identified wholeheartedly with Massis's position, the argument reveals crucial connections between the aesthetics of classicism and the politics of reaction which are frequently implicit in the romanticism/classicism debate.

It is often assumed that radical cultural criticism is the exclusive province of the left, but from the perspective of right-wing intellectuals the left, from communists via socialists to liberals, was united by an unquestioning faith in social progress. *The Criterion* created a basically right-wing platform for a more drastic form of questioning which was far from assuming that every social and technological innovation was for the good. In another attack on romanticism, Wyndham Lewis declared that 'we are the cave-men of the new mental wilderness' and claimed that in modernity the relationship between public and private life had broken down, that private life had become 'powerless, unsatisfying, circumscribed'.[31] Lewis went on to criticise his contemporaries for accepting this state of affairs rather than questioning it: 'It would not be easy to exaggerate the naiveté with which the average artist or writer to-day, deprived of all central authority, body of knowledge, tradition, or commonly accepted system of nature, accepts what he receives in place of those things.'[32] The artist or writer who sets out to document 'subjectivity' has ceased to respect the ability of thought to interrogate the conditions which form that subjectivity, and the consequence is a commodified and fashion-dependent art which has foregone its capacity for truth-telling.

Lewis's questioning of the contemporary environment is more fundamental, less complacent about 'human nature' and the possibility of knowing and fulfilling human desires, than anything in contemporary socialism:

> The kind of screen that is being built up between the reality and us, the 'dark night of the soul' into which each individual is relapsing, the intellectual shoddiness of so much of the thought responsible for the artist's reality, or 'nature', today, all these things seem to point to the desirability for a new, and if necessary shattering, criticism of modernity, as it stands at present.[33]

Lewis anticipates Adorno's use of the term 'technological veil' as a description of the process by which reality is masked not simply by ideology (in Lewis's terms, a 'reality' or 'nature' determined by shoddy thought) but by the very processes of communication which might be expected to create transparency, rather than bring about the closure of the individual in a world of personal experience: the social reality is not an inevitability, but presents itself, in the terms of both Lewis and Adorno, as a nature which deprives the individual of meaningful social interaction. What presents itself to the subject as a 'dark night of the soul' is, Lewis's quotation of the phrase implies, nothing of the sort. Rather, the individual is plunged into an

isolation by the encroachment of an increasingly technologised modernity, which, be it capitalist or communist, it is the true function of art and intelligence to resist. In his novels and satires Lewis parades anti-Semitic conspiracy theory and a denunciation of the process of 'feminisation', substituting a misguided defence of the West for the transvaluation of all values for which his *Criterion* essay calls. It is to the work of Adorno that we must turn for a version of this radical cultural pessimism rooted in the best tradition of progressive theory. The contemporary reader of *The Criterion* must regret that so much critical and resistant thought was eventually channelled so badly. Eliot, publishing an essay of Charles Maurras which argued against the primacy of creative over critical work, endorsed Maurras's views and noted the emergence of a new type of figure who was called into existence by the social crisis and replaced the established figure of the 'man of letters': 'Mr. Lewis is the most remarkable example in England of the actual mutation of the artist into a philosopher of a type hitherto unknown'. Referring as much to himself as to Lewis, Eliot argues that the 'man of letters' cannot now remain a merely 'creative' figure – the romantic notion of 'creativity' is in any case under attack by classicism – instead, 'the study of his own subject leads him irresistibly to the study of others'.[34] *The Criterion* thus announced the birth of the theorist.

The struggle between romanticism and classicism was not wholly one-sided. John Middleton Murry's *The Adelphi* provided a convenient foil to *The Criterion*'s polemics, and Murry rose to Eliot's challenge with articles printed in both journals. Murry's journal was not set up as a 'romantic' journal, and in fact he argued that the net distinction between romanticism and classicism was an artificial one in the context of English literature. Nevertheless, his object in setting up *The Adelphi* was romantic in the sense that the journal represented a personal, proselytising and healing mission. Again, the object was cultural, far removed from the niche marketing of journals of our own time. The principal impetus behind the establishment of the journal was the death of Katherine Mansfield, already famous for her short stories, and Murry's sometime partner. Shortly after Mansfield's death Murry experienced a revelation of God and decided to establish a journal to make known her unpublished work including her journal, as well as to promote life-affirming writing. Alongside Mansfield's work, *The Adelphi* regularly published material by Lawrence, conceived by Murry as the journal's second beneficiary. The title of the journal, which means 'brothers', was a homage to

Lawrence, who had offered Murry blood-brotherhood and made his refusal the subject of the novel *Aaron's Rod*. Murry's frequent affirmation of the value of 'life' in the pages of the journal are in part an acceptance of an agenda which Lawrence had defined many years earlier but which Murry had previously been unable to embrace. This is the individual aspect of the journal, yet its mission was a public one and its audience definitely conceived, even if Murry could have little idea how it would be received. *The Adelphi* was pitched at a broader audience than *The Criterion*, but not at a mass readership – in the terms of the day it was middlebrow. Murry entitled his first editorial 'The Cause of It All', and wondered aloud what the relationship might be between his own inquiry into the meaning of life and the concerns of the average person, conceived as a 'betting man': 'His betting and my preoccupations are cousins at least. The chief difference between us, I suppose, is that his particular kind of dope, like insulin, needs to be injected every twenty-four hours, except on Sunday when there is the *News of the World* […]'.[35] Murry alights on the betting man as the representative of the new culture of aimless 'leisure' (spectator sport) and pointless 'information' (the betting form) which mitigated against the type of spiritual reflection which is Murry's 'dope'. By defining himself as much an addict as the betting man, Murry is doing no more than acknowledging the post-war need for narcolepsy. At the same time, his ambition to communicate with a broader audience and perhaps challenge mass reading habits simultaneously recognises the dangers of the culture of distraction while refusing to join in with the highbrow panic. In order to keep its price at 1/- (compared to 3/6 for *The Criterion*) *The Adelphi* accepted a large number of advertisements, even allowing its cover to be taken up with a plug for the Remington portable typewriter. Apart from work by Mansfield and Lawrence, it featured a number of distinguished reviewers, including Bennett, Wells and Galsworthy, as well as a number of mediocre short-story contributions. One concession to extra-literary experience is made by the serialisation of excerpts from the pseudonymous Roger Dataller's 'From a Miner's Journal', later published in book form by Cape. The most consistent thread in *The Adelphi* is Murry himself, especially in his battle with Eliot, and his robust advocacy of Dostoevsky, Tolstoy and Shakespeare, later joined by Keats, as the great modern romantics.

'The essential attitude of Romanticism is an obedience to an external spiritual authority', a maxim which led Murry to an acceptance of

God but the refusal of religion.[36] Its combination of cheapness and Murry's frankness and occasional populism made *The Adelphi* a success: the first number sold three times the anticipated number and by the fourth issue Murry had set himself a target circulation of 20,000. Editorially at least, *The Adelphi* offered an alternative to *The Criterion*, but the debate about romanticism was never a debate about the direction of contemporary politics as far as Murry was concerned – he simply did not accept that romanticism was 'libertarian or egalitarian', while he viewed the classicists, including the author of *The Waste Land* himself, as merely 'incomplete Romantics'.[37] *The Adelphi* remained spiritual and apolitical. Its readership was certainly wider than that of *The Criterion*, and Murry's contributions to criticism both within its pages and without represent an advance on prevailing standards, but intellectuals at the time felt that Murry had gone down-market and that, as a journal of critical theory, his publication could never deal convincingly with the international squad of right-wingers assembled by Eliot.

Hunting the Highbrow: Q. D. Leavis and the Disintegration of the Reading Public

Alongside the Northcliffe press, advertising, the BBC and cinema, it is the bestseller which embodies the specifically literary dimension of the emergent mass society. The bestseller had emerged before the war, with the work of Marie Corelli boasting unprecedented sales figures, while the novels of Elinor Glyn offered new levels of sexual titillation. The rapid expansion of the bestseller market and its professionalisation along the lines of tabloid journalism and advertising during the 1920s came in parallel with the establishment of English as a University subject, making its début at Cambridge during the war. The pessimistic analysis of this decade shared by many cultural 'highbrows' fed into the development of English as a modern university subject through the work of Q. D. and F. R. Leavis, Cambridge academics who formulated an agenda for English which has dominated the subject until the present day, in spite of numerous but partial challenges.

One of the founding documents of Leavisism is Q. D. Leavis's *Fiction and the Reading Public* (1932), a book which laments the triumph of a professionalised urban print culture over an oral culture rooted in the soil of pre-industrial England. Although Leavis claims that it is a work of 'anthropology', it is also a polemical work which aims to rally the cultured 'minority', a group which she regrets is now to be distinguished from the powerful minority, since 'the people with power no longer represent intellectual authority and culture'. (Leavis, 1965: 191) What she constantly refers to as the 'minority' is that fraction of the dominating class which has invested in 'sensibility' rather than in power, a group which now has little influence on a ruling class principally interested in business values, and concerned not to cultivate a people but to massify and exploit them:

> The effect of increasing control by Big Business – in which it would hardly be unreasonable [...] to include the film interests – is to destroy among the masses a desire to read anything which by the widest stretch could be included in the classification 'literature'. (17)

In the opinion of Leavis, and similarly her equally famous and influential husband, it is literature and not any other medium which must carry forward cultural tradition and establish cultural continuity, although the actual content of this culture and its meaning as a practice is left somewhat vague, defined as a generalised 'sensibility', which is intended to mean a sensitivity to meanings and contexts of which the greatest literature (and not film, philosophy, journalism or business manuals) is the custodian. Leavis shares with D. H. Lawrence and Wyndham Lewis a dislike and fear of the mass which she occasionally characterises as the 'herd'. This term was derived from Nietzsche, whose account of Zarathustra as an *Übermensch* who has withdrawn from the herd and the market-place to live like a hermit was so influential among the cultivated that Lewis denounced him as a vulgariser of disgust.[38] Lewis, who had no wish to be part of the masses, also realised that an off-the-shelf nineteenth-century posture of Nietzschean contempt was inadequate to the deepening catastrophe of the twentieth century. Lawrence and Lewis alike had no belief or interest in education, yet it is in this area that the apparent élitism of the Leavises, as educators, differs from that of the artists.

Leavis's regret is that although literacy has been greatly extended since the Education Act of 1870 there have been few corresponding educational gains since people are using their new-gained literacy to consume novels, and these only of the worst, bestseller variety. 'In twentieth-century England not only every one can read, but it is safe to add that everyone does read' (3). Leavis points out that there are few bookshops, and that reading is conditioned by the newspapers – the eight leading Sunday newspapers were selling ten million copies a week in 1929 – and by the lending libraries (that is, the Public Libraries, the circulating libraries of W. H. Smiths and Boots, and the more exclusive postal services of the Times Book Club and Mudie's Library). These libraries rarely stocked 'what is considered by the critical minority to be the significant work in fiction – the novels of D. H. Lawrence, Virginia Woolf, James Joyce, T. F. Powys and E. M. Forster', nor did they stock important non-fiction, except for technical manuals. Rather, in a climate in which 'for most people a "book" means a novel'(5–6),[39] these libraries were awash with the so-called bestsellers, of which the crime novels of Edgar Wallace are held to be the most representative. The inclusion of T. F. Powys (whose *Mr Weston's Good Wine* is always invoked by the Leavises as a touchstone of literary sensibility) and the exclusion of Wyndham Lewis (consistently disregarded by them) alerts us that the Leavisite canon is about the continuity of a great novelistic tradition – which they insist is 'English' – and not about the Modernism which is the staple fare of the University in our own time. This is explained by Leavis's argument that in Elizabethan times the highest culture had reached the lower social strata, especially as theatre and music, in a climate in which everyone shared an active verbal sensibility and even a taste for literary pyrotechnics. At this time, it is claimed, journalists did not write down to the masses, much less cultivate a cheapened and patronising style of writing specifically aimed at an under-cultivated public with a view to further lowering their cultural level. In this culture, 'conversation was an art', (93) whereas 'popular taste is largely bound up with the discovery by the writing profession of the technique for exploiting emotional responses' (90). The difference for the Elizabethan 'masses' is that they were 'receiving their amusement from above (instead of being specially catered for by journalists, film-directors, and popular novelists as they are now)'. That these 'masses' might have gained little conscious education through the process of trickle-down cultural economics is irrelevant in Leavis's account, since 'education of ear and mind is none the less valuable for being acquired unconsciously,' or, as she puts it in relation to a later public, 'to read Bunyan and Milton for religious instruction, as to attend Elizabethan drama for the "action", is to acquire an education unconsciously' (85, 97).

Q. D. Leavis's view is then that even as recently as the Victorian epoch there has been a reading public which has been homogeneous as a readership even while it has been socially heterogeneous, and that the lower classes hence belonged to a cultural tradition which they assimilated unconsciously and organically. This vision of a nation at ease with itself is a form of one-nation Toryism which has resonances in the 1990s as well as with the Fascist nostalgia which was on the rise in contemporary Germany, but is founded on a comforting fantasy of the organic identity of an unalienated village life in which the only desires which arise are natural needs which can be met by a nature and economy ready to hand. When Leavis refers to the 'disintegration' of the reading public she is invoking a vision of the destruction, again in Tory vocabulary, of the fabric of the nation, a continuity of traditional sensibility rooted in an oral culture and in uncomplicated (if somewhat hierarchical) social relations. We need not, however, embrace the Leavises' vision of cultural tradition (for all that we continue apparently unavoidably to educate ourselves according to its precepts) to feel the force of Q. D. Leavis's description of this disintegration, which resonates in important ways with the differently articulated pessimism of Eliot, Lawrence and Lewis, amongst others.[40] Her account gives us some sense of the ways in which the widespread marketisation of literature in its by now well-established modern form appeared to people who felt that they were witnessing something like a permanent cultural closure, the beginning of a dark age in which the minority, as artists or as University English teachers, must carry the torch.

The key feature of the new literary dispensation is that, in contrast to Leavis's version of the Elizabethan past in which oral and written culture cut across social divisions, there is now a market-led polarisation of readerships. Whereas once literate members of the lower-middle and working classes had aspired to read intellectually central texts of theology, literature and philosophy, including the famed translations of Greek and Latin classics, the increasingly literate masses are now said to be diverted from serious reading by the products of the new mass culture. The circulating libraries had already turned fiction into a narcotic – 'the reading habit is now often a form of the drug habit' (7) – and by the nineteenth century 'the readiness to read a good novel had become a craving for fiction of any kind' (136). When the one-volume novel replaced the three-volume novel in the 1890s, 'the sudden opening of the fiction market to the general public was a blow to serious reading' (161). The effect of increased public literacy was to create the triumph of the mass market over taste in the wake of the Education Act of 1870, 'the only effect of which on the book market was to swell the ranks of the half-educated half a generation later (until then educated taste had managed to hold its own)' (163).

Leavis's account has important elements in common with Wyndham Lewis's *The Art of Being Ruled* (1926), which it nevertheless fails to acknowledge, perhaps because of crucial ideological differences. Lewis took the more conspiratorial view that it was in the ruling interest to divide the population according to various categories that wasted their energies in what he perceived as futile debate. Of course, the sex war and class war described by Lewis had a progressive autonomy which he declined to acknowledge. At the same time, his sense that the press in particular were responsible for building up imaginary class conflicts is best epitomised in his identification of the specious 'age war' which accompanied what he called the 'cult of youth'. In *Doom of Youth* (1932) Lewis set out to show that the press, in a spirit of divide and rule, and with the aim of infantilising the general population, has set about worshipping the values of 'youth' and denigrating the accumulated values of 'age'. Lewis is documenting the emergence of 'youth culture' in its present modern form – an element that is missing from Leavis's account – demonstrating an attempt to valorise the simple tastes of the adolescent as the mainstream culture, a process which has continued to unfold vigorously until our own time. Leavis's picture of the modern reader as an addict of ready-made sentiment is very similar to Lewis's vision of the new role of culture as the agent of a process of infantilisation based on scientifically calculated principles.

Lewis's account encompasses not only the press, cinema, radio and bestseller of Leavis's account, but even the bastions of Modernist culture itself. Indeed, Lewis penned vigorous denunciations of the leading lights of Modernism, accusing them of effecting the same kind of psychological effects as cinema, and creating an art which betrayed the values of contemplation and substituted one of effect in which the thinking subject was overwhelmed by the flux of time. Gertrude Stein, James Joyce and Ezra Pound are each severely criticised by Lewis as adherents of a new 'time-cult' which in the end serves only the interests of business with its ideology of perpetual false novelty.

Leavis and Lewis agree in seeing 'educated taste' or 'intellect' as the deliberate victim of the new dispensation. Having witnessed during the war the willingness of the press to drum up vulgar nationalism and vilify pacifists, there is a sense shared by Leavis and Lewis that the same forces were being turned against intellectual and artistic culture, that members of all classes were being roused to a contempt of the 'highbrow'. Leavis also echoes the claims of Lewis and other neo-classicists that all critical distance is being obliterated: the modern novel like the cinema is intended to wash over the reader, creating emotional effects and excitement through uncon-ditional identification with the hero, the author no longer being felt as the detached and rational companion of the reader who is instead caught up in the narrative adventure (235). Lewis's response to this pessimistic scenario was to formulate a Nietzschean 'politics of the intellect', urging what he thought of as the few remaining 'individuals' to resist massification and the politics of permanent revolution and stand outside the herd. Lewis differed from Leavis in the crucial respect that he believed the most serious contemporary writers to be saturated by the same literary politics of romantic novelty as the bestseller.[41] Leavis continued to see serious literature as a bastion of cultivation, but eschewed Lewis's essentially romantic, Baudelairean stance of the artist as outsider, and looked instead to the University and English teaching to preserve taste and sensibility through the new Dark Ages.

Because Leavis views educated taste as having a kind of potential for universality, inasmuch as it can trickle down across class barriers in the context of a parentalistic class society, *Fiction and the Reading Public* offers an account of the history of taste rather than of literary form, and defends a generalised notion of the critical intelligence which might be acquired through reading, rather than examining the historically grasped orientation of the novel form as such. For this, as for much else which Leavis and Lewis cannot supply, we would have to turn to the traditions of Western Marxism which had a parallel genesis in a Europe which was not so much post-war as post-Russian Revolution. Leavis and Lewis note many of the phenomena which are dwelt on by Benjamin and Adorno.

While Adorno's account emphasises the polarisation of high and low culture, described as autonomous and dependent art with all of the attendant problems for the former which his work explores, Q. D. Leavis produces a three-tier model in which the middlebrow plays a key role. The distinction between high and middlebrow is not clearly enunciated by Leavis because it is a question of gradations of taste rather than the sharp distinction which Adorno's model allows for. However, Leavis's account identifies the way in which the serious literary world has become divided in itself. Her example of a middle-brow journal is the *Times Literary Supplement*, while Arnold Bennett is held up as the archetypal middlebrow reviewer. The *TLS* is considered 'safe' and will give a convenient plot summary of a new novel, while the quotable remarks of reviewers such as Bennett are directly adopted as advertising or packaging: 'an enterprising publisher will reissue the novel with a band or new dust-jacket exhibiting the caption' (22). Bennett was the single most powerful reviewer of this period whose comments could make or break a new novel, and Q. D. Leavis was not alone in regretting the establishment of a middlebrow culture passing itself off as the highbrow, a process which Bennett embodied. Virginia Woolf, of course, famously rejected the middle-class materialism of Bennett's fiction, along with that of Wells and Galsworthy, in 'Modern Fiction' (1919) and 'Mr Bennett and Mrs Brown' (1924), while Ezra Pound attacked Bennett as 'Mr Nixon' in *Hugh Selwyn Mauberley* (1920), representing Nixon as part of the stifling culture which caused Pound to leave England. In this account, then, the emergence of mass culture is accompanied by the parallel development of a middlebrow public sphere, a further fragmentation of the reading public which serves all the more thoroughly the eclipse of highbrow sensibility by arrogating to itself an inflated authority.

That so much of the teaching of modern English is based on a conservative and pessimistic reading of the 1920s as the era of the emergence of a new mass culture is worth dwelling on. For all that the influence of F. R. Leavis is widely excoriated among younger English academics today, his project, based as it is on the analysis of Q. D. Leavis's *Fiction and the Reading Public*, is strangely consonant with their own. *Fiction and the Reading Public* denies that individual effort can challenge the 'monstrous impersonality' of the 'economic machinery'. 'All that can be done, it must be realised, must take the form of resistance by an armed and conscious minority.' This minority must operate in two ways. First, as researchers, not of the history of great texts but of 'the history of the reading public [...] in these days when mass-production conditions determine the supply of literature'. Second, 'it would mean the training of a picked few who would go out into the world equipped for the work of forming and organising a conscious minority' serving to carry out 'educational work in schools and universities'. The aim would be to fire the young with a sense of the 'necessity of resistance' and a 'missionary spirit'. 'In fact the possibilities of education specifically directed against such appeals as those made by the journalist, the middleman, the best-seller, the cinema, and advertising [...] are inexhaustible; some education of this kind is an essential part of the training of taste' (270–1). Leavis's minority activist is a synthesis of the missionary and the revolutionary. That her or his objective is not salvation or liberation but the 'training of taste' bespeaks a profound pessimism about human possibility which is common to writers and intellectuals of the period. It was a feature of the subsequent decade that creative writers began to look towards communism as a source of cultural optimism, although communism was, of course, very much a part of British culture in the 1920s, a feature that the Leavises were in reaction against.

Bloomsbury and the Miners: Ellen Wilkinson's Clash

So much of the literature of the 1920s speaks from pessimistic, socially conservative, even regressive political positions that any apparent exception to the rule invites close scrutiny. Ellen Wilkinson's *Clash* (1929) which deals directly with the General Strike of 1926 is one of the period's most striking anomalies in this respect. It is a frankly partisan piece of socialist realism, focused not on the strike itself but on a semi-autobiographical romantic plot which takes place against the background of the strike. While many authors discussed in this study accepted and embraced marginality and political ineffectiveness, the author of *Clash* was a sitting Labour MP.

Ellen Cicely Wilkinson (1891–1947) first became politically active in 1910 while taking a degree in history at Manchester University. She joined the Independent Labour Party and became active in the 'Votes for Women' movement. In 1913 she became the Manchester organiser for the National Union of Women's Suffrage Societies (NUWSS) and was noted for her striking appearance and her impressive capability as a public speaker. Wilkinson joined the Communist Party in 1920, and left in 1924, rejecting its revolutionary goals, but not socialist and feminist activism. She stood as Labour Party candidate for Middlesborough East in 1924 and was elected, keeping her seat until 1931. During the strike she raised funds for the miners on a trip to the USA.[42]

Wilkinson was a committed activist who became a professional politician, yet maintained a firm commitment to and identification with the working class throughout her political life.[43] Like any socialist activist of the period, she was aware that the dominant ideas of a time are the ideas of the ruling class, and would have understood that this applied not only to the dissemination of news (which became an immediate issue in the General Strike as the novel documents) but to the writing of history and the shaping of the collective imagination in fiction. Before publishing the novel, Wilkinson had contributed to a volume called *A Workers' History of the General Strike* published by the Plebs League. The main sections of the book detailed events in the 'provinces', and were assembled from material sent in by correspondents nationwide, while the shorter sections co-authored by Wilkinson detailed political events in the capital.[44] Perhaps sensing that popular fiction was more likely than a dry political history to reach a wider audience, Wilkinson turned also to fiction.[45] However, *Clash* does not attempt to document the strike from the strikers' point of view. It is designed to appeal to the reader of romance by having a strong central heroine who is faced with a relatively conventional romantic choice about whether she should become the mistress and perhaps wife of a man who is already married. Two social issues are attached to this question, each of which would have confronted Wilkinson in her own life. The protagonist Joan Craig is of a working-class background, and is of rising fame as a trade union organiser who may eventually have the prospect of standing for Parliament. Marriage or an affair as envisaged by the upper-class writer Tony Dacre would involve her giving up her political work in favour of becoming his permanent companion and, in the event of marriage, bringing up his children. The novel does not automatically resolve this question in favour of independence, but shows that Joan is attracted to the role of lover and wife. The second issue is attached to the first: the question of social class and of the politics that go with class.

Joan is a provincial working-class girl, but her trade union activism takes her out of her familiar environment to London, where she has a rich friend, Mary Maud:

> Mary Maud was a wealthy bachelor woman, an intimate of an exclusive Bloomsbury circle who bestowed fame on themselves by writing reviews of each other's books. As each slender work appeared it was greeted as a new Tchehov [sic], a more sensitive Dostoievsky, a respringing of the fountain of Shelley's genius. Most people read the reviews and not the books, and as all they wanted was to be told which was the book of the hour the circle was accepted as the last word in literary genius.
>
> (Wilkinson, 1929: 17)

This passage is not merely an attempt to knock the potential rivals and reviewers of *Clash*, but signals that upper-class culture and the protagonist's relationship to it will be a central concern. For Wilkinson and Wyndham Lewis alike, a sectional 'Bloomsbury Group' comes to stand synechdochically for the condition of the metropolitan ruling class. In *The Apes of God*, Wyndham Lewis had claimed to be writing a 'non-moral' satire of Bloomsbury which was not politically partisan. In spite of his claim, he produced a right-wing critique concerned with decadence, while the representational criteria adopted within his satirical method belong to a profoundly anti-human aesthetic. Wilkinson's critique of Bloomsbury is designed to show the ambiguous nature of liberal left-wing sympathies as expressed by this group, sympathies which are limited in the context of the strike not only because members of this class have no experience of oppression and poverty, but also because their very wealth depends on investments in mining and the other capitalist industries which are the inheritance of their class. For them to support the radical claims of the workers would be to attack the basis of their own existence as a class. The liberal Bloomsburyites are shown not to have understood the meaning of their dependence on capitalist exploitation, yet Wilkinson does not portray her ruling class with the harsh and dehumanising antagonism of Lewis's 'external method'. Rather, she depicts individual members of the class as humane and even vulnerable, and also shows how attractive the life of this class is for her protagonist. In this respect the novel is decidedly autobiographical: Wilkinson owned a Bloomsbury flat, and was known for her enjoyment of upper-class company, including individuals completely opposed to her own politics.[46] The decision that Joan makes at the end of the novel is that she cannot exchange her conditions of life as a trade union activist for the luxury of being a kept woman in Bloomsbury without losing touch with the conditions and concerns of the working class, nor can she surrender her active, working life to be passive partner to a man. The General Strike provides not merely a background to her story, but constantly intrudes as the objectification of a condition of class conflict which is not simply cultural or intellectual but takes the form of a confrontation in which the resources of each class are, for a short period, fully mobilised.

Joan is not portrayed as an intellectual who already knows all the political answers; she is an 'organic intellectual', to adopt Gramsci's definition, a thinker whose ideas are formed in the process of class struggle and whose thought will have a constant pragmatic and experiential component. Joan's ideas are also organic with her class in the sense that, as well as sharing its experience, she is also exposed to its ideology, not only in the form of the common ideas which inform everyday life, but also in the form of ideas promoted in the mass media. Her ideas about sexual relationships are traditional, and she is capable of experiencing sexual interest across class barriers, as revealed by a remark about Winston Churchill, already notorious as an aggressive enemy of the labour movement: 'He'd make a lovely revolutionary leader,' she jokes, 'He isn't exactly a sheik, I admit, but [...] there is a touch of something daredevil in him.' (14). Joan is established for the reader very much like the protagonist of a desert romance (see below, Chapter Five). She has never been in love although she is twenty-six years old. Her friend describes her as 'virile' and thinks that 'she would go over the top like an avalanche if she really loved' (76). As with the desert heroine, a major part of her attractiveness to men is her lack of femininity and her penchant for activity – she is generally best seen in action, with an unwashed and ill-dressed appearance. It appears that she is destined to be sexually awoken and made feminine by the onslaught of some 'sheik' when she begins her affair with the Bloomsbury writer Tony Dacre.[47] The artful design of the novel is to keep this possibility alive, showing that romance and sex are a genuine attraction for Joan, only to demonstrate at the end that there is an alternative for her.

'I get half my money from coal you know', Joan's Bloomsbury friend, Mary Maud, one of the daughters of educated men, casually discloses. Mary Maud will stick to the side of the miners and becomes increasingly politicised in the course of the novel. Helen Dacre appears at first as a contrasting figure, who will lend a theatre she has hired to the volunteers who will attempt to break the strike by carrying out vital economic functions. She is highly identified with political reaction, implicitly underpinned by an outfit of 'cubist design' that features a 'red swastika' (41). Helen is universally seen as a cold and manipulative wife who has married a man whom she did not love and has now trapped. Yet by the end of the novel a more sympathetic account of this character emerges, and she has changed sides and agreed to support the miners with a charity event.

The Bloomsbury culture can identify against its own class interest on a limited basis. It is shown as being able to learn, to a degree, just as Joan on the other hand must learn what the limitation of this class is and how in terms of her own politics she must reject it. Everyone in this novel learns rapidly about the personal and the political as well as the relationship between them, and the process of learning politics through experience and gaining a capacity to develop and advance political arguments is repeatedly represented in the book. The novel is established around a two cultures thesis, which sees the working class and the ruling class as divided by a gulf of experience, which even well-meaning wealthy individuals cannot cross. This is especially so in the case of Mary Maud, who attempts to argue like Joan with her rich friends:

> She knew she had been idle and luxurious, easily generous with money easily come by, but with a generosity limited to a circle of pleasant acquaintances. [...] She could only *feel* she was right about the miners. She ought to have *known* how to put their case. [...]
> Like all rich people who join a proletarian movement on mere emotion, she did not dare to question her colleagues for fear they might think her lukewarm in the Cause, and so, when faced with the old arguments on which she had been nourished from childhood, she had nothing but feelings and emotional platitudes to offer. [...] She wanted to help the miners, but it was pleasanter to dream about Joan. (111–13)

The novel, which is after all penned by a politician, is not coy about guiding the reader's analysis, here as elsewhere, yet the point is not so much to damn even well-meaning individuals in the ruling group as to show why Joan cannot opt to join this group as a mistress or wife, as all her political motivation, and the knowledge that helps her fulfil her role, comes from sharing the experience of the working class. The turning point for her comes when she begins to feel her identification with the working class fading. Finally, she chooses not to marry Tony after a charity event at which she loses her temper with hostile questioning from the wealthy audience. Outside the meeting her other admirer, Gerry, who unlike her has known how to resist the charms of the upper class, expounds to her the novel's moral:

> Its [sic] not what their class consciously does to the workers' leaders that matters, Joan. Its easy to fight against that, but its [sic] the mass of ideas which they take for granted, and which they assume as a matter of course, that all decent people will take for granted, the atmosphere they create that is so difficult to fight against. [...] You can't convert people like these. [...] All their class privileges are bound up with not being converted. [...] You've only two things to do, keep out and fight them, or go in and accept all they have to give – and its [sic] a lot if you are worth while. But you can't go in and fight them at the same time. (294)

Although Wilkinson was a reformist politician who had little knowledge of revolutionary theory, the lesson that the novel moves towards has its direct corollary in a text of Marx with which she was probably familiar:[48]

> The ideas of the ruling class are in every epoch the ruling ideas, i.e. the class which is the ruling *material* force in society, is at the same time its ruling *intellectual* force. The class which has the means of material production at its disposal, has control at the same time over the means of mental production [...]. Within this class [a] cleavage [between the 'thinkers of the class' and the 'passive, receptive' consumers of their ideas] can even develop into a certain opposition and hostility between the two parts, which, however, in the case of a practical collision, in which the class itself is endangered, automatically comes to nothing [...]. The existence of revolutionary ideas in a particular period presupposes the existence of a revolutionary class.[49]

In the logic of the novel, Joan must learn the truth of this formulation, and she does so more at the level of experience than of abstract reasoning. The novel concentrates on this dilemma rather than on the strike itself, although the vignettes of the strike which emerge are designed to contrast not only the poverty of the strikers with the Bloomsbury socialites, but also the nature and meaning of their solidarity – the fact, for example, that one man on the verge of retirement will sacrifice his pension by coming out on strike in support of the miners. The novel is also concerned to reiterate the central conclusions of the left as represented in *A Workers' History of the General Strike*, asserting the socialist view that mining should be organised as a national asset rather than a set of private concerns, and emphasising the contrast between the betrayal of Union leaders and the unprecedented solidarity of the striking workers. The heroism of the strikers is never left in doubt, and as the passage quoted above demonstrates, ambiguities of any kind are discarded as the luxury of bourgeois fiction. This is a work of socialist realism which certainly lacks the sophistication of a Henry James, yet as a diagnostic of English class dynamics in the 1920s it is difficult to find a more serious or truthful treatment among the highbrow novels produced by the Bloomsbury culture which is here put into question. At the same time, it is a manipulative book, and as a consequence the characters are not fully dimensioned. This is true even of the protagonist, whose unrelenting virtue is irritating and unconvincing – worryingly so, as she is closely modelled on the author herself.

The New World Order: D. H. Lawrence's Kangaroo

Several of the works of D. H. Lawrence are discussed under other headings in this book. *Kangaroo* (1923) makes an appearance here because its principal theme is the relationship of the individual to mass politics. This novel is generally considered one of Lawrence's minor works, and critics who believe Lawrence's lifelong theme to have been a sexual one have generally passed over it, as they have passed over *Aaron's Rod* (1922) and *The Plumed Serpent* (1926), in a hurry to get to the more carefully composed *Lady Chatterley's Lover* (1928). *Kangaroo* was in a sense written on the hoof during Lawrence's 'savage pilgrimage', and the claim of Richard Aldington's 1950 'Introduction', that this 'is not one of Lawrence's worked-over novels' but that it was 'improvised' rather than 'planned',[50] has set the tone of much subsequent discussion. However, it is misleading to think of *Kangaroo* as simply not a very proficient or fully realised novel, redeemed in some parts but not in its whole by the quality and conviction of the writing.

On the one hand it is necessary to consider *Kangaroo* in terms of the history which stands over the text and structures its interior. On the other, it is essential to grasp that its apparent flaws owe much to the author's own perception that the novel itself has approached a kind of crisis in the aftermath of the war, much as the thesis of the novel is that the status of the individual is in crisis in mass society. Lawrence's determination that the novel should open out on to history rather than attempt to ward off historical crisis through its own aesthetic closure accounts both for *Kangaroo*'s unsatisfactoriness as a novel and for its interest as a book.

Lawrence once again uses his wife Frieda and himself as protagonists. The setting is Australia, where the Lawrences stayed for nearly three months in 1922. It is considered the most autobiographical of Lawrence's novels, because many of the scenes describing landscape and travel experiences are based on his own experience, and because the tone of the Lawrences' marriage at this time is faithfully represented by Lawrence (in a moderately self-critical manner). Furthermore, the ideas which Lawrence ascribes to his protagonist Richard Somers are very much his own. What is remarkable, though, is the rudimentary action of the novel, which is based entirely on invention, although its autobiographical and travel aspects led some readers to believe that the political world which the novel describes was also a reality.[51] Lawrence had gone to Australia believing it to be 'a place to go when one has had enough of the world – when one doesn't want to wrestle with another single thing, humanly',[52] and in the eyes of Somers, Australia at times seems an 'amorphous' and 'foundationless' physical and social environment which contrasts with the 'horrible *weight*' of 'the heavy established European way of life' (Lawrence, 1997a: 346).

However, the sense of escape from Europe and its values is temporary, as Somers has political demands made on him which exactly resemble those of the European scene. The political scene in Australia as described in *Kangaroo* is a concoction which forms Australian elements according to the Italian model. Lawrence had witnessed the struggle between Fascists and Communists in Italy between 1920 and 1922, and converts this struggle into a confrontation between 'Diggers', led by a lawyer nicknamed Kangaroo, and Socialists. Each side vies for the support of Somers, who as an established writer can greatly further the cause. Somers is divided between a desire to involve himself in collective male politics – facetiously described by John Middleton Murry as 'a sort of powerfully organised Whitmanism'[53] – and the desire, which ultimately proves stronger, to transcend the masses and exist as one of the few individuals in mass society who can remain true to his individual selfhood: 'Back to the central self, the isolate, absolute self' (280).

The context of Somers's dilemma is explained in Chapter Twelve, 'The Nightmare', an extended flashback based directly on Lawrence's own experiences during the war. This justifiably famous chapter describes Lawrence's own sense of humiliation before the national state which attempted to coerce him to fight in the war, at first through moral pressure and then through conscription or the 'call up'. Lawrence as Somers insists that he is not a pacifist or conscientious objector, but is opposed to a war brought about by official mob rule. Somers's resistance to the war is represented in terms of the 'independent soul' opposed to the 'criminal mob', and Lawrence/Somers regrets the years 1916 (the year in which conscription was introduced) to 1919 as 'the years when the world lost its real manhood' (213). The moment of his most absolute humiliation occurs when he must bend over and present himself for rectal examination before a panel of military medical examiners (245), a moment which confirms him in his resistance to submission to the masculine collective. We have noted the way in which a centralised state emerged during the war, and how the press and other propaganda organs created an atmosphere of mass hysteria. Lawrence's terms of resistance, which set the individual in opposition to the mass or herd owe much to Nietzsche. Lawrence was not a rigorous reader of Nietzsche, but frequently returns throughout his work to his own adaptations of certain Nietzschean concepts.[54] However, Nietzsche is adapted by Lawrence, as he was by Wyndham Lewis, to an entirely new social situation in which the herd is no longer a slave-like, Christianised mass (as Nietzsche saw it), but a passive and manipulated body of people who have been deprived of selfhood by industrialisation and democracy. *Kangaroo* registers a situation in which mass politics are now the norm, and European dilemmas are set to repeat themselves not only in Europe, but also in the colonised world. So while Australia, with its picturesque and non-human landscapes and its apparently informal towns and cities seems like a place where the self can gain a little space and leave everything behind, European forces are at work here too, as the *political* struggle between Fascism and Communism appears set to take the place of *national* struggle, as the period of conflict between nations is replaced by a new era of political conflict within nations. Each is a form of collective struggle between masses which demand the allegiance of individuals only in order to extinguish them as individuals.

Kangaroo registers clearly enough that the basis of Communism is workers' organisation, and that Fascism is a movement of national revival and discipline which draws initially on the disillusion of demobilised soldiers. However, Lawrence/Somers superimposes on this distinction a more tenuous one, seeing the Socialists (Communists) as valorising work and the Diggers (Fascists) as representing love.[55] These opposed forces are seen as being merely variants of each other: both work and love require the individual to submit to the collective. Somers rejects both and asserts a preference for isolation:

> The only thing one can stick to is one's own isolate being, and the God in whom it is rooted. And the only thing to look to is the God who fulfils one from the dark. And the only thing to wait for is for men to find their aloneness and their God in the darkness. Then one can meet as worshippers, in a sacred contact in the dark. (328)

Set against the anal examination, the notion of God fulfilling one in the dark acquires a promising resonance from the point of view of psychoanalytical criticism.[56] The mystical terms employed by Lawrence-/Somers here, and the home-made psychological concepts deployed elsewhere in the novel (which resemble those of *Fantasia of the Unconscious*), do not offer a convincing model of the individual.

Other passages in the novel which discuss personal power and the submission of weaker personalities to strong ones, as well as the continued attempts of Somers to get his wife to submit to his own will (again reflecting the relationship of the Lawrences), will convince few readers that there is an attractive notion of individuality at the centre of the philosophy which appears to lie at the centre of the novel. However, this novel has no philosophy at its centre – it is described in the authorial voice as a 'thought adventure', and we might therefore expect inconsistency or lack of conclusiveness in the idea represented. This lack of philosophical centre, though, is very much the subject of the book. As the increasingly Western world shifts from one form of global organisation to another, the notion of the individual loses its ground. So the notion of selfhood becomes negatively defined, the space of a still vaguely conceived utopian possibility. It is constituted as an evasion of the external masses, not an answer to them. It articulates itself in terms which are mystical and opaque, so as not to give itself away. The self may already be lost, may be a fiction, but Lawrence/Somers refuses to surrender the spirit of resistance which is both the last residue of the self's former existence and the potential space for its future emergence.

The form of the novel can be understood as the expression of this dilemma. The author knows well enough that conventional demands for plot action are not being fulfilled in a novel more interested in thought, conversation and landscape. 'Chapter follows chapter, and nothing doing' (284). This is the opening of Chapter Fifteen, which goes on sardonically to recapitulate the plot before continuing, a mocking concession to conventional readerly expectations. Plot itself instrumentalises character, especially in the world of the popular thriller, and Lawrence is determined that his characters, if they are to be preserved as ends in themselves, will not become mere puppets, the means to an action determined by the criteria of mass entertainment.

Lawrence's conception of an individuality which is prior to the social is in itself a flawed one. Yet *Kangaroo* is a clear and early warning that the process of massification did not end with the war. Further, in the very moment when, with the ending of the war, romantic escape through travel became possible on an unprecedented scale,[57] *Kangaroo* shows that the traveller must go far afield to escape a political process which colonisation has already spread through much of the world. Murry called *Kangaroo* 'one of the most profound political treatises of modern times', which showed 'the complete moral demand of conscious politics upon the modern man'.[58] *Kangaroo*, in its ideas, in its rejection of fictional norms, and even in its confusions, is an early and in some ways remarkably subtle fictional response to the encroaching demands of the nascent totalitarian epoch. The problems which it sets forth define the trajectory of Lawrence's subsequent work, as the discussion of *The Plumed Serpent* and *Lady Chatterley's Lover* in the following chapters aims to make clear.

Notes

1. For recent work in this area, see Michael Tratner, *Modernism and Mass Politics*, and John Carey, *The Intellectuals and the Masses*.
2. For near-contemporary comment on 'Sport and Spectacle', see John Collier and Iain Lang, *Just The Other Day*, pp. 113–18. For a recent academic overview, see Stephen J. Jones, *Workers At Play*.
3. Douglas Goldring, *The Nineteen Twenties*, p. 27.
4. See Bernard Waites, *A Class Society at War*, pp. 8–10.
5. See Waites, *Class Society*, pp. 37–42.
6. See Waites, *Class Society*, pp. 47–54.
7. See Waites, *Class Society*, pp. 49–52, and Charles Masterman, *England After the War*.
8. The figures are taken from Charles Loch Mowat, *Britain Between The Wars*, pp. 126, 357. For higher contemporary estimates see Irene Clephane, *Ourselves*, p. 155.
9. Clephane, *Ourselves*, p. 155.
10. Collier and Lang, *Just the Other Day*, p. 65.
11. Clephane, *Ourselves*, p. 163.
12. Quoted Goldring, *The Nineteen Twenties*, p. 222.
13. D. H. Lawrence, *Phoenix II*, pp. 257–66.
14. For a comprehensive account of publishers and readerships, see Joseph McAleer, *Popular Reading and Publishing in Britain 1914–1950*.
15. For a short discussion of the significance of the eighteenth-century public sphere in relation to English literature and criticism see Terry Eagleton, *The Function of Criticism: From the Spectator to Post-structuralism*, pp. 9–43.
16. Edgell Rickword, review of *The Art of Being Ruled*, *The Calendar of Modern Letters* 3: 1 (October 1926), 247–50.
17. Edwin Muir, 'Scrutinies (4) Arnold Bennett', in *The Calendar of Modern Letters* 1: 4, (June 1925), 290–6.
18. H. C. Harwood, review of Dorothy Richardson, *The Trap*, *The Calendar of Modern Letters* 1: 4 (June 1925), 328–9.

19. 'Comments and Reviews', *The Calendar of Modern Letters* 1: 2 (April 1925), 153.
20. Wyndham Lewis, 'The Dithyrambic Spectator: An Essay on the Origins and Survival of Art', *The Calendar of Modern Letters* 1: 2 (April 1925), 89–107 (see pp. 93–4).
21. See G. W. F. Hegel, *Introductory Lectures on Aesthetics.*
22. See 'Commentary' in *The Criterion*, 7 (April 1924), 231.
23. T. S. Eliot, 'The Idea of a Literary Review', *The New Criterion* 4: 1 (January 1926), 1–6.
24. T. S. Eliot, 'The Literature of Fascism', *The Criterion* 8: 31 (December 1928), 280–90 (see 288).
25. Alert to the contrast between Massis's Eurocentrism and the exoticism of Lawrence's Mexican phase, Eliot places the second instalment of Massis next to an excerpt from Lawrence's *Mornings in Mexico.*
26. Henri Massis, 'Defence of the West I', translated by F. S. Flint, *The New Criterion* 4: 2 (April 1926), 224–43 (see p. 225).
27. Massis, 'Defence of the West I', p. 226.
28. Massis, 'Defence of the West I', p. 231.
29. Massis, 'Defence of the West I', pp. 488–9.
30. *The Criterion* 6: 2 (August 1927), 98.
31. Wyndham Lewis, 'The Values of the Doctrine Behind Subjective Art', *The Criterion* 6: 1 (July 1927), 9–13 (see p. 9).
32. Lewis, 'The Values of the Doctrine Behind Subjective Art', p. 9.
33. Lewis, 'The Values of the Doctrine Behind Subjective Art', pp. 10–11.
34. *The Criterion* 6: 5 (November 1927), 386–7.
35. John Middleton Murry, 'The Cause of It All', *The Adelphi* 1: 1 (June 1923), 1–11 (see pp. 2–3).
36. John Middleton Murry, 'More about Romanticism', *The Adelphi* 1: 7 (December 1923), 557–69 (see p. 557).
37. John Middleton Murry, 'On Fear; and On Romanticism', *The Adelphi* 1: 4 (September 1923), 269–77 (see p. 277).
38. See Wyndham Lewis, *The Art of Being Ruled*, pp. 113–18.
39. Joseph McAleer notes that for many people at this time a 'book' is a serial fiction magazine.
40. On the differences between Eliot and F. R. Leavis, see David Gervais, *Literary Englands*, pp. 133–55.
41. See, for example, his treatment of D. H. Lawrence in *The Enemy II.*
41. For a short account of Wilkinson's life see Terence Anthony Lockett, *Three Lives.* A more detailed account appears in Betty D. Vernon, *Ellen Wilkinson*, a disturbingly wooden hagiography which assembles facts competently without ever giving the impression of getting close to its subject. Wilkinson is also celebrated in fiction as the pugnacious Sarah Burton in Winifred Holtby's *South Riding.*
43. After losing her Middlesborough seat Wilkinson became the

prospective parliamentary candidate for Labour in Jarrow, where she was duly elected, going on to take a key role in the famous Jarrow Crusade against mass unemployment.

44. *A Workers' History of the Great Strike* was 'Written, from material supplied by PLEBS correspondents in all parts of the country, by R. W. Postgate, Ellen Wilkinson M.P. and J. F. Horrabin'. Readers of the *History* were invited to subscribe to the monthly journal *The Plebs* by writing to an address in Buckingham Palace Road.

45. *Clash* was printed in a run of 3,000 (see Vernon, *Ellen Wilkinson*, p. 133) and not reprinted until after the war.

46. See Vernon, *Ellen Wilkinson*, p. 116.

47. She is not yet 'awakened' (p. 181); Tony Dacre is 'acting the sheik' (p. 227).

48. See Vernon, *Ellen Wilkinson*, p. 34.

49. Karl Marx and Friedrich Engels, *The German Ideology*, pp. 64-5.

50. Aldington, 'Introduction' to *Kangaroo*, p. 8.

51. Aldington notes: 'Yet so convincing are these imagined scenes that Lawrence was bitterly blamed for refusing to tell the dying 'Roo that he loved him – although no such person and no such scene ever existed.' 'Introduction' to *Kangaroo*, p. 9. See David Ellis, *D. H. Lawrence: Dying Game*, p. 45, for a summary of the issues around Lawrence's knowledge of Australian paramilitary organisations, and his 'D. H. Lawrence in Australia: The Darroch Controversy', *The D. H. Lawrence Review*, XXI (Summer 1989), 167–74, for a more complete account.

52. Lawrence, *Letters* IV, pp. 272–3.

53. John Middleton Murry, *Son of Woman*, p. 240.

54. See Colin Milton, *Lawrence and Nietzsche*, for a developed account.

55. The schema is again indebted to Nietzsche at the same time that it is a residue of Lawrence's earlier thinking – a pattern of thought which would take more space to unfold than is available here.

56. I do not develop the obvious psychoanalytic possibilities here, but my *Wyndham Lewis and Western Man*, pp. 30–53, contains a discussion of anti-Semitism which, amongst other elements, suggests how Freud's case study of Schreber can be used to understand the role of repressed passive homosexuality and corresponding homosexual dread in the resistance to mass politics.

57. See Paul Fussell, *Abroad*, for a general account of this phenomenon.

58. Quoted in Harry T. Moore, *The Priest of Love*, p. 446.

4

Sex, Satire and the Jazz Age

S EX AND SEXUALITY DO not only have a crucial structural role in the literature dealing with war and social change, they also generate a whole literature of their own in the 1920s which is variously cynical and progressive. The treatment of sex reflects both social realities and a renewed intellectual interest in sex, and plays a key part in the notion of this decade as the 'jazz age'.

In the popular imagination, fed largely by the new mass circulation newspapers, young women were connected not merely with Bolshevism but with sexuality itself. They seemed to undermine traditional gender roles at the level of appearance and behaviour, sporting short haircuts such as the famous bob, and wearing shorter skirts which showed an amount of leg considered indecent before the war. Many young women took to smoking in public, another sign of modernity and independence, and began to mix with men on a much more informal basis. The flattened chest of the modern young woman suggested androgyny or sexual ambivalence, and seemed to some commentators to suggest the emergence of a new sex. That marriage remained the norm in this period, and that most women took it for granted that once married they would give up whatever work they had and dedicate themselves to home and children, indicates that the apparently great shift in surface attitudes was accompanied by a slower change in underlying assumptions.

It was not only a question of shifting attitudes, however. As in any epoch of change, technology and information played a crucial role, this time in the form of great improvements in the quality and availability of contraception, and in the widespread dissemination of information about sex itself, especially in the form of Marie Stopes's bestselling *Married Love* (1918), a work which explained the mechanics of heterosexual sex to an audience which proved surprisingly ignorant of them, especially on the subject of female pleasure during intercourse. This new emphasis on the mechanics of pleasure of course suggested to some an immoral neglect either of relationship or of 'duty' – understood by some older commentators to mean a woman's duty to bear children. In opposition to this, Dora Russell's short tract, *Hypatia: or, Woman and Knowledge* (1925), is written in the defence of woman's sexual pleasure: 'To enjoy and admit we enjoy [...] is an achievement in honesty' (Russell, 1925: 33). She attacks the ideology of marriage and motherhood, and calls for relations between men and women to be based on free love, on the idealistic grounds that 'lovers know that it is through sexual understanding that they best apprehend the quality of each other's minds' (35).

The general public was also clearly sold on the idea of sexual pleasure. Margaret Kennedy's *The Constant Nymph*, possibly the bestselling novel of the decade, is a fascinating treatment of the risks associated with feminine desire and the unconventional, bohemian lifestyle. The novel registers a scepticism of the supposed new values, and resolves a complex issue with a melodramatic and simplistic conclusion, but its immense popularity clearly touched a nerve: it was staged with Noël Coward in the lead role, and filmed four times. Probably the nearest most of its readers got to the new bohemian values was in the reading of this novel.

Freud's work on sex and sexuality is commonly alluded to in the writing of the period, but little in the creative literature reflects anything more than a superficial acquaintance with his ideas. Instead, thinking about sex tends to be conditioned by work which had its roots in Victorian sexology. Richard Von Krafft-Ebing's *Psychopathia Sexualis* (1889) and the work of Karl Ulrichs form the background to the writing of Edward Carpenter and Havelock Ellis. A common assumption of these writers is that the preference of sex object is fixed by nature. Krafft-Ebing sees all forms of sexual deviancy as a disease. Contesting this pathological approach, Ellis looks to other species in nature for confirmation that same-sex preference is neither disease nor choice but biological inevitability. The underlying assumption is that heterosexual preference is normal because it is a biological given, and accounts of homosexuality, even where these are affirmative, as in the work of Edward Carpenter, look to the creation of a further natural, biologically determined category, that of the 'third sex'. From Krafft-Ebing to Carpenter, there is a tendency to think of sexuality in terms of types, and the work of scientific inquiry is to deliver descriptions of these types. There is only the faintest trace of recognition that sexuality may be fluent and various – the celebration of polymorphous sexuality belongs to a much later period – or that it may be in some ways socially determined and an instrument of social control. Friedrich Engels had been emphatic, in *On the Origin of the Family, Private Property and the State* (1884), that family organisation, and therefore the ideology of the family, were key elements in the reproduction of existing social conditions, but the connection of this insight with the study of sexuality itself had yet to be made. Nevertheless, Wyndham Lewis could write in 1926:

> It is round the question of *the family* that all the other questions of politics and social life are gathered. The break-up of the family unit today is the central fact of our life: it is from its central disintegration, both in fact and in our minds – the consequent readjustments of our psychology – that all the other revolutionary phases of our new society radiate. The relations of men to women, of the child to the parent, of friendship and citizenship to the new ideals of the state, are all controlled by it.[1]

Much of Lewis's work is dedicated to a mocking review of the effects of what he sees as the new fashion in high society for the invert – the male or female homosexual in the jargon of sexology. His work indicates that the old sexological theories had a wide general currency, and it is worth reviewing these ideas even if their sources were not widely known.

Edward Carpenter, although known to some 1920s authors, such as D. H. Lawrence and Radclyffe Hall, was generally neglected in this period. His short volume, *The Intermediate Sex: A Study of Some Transitional Types of Men and Women* (1908), was an influential attempt to legitimate homosexuality with reference to the principal work on sexology. Following Karl Ulrichs, Carpenter provides the classic definition of the third sex or 'Uranian', which would stand until displaced by the more sophisticated researches of Freud on sexuality:

> [Ulrichs] pointed out that there were people born in such a position – as it were on the dividing line between the sexes – that while belonging distinctly to one sex as far as their bodies are concerned they may be said *mentally* and *emotionally* to belong to the other.[2]

This model decisively recognises the existence of homosexuality, but it does so by crudely separating the mental and the physical. Following the sexologists, Carpenter provides a typology of what he terms the 'homogenic' man and woman, finding the homogenic man to have 'feminine' qualities such as intuition, sensitivity and an artistic nature, while the homogenic female has male qualities, being both logical and scientific as well as fiery and active. Carpenter quotes Ellis in support of the theory that inversion is natural and not pathogenic: 'Thus in sexual inversion we have what may fairly be called a 'sport' or variation, one of those organic aberrations which we see through-out living nature in plants and animals.' (Carpenter, 1908: 60). He also makes a superficial attempt to reconcile inversion with the claims of Social Darwinism that human sexual activity must be understood functionally, in terms of the survival of the race: 'It certainly does not seem impossible to suppose that as the ordinary love has a special function in the propagation of the race, so the other has its special function in social and heroic work.' (70); and makes political claims for inversion. Female inversion is central to the struggle for female emancipation because the social motives of men can no longer be trusted, while among men inversion can favour socialism by forging cross-class relationships, 'as it often seems to do' (77–8).

Havelock Ellis, in the famous chapter on 'Sexual Inversion' in his *Studies in the Psychology of Sex* (1910), makes a similar connection between inversion and work in the 'moral movements'. Having established the existence of inversion throughout nature and the culture of the 'lower races', he proceeds to connect it both to 'men of exceptional intellect' (Ellis, 1936: 27) and to criminals and tramps. Ellis makes some concessions to the theory advanced by Freud in *Three Essays on the Theory of Sexuality* (1905) that inversion is acquired rather than congenital, but concludes that the congenital theory is both the more modern and the more accurate. However, Ellis does accept the findings of physiologists that 'each sex contains the latent characters of the other or recessive sex' and rejects the systems of 'elaborate classification' of Krafft-Ebing and others in favour of a more fluid notion (82). His model is that inversion is basically con-genital but its emergence or otherwise is influenced by social factors. He continues to insist on its physiological basis, for example when arguing that invert women are likely to, but will not necessarily, have more facial hair, a more developed musculature, and arrested development of the genitals (that is, a small vagina). Ellis's conclu-sions, in many ways progressive in intention, remain mired in nineteenth-century biological thinking: 'The sexual invert may thus be roughly compared to the congenital idiot, to the instinctive criminal, to the man of genius' (317).

The now arcane ideas of sexology inform two of the works examined in this chapter: Radclyffe Hall's *The Well of Loneliness* and Wyndham Lewis's *The Apes of God*. In a lighter vein, Michael Arlen's popular novel *The Green Hat* produces a classic image of 1920s high life, setting the iconic figure of the vamp against a background of moral rootlessness; similarly central to the self-image of the jazz age, the brittle satires of Aldous Huxley are traced in their trajectory from cynicism to despondent moralism. Finally, the genesis of D. H. Lawrence's *Lady Chatterley's Lover* is examined in terms of its attempt to project a utopian alternative to old-fashioned moralism and new-fangled cynicism.

Lesbian Sexology: Radclyffe Hall and The Well of Loneliness

One work which systematically introduced sexological theory into fiction was Radclyffe Hall's *The Well of Loneliness* (1928), her fifth novel, and published by Jonathan Cape when her usual publishers refused it because of its lesbian content. Cape persuaded Havelock Ellis to add a brief 'Commentary' and sent out review copies to those newspapers and weeklies which it was felt could be trusted to take it seriously. However, the *Sunday Express* published a denunciatory editorial which had the immediate effect of causing the novel to sell out. The terms of the editorial are worth savouring:

> I am well aware that sexual inversion and perversion are horrors which exist among us today. They flaunt themselves in public places with increasing effrontery and more insolently provocative bravado. The decadent apostles of the most hideous and most loathsome vices no longer conceal their degeneracy and their degradation [...] This pestilence is devastating young souls.[3]

The editorial called for the Home Secretary to investigate whether the novel could be prosecuted, and in closing claimed to be defending literature as well as morality: 'Literature has not yet recovered from the harm done it by the Oscar Wilde scandal. It should keep its house in order.' Without reference to the author Cape sent a copy of the novel to the Home Secretary, as if to throw down the gauntlet. *The Well of Loneliness* was tried for obscenity and subsequently declared obscene. This was despite a stream of prominent defence witnesses, including Virginia Woolf and E. M. Forster, prepared to testify that the novel was not obscene and to defend the seriousness of the author's project. These witnesses were not allowed to be heard and the book was found to be 'prejudicial to the morals of the community', although female homosexuality was not illegal in England.

The Well of Loneliness is written in a workaday style and presents an overlong narrative in chronological order. If it is unremarkable as art, its ambition and even its very existence are remarkable. The author is familiar with the literature of sexology, especially the ideas of Krafft-Ebing, Havelock Ellis and Edward Carpenter, and follows them in using the established concept of 'inversion' for homosexuality, treating the invert as a 'third sex', and assuming that inversion is congenital rather than being dependent on early emotional formation or adult choice. The use of a sexology which is certainly now outmoded and to which psychoanalysis even at that time presented a possible alternative has led recent commentators to question the use of the novel in lesbian culture. The doubts are enhanced by the novel's emphasis on the necessity of suffering and sacrifice, an emphasis which owes something to the author's Catholic conversion, itself a topic in the novel; something to Carpenter's emphasis on homosexual suffering; and something to an ethic derived in part from the proto-Fascist Italian author, Gabriele D'Annunzio, whose *Trionfo della Morte* is echoed in the chapters dealing with Stephen's war experience. The conceptual substructure of the novel is not adequate to its topic, and the doctrinaire approach is unsubtle as a register of experiential realities in comparison to Radclyffe Hall's earlier work, such as *The Unlit Lamp* (1924). However, what is significant about this novel, which is sexually quite inexplicit despite its notoriety, is that it attempts to describe the confusion of feeling of a young woman discovering her sexuality, and of an older woman finding a way to realise her desires – even if only, in the end, to renounce them. Contemporary readers may justifiably query the novel's ethic, but as an attempt to represent and document sexual feeling, and offer some model of self-understanding to an unrepresented group, *Well of Loneliness* is a considerable innovation, has far more integrity than the diet of fantasy offered to young women by the desert romancers and their ilk, and is at least as sustained, and at points more persuasive, as the examination of sexuality in the work of Hardy and Lawrence.

The novel presents the story of a young woman in a wealthy

country family who is brought up almost as a boy and bearing a boy's name, Stephen. Her father, because he has read Krafft-Ebing, has an early intuition that she belongs to the third sex on account of her masculine physique, and treats her with understanding because his sources tell him that inversion is an inevitable biological fact: she is a male person in a female body, a fact reflected by her height and muscularity. Consequently, he allows her to learn male skills such as riding and fencing and does not pressurise her to marry. The possibility that her father's assumptions about her sexuality, conditioned by his desire for a male child, are the cause of Stephen's inversion is allowed for by the novel, but not systematically developed. In contrast to this somewhat idealised father-figure is Stephen's mother, who rejects her daughter when her sexuality is eventually revealed. Stephen has a long-standing servant, a mother-substitute, who also 'understands' her sexuality and provides the support which her mother does not. Again, the possibility is left open that maternal rejection has also conditioned Stephen's sexuality, although the novel's prior commitment to biologistic inversion theory appears to preclude development of this more Freudian strand of analysis. In terms of psychological realism, these relationships are all idealised, and it is the trajectory of Stephen's two love affairs which are of more central narrative interest. The first is with a married woman, who exploits Stephen's interest and even kisses her in an experimental fashion, but who does not return her love. It is in this context that the novel unfolds its doctrine of transcendent suffering:

> She loved deeply, far more deeply than many a one who could fearlessly proclaim himself a lover. Since this is a hard and sad truth for the telling; those whom nature has sacrificed to her ends – her mysterious ends that often lie hidden – are sometimes endowed with a vast will to loving, with an endless capacity for suffering also which must go hand in hand with their love. [...]
>
> Her physical passion for Angel Crossby had aroused a strange response in her spirit, so that side by side with every hot impulse that led her at times beyond her own understanding, there would come an impulse not of the body; a fine, selfless thing of great beauty and courage – she would gladly have given her body over to torment, have laid down her life if need be, for the sake of this woman whom she loved.   (Hall, 1992: 145)

Such passages closely reflect a reading of Carpenter on the subject of love:

> Anyone who realises what Love is, the dedication of the heart, so profound, so absorbing, so mysterious, so imperative, and always just in

the noblest nature so strong, cannot fail to see how difficult, how tragic even, must often be the fate of those whose deepest feelings are destined from the earliest days to be a riddle and a stumbling-block.

(Carpenter, 1908: 24)

Those sections of the narrative which deal with Angela's manipulation of Stephen perhaps do little more than adapt a conventional heterosexual nexus to a lesbian content, but the very conventionality of the love triangle format serves to legitimate and make recognisable lesbian feeling in an important way. At the same time, the convention closes down any exploration of the complexity of desire. As Stephen's is a male mind in a female body, her object choice is female because she is man-like and can therefore adopt the position of the man in the situation of unrequited love. The convention also brings with it an understanding of unrequited love in the terms of Christian suffering: the masochistic desire for the flesh to be tormented so that it can be transcended. The desire for suffering is made a defining feature of Stephen's inversion: she wishes to maim her own body and is wounded in the war working as an ambulance driver, acquiring a symbolic scar on her cheek. She experiences a desire for religion, acknowledged to be a paradox and a problem:

And what of the curious craving for religion which so often went hand in hand with inversion? Many such people were deeply religious, and this surely was one of their bitterest problems. They believed, and believing craved a blessing on what to some of them seemed very sacred – a faithful and deeply devoted union. But the Church's blessing was not for them. (Hall, 1992: 412)

Although Christianity promises reconciliation with the Father – and the understanding and forgiveness of Stephen's own father is therefore a crucial feature of the novel – it is to an almost medieval version of Christianity, in which the gap between Man and God cannot be closed, that the novel makes its appeal.

Stephen's second love affair is with a woman ten years her junior who arouses in her feelings of protection and cruelty. As with the first affair, this relationship is given a sustained and recognisable psychological development, although the characterisation of the Welsh Mary in terms of her 'Celtic soul' (286) is indebted to the stereotypes of, amongst others, Matthew Arnold. Despite having become a successful author, and having gained acceptance in Paris, Stephen is still not accepted in English county society, and she finally decides that she cannot allow Mary to live the life of a lesbian outcast with her. Mary is in any case not an invert – the very model of inversion central to the novel does not allow that two inverts can love each other – and Stephen's final sacrifice of the novel is to force Mary into the arms of a man by allowing her to believe that she no longer loves her. Stephen has made the ultimate sacrifice – she has told Mary that 'you are my life' (429) – and her suffering is identified with the redemptive suffering of Christ. The novel closes with an appeal to God to recognise the existence of the generations of inverts who have believed in him but whose existence he does not acknowledge. So, despite its commitment to providing a recognisable account of the psychological and social dilemmas of lesbianism, the novel remains committed to a model of inversion as congenital and tragic, and recommends courage in the face of inevitable suffering.

In retrospect, *The Well of Loneliness* seems destined to have become a *cause célèbre*, a year earlier, in *The Hotel*, Elizabeth Bowen had attempted a treatment of lesbianism which was a good deal more subtle and unlikely to attract the attention of the law. *The Hotel* shows how the new post-war knowingness about sexuality and marriage can still create only the most slender opportunities for the recognition of lesbian desire. Her young protagonist, Sydney Warren, 'at a probable twenty-two', is characterised by her 'nervous swagger' (Bowen, 1981: 14), but despite her name, she is not simply a man in a woman's body, nor does she recognise the nature of her own 'strangeness' to others of which she herself is only dimly aware. Her brief relationship is with an older woman holidaying alone, known only as Mrs Kerr, an appellation which signifies her marriage, aloofness and respectability, and also an anonymity which, as only slowly becomes clear, is related to the conscious suppression of her own lesbian tendencies. Neither Mrs Kerr nor Sydney acknowledges their love, and they part at the end of the season with everything unspoken. Bowen's treatment is a subtle one, intended to highlight the discrepancy that, while modern marriage has acquired a 'cynical' discourse all of its own, one which denies any mystery in sex, desire remains largely denied, marriage remains even more than before a matter of calculation, and same-sex desire remains a matter of painful isolation for the older woman, who can only acknowledge it after marriage, and a matter of confusion for the younger woman who cannot recognise it at all. However, so excessively 'subtle' is the treatment that the novel itself seems finally to consign to an unapproachable 'complexity' a love which it, as much as its protagonists, are, right to the end, unwilling to name.

Brief mention should also be made in this context of Rosamond Lehmann's *Dusty Answer* (1927), a partially autobiographical novel which explores the emotional experiences of its protagonist during her youth and her time at Cambridge (Lehmann attended Girton College). A shy woman, Judith Earle develops a close but not sexual relationship with another woman who is snatched away when her former lesbian lover appears, a woman whose appearance blends features of the modern, mysterious vamp and the archetypal masculinised lesbian:

> The hair was black, short, brushed straight back from the forehead [...] The eyes were long slits, dark-circled, the cheeks were pale, the jaw heavy and masculine. [...] She was tall, deep-breasted, with long, heavy but shapely limbs. She wore a black frock and a pearl necklace, and large pearl earrings. (Lehmann, 1936: 161)

This description exploits the by now stereotypical vocabulary of the period to announce both her sexual orientation and her depth of experience and sophistication. The inexperienced Judith loses her new friend to the older woman, and is left to contemplate her own emotional confusion. She contemplates but rejects marriage, and continues to prefer her lost friend to men, but her sexuality remains inexplicit. Like *The Hotel,* and in sharp contrast to *The Well of Loneliness, Dusty Answer* explores same-sex infatuation, but does not tackle lesbian sexuality directly, even although in both novels it remains obscurely in the wings.

Inverted World: Wyndham Lewis and The Apes of God

Wyndham Lewis, a painter as well as the author of numerous fictional and theoretical works, devotes much space to attacking what he sees as the fashion of inversion. His work may appear to have much in common with the reactionary hysteria of the *Sunday Express* and the Home Secretary, but it differs in its impulse to give systematic shape to the analysis of sexual and family politics in terms of the developing encroachment of the state. The editor of the *Sunday Express* sees 'inversion and perversion' in Victorian terms of decadence, degeneration and degradation; Wyndham Lewis concurs in connecting the 1920s to the 1890s, but his analysis differs sharply. While newspaper commentators are defending family values which they perceive to be identical with the values of the state, Lewis argues that inversion is the new value of the state, which wishes to advance its totalitarian agenda by infantilising the male citizen in order to rule him more effectively. This is a very different view from that of the left-wing author Douglas Goldring, who describes 1927–9 as 'the heyday of the Bright Young People, the Wild Party's Crescendo, the final binge before the slump'. 'There were, perhaps, a couple of thousand of them all told, with a fringe of socialites and intellectuals of the kind portrayed in the novels of Michael Arlen, Aldous Huxley and later, Evelyn Waugh.' For Goldring, the importance of this phase lies not in the personal activities of the small and transient group which it comprised, but in its function as the avant-garde of a general moral revaluation which led to a more widespread liberalisation of human sexual behaviour, in that 'it brought into the open tendencies which had previously been politely ignored'.[4] Lewis's contrasting, and many-faceted, view is advanced in two discursive works, *The Art of Being Ruled* (1926), which deals with political philosophy, and *Time and Western Man* (1927), which analyses the role of the arts and philosophy in supporting the agenda of the centralised state. Lewis's novel *Tarr* (written 1917–18; rewritten and republished 1928), and his satire *The Apes of God* (1930), are organised around his pessimistic analysis of the nature of sex and sexuality. His ideas are in the end obviously 'wrong' – indeed, his work, despite the stylistic and organisational brilliance of his fiction, is a sobering example of thought gone wildly wrong – but his writing is a provocative attempt not to take contemporary beliefs at face value. If, as I have argued elsewhere, its central current is a now overt, now covert anti-Semitism, which locates in the figure of the 'Jew' a whole series of values which Lewis wishes to stigmatise (including inversion in particular and the feminine in general), this should not prevent us from recognising the innovativeness and boldness of his attempt to account for the emergent modern condition.

> The family as it is, broken up on all hands by the agency of feminist and economic propaganda, reconstitutes itself in the image of the state. The government becomes an emperor disguised as Father Christmas, an All-father, a paterfamilias with his pocket full of crystal sets, gramophones, russian [sic] books, and flesh-coloured stockings, which he proceeds to *sell* to his 'children.'[5]

The state is intent on infantilising its citizens, and inversion unwittingly reinforces this process: 'the present widespread invert fashion [...] is an instinctive capitulation of the will on the part of the ruling male sex' (Lewis, 1989: 239):

> So a revolution in favour of standards unfriendly to the intellect, and friendly to all that had been formally subordinated to it, is the first and most evident result of sex-transformation. The 'passions', 'intuitions', all the features of the emotive life – with which women were formerly exclusively accommodated – are enthroned on all hands, in any place reached by social life; which is increasingly (in the decay of visible, public life), everywhere. (216)

The entertainments of the new mass society, especially cinema and the romantic novel, serve to bring about this capitulation of the will, especially by generating an obsession with sex in particular, and the private, psychological world in general. The social subject is encouraged to retreat into its private, mental domain, where it is fed a constant diet of consumer sensation, while outside any form of public life breaks down. Lewis concludes pessimistically that most people prefer this inarticulate dependence on the state to any form of responsibility. He finds that highbrow literature and philosophy also contribute to this process, as if the intellectuals were themselves capitulating, and finds what he calls High Bohemia, peopled by millionaire inverts, to be at the centre of this process. His conclusions owe something to his reading of Proust, whose *Sodome et Gomorrhe* he praises for its 'analysis of the powerful instinctive freemasonry of the pederast' (362), and it is to Proust he alludes when he announces the purposes of his literary criticism in the first part of *Time and Western Man*:

> The art that I am attacking here is the art of this High-Bohemia of the 'revolutionary' rich of this time. That is the society the artistic expression of whose soul I have made it my task to analyse. That a glittering highly-intellectualist surface, and a deep, sagacious, rich though bleak sensuality make its characteristic productions appear, as art, a vast improvement on the fearful artlessness, ugliness and stupidity that preceded it [...], is true enough. That Marcel Proust (the classic expression up-to-date of this millionaire-outcast, all-caste, star-cast world, in the midst of which we live) is more intelligent, and possesses a more cultivated sensuality, a sharper brain, than his counterpart in the age of Tennyson, must be plain to everyone. But it is not with the intellectual abyss into which Europe fell in the last century that you must compare what we are considering.[6]

The allegedly 'highbrow' art of Modernism, now based principally in Paris, is not to be compared to the nineteenth-century art which it displaced, but with the contemporary 'lowbrow' culture to which it is invisibly connected and which it mirrors in its use of the star-system of cinema advertising: it is to be understood as part of the insidious massification process of the modern state. Literary Modernism is not seen by Lewis as a marginal, alternative, or élite activity. The pathos of marginality and a rhetoric of intellectual irony are seen as part of the literature's marketing technique: it offers its readership a flattering view of itself. Lewis brings to the fore the class origins of a literature which markets a certain kind of sophistication but has become irresponsible, in his terms, and uncritical. This account seems consistent with at least some of the facts when he makes passing reference to an advertising slogan which defines 'The Sophisticated School of Literature' to include figures such as Michael Arlen, Ronald Firbank and Aldous Huxley,[7] a type of advertising which is evidently a feature of newly aggressive book-marketing strategies (Lewis did not fail to ensure that his own books were advertised in a similar way, no doubt with a sense of irony). However, the Modernism which Lewis criticises at length at this time includes the work of Pound, Joyce, Stein and Lawrence, and later Eliot and Woolf. Of these, only Stein could have been considered an invert, so there is clearly more than inversion at stake, and most were, as Lewis well knew, far from wealthy, a further contradiction in his account. Nevertheless, one of the major functions of his creative writing is to dismantle what he sees as the dominant model of sexuality, attack the 'instinctive freemasonry' of invert society and provide an alternative to High Bohemian literature.

The Apes of God is a satire on the High Bohemia of Bloomsbury, set on the eve of the General Strike, in which sexual perversion and inversion play a key role. There is a significant debt to Proust, whose *Sodome et Gomorrhe I* (1921) contains an extended description of the workings of homosexual society. Proust uses the term '*inverti*' and '*homme-femme*' to designate the homosexual, maintaining the notion of the sexologists that inversion is a biological fact; indeed, he concurs in referring to it as disease which cannot be cured. Inversion is so biologically rooted that a man who does not even know he is an invert may, when he falls asleep, reveal himself to others as having a woman's soft face. Lewis rejects the theory that inversion is biologically conditioned in favour of a model of social determination; but what he does take from Proust is the model of inverts as a race or colony connected by common interest in bonds that resemble freemasonry. So in Proust's description the inverts belong both to the general society, in which they usually disguise their inversion, and to a secret society when they meet in private. Many social and professional clubs are dominated by inverts, and their covert role in upper-class society is, claims Proust's narrator, similar to that of the Jews. Jews and homosexuals are alike in being each a race apart, each marked by a form of original sin, unable to escape the disgust of the rest of society, and each therefore covertly grouping together within and against the general society to which they belong. *The Apes of God* attempts something like an exposé of this situation, in its extensive parade of Jews and homosexuals.

Satirical and frequently highly visual description is one of the principal modes of *The Apes of God*. The description of a mannish lesbian in Part VIII 'Lesbian Ape' could not contrast more starkly with the portrayal of Stephen Gordon in *The Well of Loneliness*. The dress and mannerisms of this character are meticulously detailed, right down to the 'Radcliffe-Hall collar' [sic]. While Radclyffe Hall, herself a cross-dresser, used conventional narrative form to explore her character's psychology, there is little sustained description of clothing in her work. Lewis's style is to focus in detail on externals and on the present moment, denying conventional narrative identity altogether. His description of the lesbian artist Miss Ansell is thus impressively documentary:

> She was wiry and alert with hennaed hair bristling, en-brosse. In khaki-shorts, her hands were in their pockets, and her bare sunburnt legs were all muscle and no nonsense at all. [… S]he was bald […] on the top of her head [and] had a peculiar air of being proud of it all the time (to be bald, like the ability to grow a moustache, was a masculine monopoly). A march had been stolen, with her masculine calvity. But a strawberry-pink pull-over was oddly surmounted by a stiff Radcliffe-Hall collar, of antique masculine cut – suggestive of the masculine hey-day, when men were men starched up and stiff as pokers, in their tandems and tilburys. The bare brown feet were strapped into spartan sandals. A cigarette-holder half a foot long protruded from a firm-set jaw. It pointed at Dan, sparkling angrily as the breath was compressed within its bore.
>
> (Lewis, 1981: 222)

The Apes of God embodies a decisive rejection of the explanatory claims of the novel. Lewis's work rejects the notion that the self is something that develops in explicable ways, which it is the task of the novel to unfold according to the logic of the *Bildungsroman* (the novel of education or development) or the conventional plot-driven romance, or in line with psychological theories and fictional practices which emphasise memory and childhood. Here, everything is stark irreducible presence. The refusal of narrative psychologism and the creation of an alternative style which owes something to pre-psychological (seventeenth- and eighteenth-century) models is in effect a resistance to certain types of explanation. What so many readers have found problematic in *The Well of Loneliness* is the combination of a variety of narrative and explanatory models which, while they may have served the strategic purposes of publishing the novel, finally straightjacket and fail to explain their object. Lewis's resistance to the novel and its psychology in *The Apes of God* predicts more recent dissatisfactions with these modes, even though the world-view which he models is in so many respects unacceptable.

The narrative of *The Ape of God* is picaresque, centred on one Dan Boleyn, in part modelled on the young Stephen Spender, who is the protégé of Horace Zagreus (Horace de Vere Cole), an ageing invert who shares the passion of the period for everything youthful. There is also an analogy with the relationship between Marcel and the Baron de Charlus in Proust. Dan is portrayed as a *naif* who cannot understand the intentions, frequently sexual, of the people with whom he is brought into contact. In a series of discrete episodes, he is introduced by Horace, who is guiding his education as a future artist, to a number of figures in the wealthy artistic circles of Bloomsbury. Indeed, in its encyclopedic scope and positioning of these figures as exemplary 'apes', *The Apes of God* distantly resembles the typology of sexual pathologies of the early sexologists. Dan himself is infantile and fundamentally asexual, although he unwittingly loses his virginity to the masturbatory attentions of a predatory older woman in Part II 'The Virgin'. This chapter presents the figures of Matthew Plunkett and Betty Bligh (modelled on Lytton Strachey and Dora Carrington), concentrating on the sexual psychology of Plunkett (who has been treated by the Freudian Dr Frumpfsusan in Vienna). In line with Lewis's analysis of High Bohemian literature, Plunkett is defined as a 'feuilletonist, of the highbrow-lowbrow purple-passion' (67). Plunkett has a sexual interest in Dan, who stays at his house, but under the direction of Frumpfsusan is attempting to become more manly. Lewis draws on the popularised notion of the inferiority complex in his depiction of Plunkett's treatment. Plunkett must break his inferiority complex by selecting an unusually short female partner, one whose size can in no way make him feel unmanly, and he enhances the treatment of his sexual neurosis – that is, his homosexuality – by seeking to act in the most stereotypically masculine way possible. The chapter opens with Plunkett shaping up to go out for lunch at the local working-class pub, where bluff manly rituals of shoves and matey apologies are in order, although he would rather stay at home with his collection of shells and muse over 'a few scraps of a feast of reason of Eminent Victorians', an allusion to the attitude of Strachey, and indeed Woolf, to the Victorian patriarchs, the source of Plunkett's inferiority complex. Woolf is a presence in the chapter's stylistic parodies: Plunkett twice sees a van bearing the advertising slogan of an oil company, 'SHELL IS SO DIFFERENT', an episode which parodies the car and aeroplane of *Mrs Dalloway*, as does the striking clock which marks the time for Clarissa (itself a Joycean device). Plunkett's shells are the occasion for a *recherche du temps perdu*, again recalling Woolf's frequent use of her Cornish beach experiences as an idyll of memory, as well as Marcel's famous involuntary recollection in *Du côté de chez Swann*.

> At random he took up the shell of the pearly Nautilus. Then he surveyed the miniature landscape. He lay down on the beach, kicking his heels, it was midsummer holiday, he was the callow schoolboy – today was a holiday. Fixing his eyes in big subaqueous Bloomsbury stare he was soon sufficiently mesmerized: they were directed upon the landscape, rather than upon the specimens. (79)

The depiction of Plunkett as a representative of Bloomsbury aestheticism incurs a paradox. On the one hand, the Proustian/ Woolfian use of memory is satirised as a type of regressive dreaminess and an inability to observe the present, a phenomenon which *The Apes of God* resists at the level of its own style which obsessively documents sheer physical presence. On the other hand, the growing interest in Freudian analysis is satirised, not merely as faddish, but as in itself a regressive dependence on external authority which reflects an inability to take responsibility for oneself. The paradox is that while the Freudian diagnosis of Plunkett is satirised, it is actually accepted and employed by Lewis who does indeed depict Plunkett/ Strachey's inversion in terms of the inferiority complex.[8] Plunkett's stuttering attempt to behave 'like a man amongst men' in the local pub, where he is almost too nervous to get himself served in the bluff manner required in such a place, confirms his effeminate inversion as the product of an inferiority complex which is in fact inverted. His feelings of inferiority in the company of working-class men are a form of inverted snobbery. His inferiority complex has led him to reject his own once eminent class, but in the company of the working class it reappears.

The Apes of God culminates in a long section which describes a party at the house of the Finnian Shaws (modelled on the Sitwells), an opportunity to depict the decadent childishness of the ruling class and its culture: 'The barriers that will soon be *thrown* down are already down in fact' (429), remarks Zagreus, whose function in the narrative is in part to provide Lewis's own analysis. The guests at the party are principally men – Lewis follows his reading of Proust in depicting the 'instinctive freemasonry of the pederast' – although it is willed childishness rather than homosexuality which is the shared trait of the characters. The guests at the party do not behave but rather act. This culture lacks the possibility of an authentic way of being and its members are condemned to play at living. Everything is done to be seen and heard, to become the stuff of gossip. The Finnian Shaws themselves are shown to be throwbacks to the 'naughty nineties', with its associations of aestheticism, decadence and the Oscar Wilde trial. Inversion is viewed not as biological inevitability, but as socially determined by developments in the general culture. A brief dialogue on the fashion for homosexuality in Paris sets the scene for Lewis's analysis:

> '[T]he *Grain Qui Meurt* leads to the *Faux-Monnayeurs*. An outcast-status leads to a *brotherhood* – reaching from the gallows to the rubber-shop. Laws against sex-perversions like dry-laws make criminals of harmless sex-oddities. But everybody is driven into a league against Law. [...] Jacques Coq d'Or [Jean Cocteau]. [... F]or years with him it was common-or-garden homosexuality, not very exciting (we had our poor old Oscar under Victoria) but new in France and very exclusive. [...] It afforded Jacques the necessary advertisement for a rising critic for many years. Now times are different. Homosexuals are as common as dirt.'
> 'It is now the non-homosexual who is abnormal.'
> 'That is so.'
> (409)

The two French works referred to are by André Gide, known for his celebration of the *acte gratuit*, the motiveless crime at the centre of his novel *L'Immoraliste*. *Si le grain ne meurt* (1920) is an autobiographical work which details Gide's sexual development and his experience of the literary *salon* culture, and includes an account of his night of passion with Oscar Wilde in an Algerian hotel, shortly before Wilde's trial. *Les Faux-Monnayeurs* (1925) contains a brotherhood of schoolboys passing counterfeit money and a novelist who disbelieves both in selfhood and in social meanings. The topics of a criminal brotherhood of juveniles and the society of counterfeit in the novel of a homosexual writer emerge in Lewis's own schema of post-war High Bohemia. Cocteau's *Les Enfants Terribles* (1929) depicts criminality as a social game, and Lewis goes on to refer to Cocteau's own deliberately cultivated reputation for petty crime. The fascination of homosexual authors with crime is connected to the upsurge of interest in the detective novels of Edgar Wallace. His point is that crime and homosexuality are forms of anti-authoritarian behaviour which situate the offender as the 'naughty' child in relation to a powerful parent. In the modern world, the parent is the state and its agents are the police. At Lord Osmund's party, an unexpected knock at the door is interpreted by the guests as the arrival of the police. They fall into a silence which is marked by an erotic *frisson*:

> So the world-hush of the universal *Speak-easy-soul* of the Post-war, was in this company prolonged until the knocking abruptly ceased. [… T]his Theoretic Underworld still shook in its criminal shoes, its Edgar Wallace teeth never ceased to chatter, its Potemkin heart was in its throat. The World that had become fashionably Underworld wilted deliciously, at the bare prospect of wholesale detection: half-amorously it fluttered at the shadow of Authority (a child shrinking from the birch-armed Dad) – all breathing one big bated breath of fond fellowship of romantic Revolt, of elect Criminality. (376)

The references to Russian communism (the revolt of the crew of the battleship Potemkin) and to the fashion for all things American (the culture of the American bar, as well as crime fiction and, elsewhere, jazz), complete the frame of analysis which connects inversion or its affectation to the industrial future and its need for a passive population which believes in its own subjective freedom but cowers in infantilised erotic subjection before the parental state.

The Apes of God uses four principal modes. The most noted is the highly visual descriptive mode, which preternaturally breaks down appearances and actions into small components which would not be noticed by a participating observer. Second is the mode of direct presentation of conversation. As in the satires of writers such as Huxley and Waugh, conversations in the novel are frequently used to characterise the personages in terms of their triviality or venality. At other times conversations are used to announce important thematic topoi. The third mode is that of the interior monologue. These two modes overlap, in that the 'interior' monologue is sometimes presented in spoken form. The point of these interior monologues, as of much of the conversation, is that the verbal content of consciousness, whether spoken or otherwise, consists of a kind of childlike, self-comforting chatter, a sort of inarticulate 'stutter' which is associated by Lewis with the work of Gertrude Stein.

> Miss Gertrude Stein in her *Melanctha* is giving the life of a poor negress, not in the negress's own words, but in her own manner. Then the mannerism is intended to convey, with its ceaseless repetitions, the monstrous *bulk* and vegetable accumulation of human life in the mass, in its mechanical rotation. Creaking, groaning, and repeating itself in an insane iteration, it grows, flowers heavily, ages and dies. [...]
>
> [T]his kind of doll-like *deadness*, the torpid fatal *heaviness*, is so prevalent, in one form or another, as to dominate in a way the productions of the present time.[9]

The fourth mode is the privileged discursive mode in which Lewis's own analyses of the contemporary situation are presented. This occurs in some of the monologues of Horace Zagreus, and always in the words of Pierpoint, a mysterious figure whose words are quoted or written but who never makes an appearance, who appears to be, as is the novelist, outside the frame of the society which he analyses. This mode is used to present Lewis's own views then, although the figure of Pierpoint is presented in such a way as to ask whether any purely external, purely objective viewpoint can be established outside the 'deadness' of that which passes for contemporary life.

These then are the narrative modes in which *The Apes of God* presents its view of the human. In its attempt to describe human reality, *The Well of Loneliness* settled for an analytical frame derived from sexology and a narrative mode derived the romantic novel. *The Apes of God* is an anti-novel which resists the claims of the novel to explain human society. That is not to say that its own concatenation of narrative modes form a truly explanatory picture. Radclyffe Hall may well have selected the romance as a genre for strategic reasons, in order to engage readers with an easily recognisable form and thereby to communicate better the lesson that the invert is human within received notions of what constitutes the human. By contrast, Lewis's method asks more probingly whether the human is at all that which the novel, or indeed other contemporary discourses, takes it to be. Lewis queries the explanatory power of psychology, whether of the novel or of the newly fashionable psychoanalysis. A person's life story is not that which explains who they are or why their life is shaped in the way it is, but is a story which individuals tell themselves in order, in Lewis's frame, to apologise for their inability to become adults. This is so in the case of the Finnian Shaws, who constantly relive their relationship to their father, nicknamed 'Cockeye' in a condensed allusion to the Father of the Gods in Norse mythology and an association of adult masculinity and the all-seeing eye (551–7). It is also the case for Plunkett who is equipped by psychoanalysis with an understanding of his 'inferiority complex' and inability to achieve masculine adulthood. It remains a contradiction of *The Apes of God* that, while it ostensibly rejects the explanations of psychoanalysis, it embodies assumptions which are akin to those of Freud in its mapping of the arrest of what it posits as normal psychological and sexual development. However, the descriptive passages do not embody a Freudian perspective. Rather, they are concerned with viewing the human being as a behaving body. So, although inversion is not perceived as a biological inevitability, human beings are produced by the text as biological rather than psychological entities. Human beings are therefore not to be perceived as that which they narrate themselves to be in their own psychological subjectivity. Speech, then, becomes as much a physical fact as the body, and the author is positioned as scientific observer, an anthropologist or behavioural scientist, whose subjects are not longer human but laboratory monkeys – the 'apes' of the title.

Lewis's description of Stein's work as an embodiment of 'the monstrous *bulk* and vegetable accumulation of human life in the mass' might equally be applied to *The Apes of God*. Human sexual activity is not seen here as a potential zone of liberation. Sexuality is overdetermined by general social processes which are viewed deterministically: 'We are all rats caught in a colossal mechanical trap' (405). Because Lewis's anti-humanism finds its principal subjects among homosexuals, Jews and the Irish, few readers, then or now, have warmed to a perspective which can be read as merely intellectualised bigotry, even though Lewis can be found at one point or another explicitly rejecting racism, anti-feminism, and homophobia.[10] Yet *The Apes of God* contains some of the most consistently brilliant writing of its period, and its attempt to interdict the contemporary treatment of sexuality and propose itself as an alternative is perhaps no less contradictory than some of the apparently more benign accounts – the vitalism of Lawrence or the psychologism of Woolf – which have historically secured a broader assent.

Mention should be made in this context of the work of Douglas Goldring. Goldring had been politically radicalised by the Easter Rising of 1916, and had transferred to Dublin to witness the effects of British rule for himself.[11] Two of the books which he produced in this period and attributed anonymously to 'An Englishman' – *Dublin: Explorations and Reflections* (1917) and *A Stranger in Ireland* (1918) – were intended to communicate the realities of Irish politics to the British. In subsequent work, Goldring combined his pacifism and radicalism with his opposition to the culture of Bohemian sexuality and followed Lawrence in his inquiries into the possibilities of human sexual relationships, although from the very different perspective of a loosely, though fervently, adopted Communism. Goldring's play, *The Fight for Freedom* (1919), written in Dublin and performed in Germany and Hungary, is a verbose drawing room drama which places the liberated Leninist Oliver amongst a variety of types representing the English establishment – the Vicar, the returned soldier, the civil servant. The central event is the rape by the returned soldier of the fiancée who has changed her mind about marrying him, and the play concludes with a chorus of The Internationale. Goldring's introduction to this play outlines an unrealised ambition for an international workers' theatre:

> In Russia, in Germany, in Austria, in Holland the theatre is the great medium through which the unifying ideas of internationalism, brotherhood, and detestation of war are receiving full and free expression. When is English Labour going to recognise its importance, and start a theatre of its own? (Goldring, 1919: 9)

Goldring's novel *The Black Curtain* (1920), dedicated to D. H. Lawrence, follows the path of a partially autobiographical figure, a journalist and unsuccessful novelist called Philip Kane, who must decide between the culture of London, and specifically that of the pre-war Bohemia, and the path of pacifism and internationalism conveniently embodied in the person of a young woman. Because the plot organisation is romantic, and because the novel concentrates on the slow mental evolution of the protagonist towards Leninism, the actual political content is relatively slight. Goldring routinely denounces the culture of Bohemia in his writing. His essay on 'Clever Novels' collected in *Reputations* (1920) denounces a series of novels for their depiction of Bohemian sets which he finds tedious: the targets include Clemence Dane's *Legend* (1919), the novels of Gilbert Cannan, John Middleton Murry's *Still Life* (1916) and Romer Wilson's *If All These Young Men* (1919). A further essay on 'The Author of Tarr' criticises Wyndham Lewis for his interest in Bohemians. However, *The Black Curtain* suffers exactly the same fault: the Bohemian world which Kane rejects is modelled very closely on the pre-war Vorticist ambit of Ezra Pound, who provides the model for one Ephraim Stork, described as 'the poet and high priest of the newest art movement' (Goldring, 1920: 30), and Wyndham Lewis, who is the model in all but physical appearance for Hawkins Moss, the painter, who is editing a journal called *Kosmos* which is intended to be 'the great organ of rebel art in England,' (31) and contains denunciatory manifestos which correspond to those of Lewis's *Blast* (1914–15). The portrayal of Moss/Lewis is in itself fascinating, and serves Goldring as the counterpart to the choice of socialism represented in the novel by Anne Drummond. 'Moss stood for the barbaric, the untamed in modern life. He came into the room with his hat on and left it there; he was the superman, not stooping to the small bourgeois civilities' (43).

There is much more in this vein, as Goldring goes on to describe an evening in a gallery in which Moss's new movement is launched, to the acclaim of wealthy patrons and journalists.[12] The point is to expose the radicalism of Bohemian culture as sham, as becomes apparent when this group fails to oppose the war. Moss is developed as a formidable and intelligent figure, only to have his alternative credentials ruined by his decision to sign up and go to the front. The alternative to Moss is the revolutionary Anne Drummond, member of the radical Independent Labour Party. Her manifesto represents an abrupt alternative to the aesthetic manifesto of the *Kosmos* group: 'We must have a complete change, a communist revolution, and the only way to get rid of the present gang of oligarchs is to have a communist republic' (58). However, the social and political background is not extensively developed by Goldring, who emphasises the personal relationship and the tragic death of Anne, ill and in prison, on the day of the Armistice.[13] The melodramatic conclusion has Kane acknowledge Lenin as the secular saviour, and the final passage is a wooden evocation of the coming Red Dawn – 'cold, terrible, relentless, but bearing with it the promise of a new day' (240). Although left-wing politics are frequently evoked in Goldring's work, it is the consequence of changing mores for personal relationships which preoccupies him in his novels. Kane passes much of this novel simply 'missing Anne' in the context of his developing resistance to the climate of war hysteria. When he becomes firmly anti-war he 'finds' Anne again.

Goldring never properly integrated politics and art, and on his own account, *The Black Curtain* 'marked the end of my revolutionary pacifist preaching through the medium of fiction',[14] as he came to

157

find the climate of left-wing activism increasingly alienating. A subsequent novel, *Nobody Knows* (1923), is therefore basically focused on the sexual relationships of its protagonist, another unsuccessful novelist, and follows *Aaron's Rod* (even to Florence) in asking whether a man should prefer chastity to the complex demands of modern heterosexual relationship. This is the first in what Goldring later defined as 'a trilogy of studies of contemporary "love among the artists".'[15] Goldring's continued independent radicalism is reflected in the remarks from his survey of the decade quoted elsewhere in this study, and after *The Black Curtain* it continued to take the form of opposition to the sexual and artistic mores which he associates with his recurrent target, contemporary 'Bohemia'. The partly autobiographical protagonist of *Nobody Knows* probably reflects Goldring's own view: 'Bohemianism was a disgusting thing erected upon something real and obscuring it. That something real was the artist's contempt for all forms and kinds of "furniture"' (Goldring, 1923: 25). It is interesting and important that this decade produced an avowedly, if temporarily, communist novelist, but the focus of Goldring's work is predominantly personal and in the end romantic, in certain moments simply lamenting the loss of sexual constancy, while 'Bohemia' as a target is both a narrow and insufficiently analysed topos for the critique of contemporary gender relations. As a consequence, despite the element of a progressive and critical outlook, Goldring's work has little of the quality of sustained negation which is to be found in the relentless querying of sexual mores to be found in Lewis and Lawrence.

Enigmatic Femininity and English Myth: Michael Arlen's The Green Hat

Michael Arlen's *The Green Hat* (1924) was an instant bestseller, always remarked in literary surveys of the period, was filmed with Greta Garbo as the heroine Iris Storm and, in the minds of its readers, clearly evoked something of the essence of the period just as the fiction of F. Scott Fitzgerald appeared to do for the USA. Indeed, *The Green Hat* shares several features with *The Great Gatsby* (1925): an atmosphere of wealth and freedom; a first-person narrator whose role depends on the use others make of him; expensive cars and a fatal car crash; an element of licentiousness and amorality – although this latter is more apparent than real as the melodramatic plot is resolved in a denouement which reveals the apparently destructive *femme fatale* at the narrative's centre to be herself a wronged innocent. Iris Storm is probably based on Nancy Cunard, a wealthy socialite and herself a poet and publisher, who has also been claimed as the model for similar figures in Huxley's *Antic Hay* and *Point Counter Point*, and Waugh's *Decline and Fall*. Unlike *The Great Gatsby*, *The Green Hat* is generally clumsy and the would-be sophisticated dialogue is anything but. However, its principal disappointment is prepared by the type of expectations which Lewis's passing reference arouses – a general hope that this novel might capture a 1920s full of *risqué* fun and morally ambiguous behaviour punctuated by high-speed car journeys and unexpected telephone calls against a background of jazz music and naked ladies in public places. And, in fact, *The Green Hat* itself goes some way towards arousing these expectations by providing a modicum of cars, telephones, jazz and fleeting nakedness. However, the genuine risk and surprise which gives *The Great Gatsby* its appeal is merely faked here, and the melodramatic and over-manipulated plot conclusion simply restores a moral order which the opening of the novel had tried to persuade us was in abeyance. We are shown a heroine who seems to destroy men in a pattern based on complex and unrevealed desires, and are left with a woman who has done all for love – separated from her childhood sweetheart and unable to love other men. A number of perhaps unintentionally funny plot manipulations are involved in getting from the former to the latter – better left to the discovery of the interested reader – and neither plot nor character carry much conviction.

The disappointment is not what we had been led to expect by Lawrence's depiction of Michaelis in *Lady Chatterley's Lover*, which is based on Arlen. Michaelis is an Irish outsider who has made money through his plays which flatter and satirise London society; with his expensive car and Bond Street clothes he appears the wealthy English man without being it. Arlen was not Irish but Armenian, and it was *The Green Hat* alone which brought him wealth and fame. He helped Lawrence to publish *Lady Chatterley's Lover* even though he is in effect criticised, indeed abused, in it for courting easy commercial success. Michaelis is not present merely as a representative of commercial success. He offers Connie her first sexual alternative to Clifford and is therefore the unsuccessful precursor of Mellors. In Lawrence's terms, Michaelis is equated with the modern attitude to sex: discursive, mechanical, inauthentic. A modern 'sophisticated' attitude to sex might then be expected from *The Green Hat,* but instead, amidst all the apparent nervous fragility which Lawrence identifies with this ambience, we are presented with the image of a heroine who wants eternal love and a child, and has been denied both by family history. This is the clue to the parallel with *Lady Chatterley's Lover,* which keeps feminine desire as an allotropic and open-ended phenomenon firmly in the frame, and links sex and sexuality to broader questions of human possibility.

Lawrence then reacted against *The Green Hat* in a manner which was fruitful for his own work, yet some account of the success of Arlen's novel is needed. Satirical descriptions such as that of the dandy and other potentially identifiable literati are only part of the novel's attempt to situate itself in the *beau monde* and are not its principal offering. Its appeal clearly has something to do with the elusiveness and enigmatic nature of its heroine. Here is a woman whose actions are not determined by propriety but by desire, and moreover a desire which results not in satisfaction but which seems bound up with a capacity for infinite and affecting if unarticulated sadness. These are the qualities which attract the narrator and are intended for the consumption of the reader. When Arlen raises his prose to its highest emotional and nostalgic pitch, as here in the evocation of a car journey by night, the effects are merely mawkish:

> Silence marches with the thoughts in your mind. Maybe a word or two will drop, hesitate in the wind, fight with the dying hosts of midgets, perish on the road. Small flying things brush by your face, and a dry unsweet scent, as though England is sleeping with her windows closed.
>
> (Arlen, 1991: 194)

That England is asleep while stifled desire suffers is a topos revisited several times: 'I despise your England' (230) proclaims Iris, denouncing the tradition that has seen her married off to a man she could not love, a sentiment endorsed by the hero – divided between his wife and his childhood love Iris – in the novel's melodramatic conclusion:

> You sacrificed my happiness to the ghastly vanity of making our name something in this world. [...] Here I am at thirty [...] a nothing wrapped round by the putrefying rules of the gentlemanly tradition. And my God they are putrefying, and I bless the England that has at last found us out.
>
> (237)

Iris's betrayal of the English tradition is represented by the death of her first husband, 'Boy Fenwick of Careless-Days-Before-The-War fame' (47), a type of Rupert Brooke figure who represents the naïve ideals of mystical English nationalism. However, the whole theme of Englishness, while it is adumbrated, is explored only superficially by Arlen – for this we must turn to *Parade's End* – and the cultural commentary is buried in the plot. This is something of a pity, since 'Boy' is set up for an entertaining fall. His fall from a hotel window in the pre-war is blamed on Iris – did he jump when she revealed some awful sexual secret, the wickedness of a woman's heart? His death hangs over Iris and links her to the demise of the old ideal England, the culture again blaming the modern woman for the post-war changes – a blame which the novel's plot is intent on removing. Entertainingly enough, the prolix denouement reveals that the probably drunken fall of the misty-eyed Edwardian idealist 'Boy' coincided with his own guilty revelation to Iris that he has contracted syphilis and may have given it to her. Modern England should not succumb to the myth of the pre-war Eden, is the message.

'I am a house of men', declares Iris: 'Of their desires and defeats and deaths.' (24) Certainly, as the daughter of a wealthy family she has been married off for property and not for love, but the simplistic way in which love and her desire to have a child are put into place as her true 'desire' does little to unravel the enigmatic nature of the feminine which the novel explicitly claims as its topic:

> I am trying, you can see, to realise her, to add her together; and, of course, failing. She showed you first one side of her and then another, and each side seemed to have no relation with any other, each side might have belonged to a different woman. (14)

> She was, you can see, some invention, ghastly or not, of her own. [...] You felt she had outlawed herself from somewhere, but where was that somewhere? You felt she was tremendously indifferent to whether she was outlawed or not. In her eyes you saw the landscape of England, spacious and brave; but you felt unreasonably certain that she was as devoid of patriotism as Mary Stuart. (15)

We are told this by a narrator who, knowing the end of his tale, already knows better, and the Iris of the denouement is suddenly more explicable in conventional terms than the elusive nature outlined here. So here is the novel's appeal – it will expose English myth, hint at an enigmatic feminine beyond patriarchal social rules, and in the process reflect the mood of mingled excitement and sadness of a jazz age generation still in mourning. The novel's agenda has an appeal which in the event is as palpable as its shortcomings, and it is left to Lawrence to attempt a more radical and questioning treatment of feminine desire in relation to English values in *Lady Chatterley's Lover.*

Sexual Cynicism and Intellectual Despair: Aldous Huxley

Aldous Huxley emerged as the foremost satirist of his age with the widely-acclaimed *Crome Yellow* (1921) and *Antic Hay* (1923), works which represented the new cynical post-war mood of England to the world, attracting the praise of Scott Fitzgerald and H. L. Mencken, and even earning Huxley, alone among contemporary English novelists, a favourable reference in *A la Recherche du temps perdu.* In *Crome Yellow*, Huxley appears as the maladroit Denis, a recent graduate and aspiring Symbolist poet, the guest at a house party in which some of the manners of his class are put on show. Denis's poetry reveals him to be not quite of his age, but a romantic looking back to the 1890s: 'He felt, like Ernest Dowson, "a little weary'. He was in the mood to write something rather exquisite and gentle and quietist in tone; something a little droopy and at the same time – how should he put it? – a little infinite.' (Huxley, 1977: 125) Denis's thinking is contrasted with that of Scogan, an older and more pragmatic man whose ideas resemble those of Bertrand Russell, advocating the coming of the rational state and of eugenic control – the eventual theme, of course, of *Brave New World.* Subjects of passing satire include the Church, the post-war fashion for horoscopes (Scogan's appearance in drag as 'Sesostris, the Sorceress of Ecbatana' gave Eliot his famous 'Madame Sosostris'), and ragtime (which 'came squirting out of the pianola in gushes of treacle and hot perfume' [50]). The tone is light and brilliant and the satire never over-emphatic. There are several women at the party who appeal to Denis, but what narrative there is highlights his inability to grasp modern sexual mores. One of the women has read Havelock Ellis and apparently Freud – dreams of falling lead her to conclude that she is repressed, a situation she logically and passionlessly sets out to remedy: 'Sex isn't a laughing matter; it's serious', she informs her friends (83). Her plan to find a man is a parody of the beliefs of the modern woman:

> It must be somebody intelligent, somebody with intellectual interests which I can share. And it must be somebody with a proper respect for

women, somebody who's prepared to talk seriously about his work and his ideas and about my work and my ideas. It isn't, as you see, at all easy to find the right person. (38)

These are the criteria for sex, *à la* Dora Russell, not for marriage.

Antic Hay pits Theodore Gumbril (Huxley), an Oxford graduate who renounces teaching to take up a business scheme (he invents inflatable underwear for people in sedentary professions), against the committed Dostoevskyan artist, Casimir Lypiatt, in competition over the femme fatale Myra Viveash (probably modelled on Wyndham Lewis and Nancy Cunard: the situation had a biographical basis). To compete with Lypiatt, the unworldly Gumbril acts on advice that women are more easily seduced by bearded men, and acquires a stick-on beard from a wig-maker:

> The effect, he decided immediately, was stunning, was grandiose. From melancholy and all too mild he saw himself transformed on the instant into a sort of jovial Henry the Eighth, into a massive Rabelaisian man, broad and powerful and exuberant with vitality and hair.
>
> (Huxley, 1990: 94)

He becomes, in fact, 'Complete Man' and finds instant success in business and sex, seducing a lone woman who turns out to be a friend's wife. Gumbril renounces the disguise and returns to being himself: he cannot accept sex without love. Myra Viveash, the vamp who apparently can, is depicted as bored and saddened by her own promiscuity as she leaves his room:

> When it came to the point, she hated her liberty. To come out like this at one o'clock into a vacuum – it was absurd, it was appalling. The prospect of immeasurable boredom opened before her. Steppes after steppes of ennui, horizon beyond horizon, forever the same. (155)

Her promiscuity is now moralised and explained: she has lost her lover in the war and feels unable ever to find love. The 'cynicism' of Huxley's world is thus only apparent. This novel at least retains a humanist and humane basis: the new sexual mores are shown to be simply a surface hardening in response to so much grief.

Point Counter Point (1928) is a more sombre creation by far than its predecessors. Like *Antic Hay* it is partly a *roman à clef*: Huxley himself is divided between the novelist Philip Quarles and Walter Bidlake, who lives with his pregnant mistress but pursues an affair with the glamorous Lucy Tantamount, who seems again to be loosely based on Nancy Cunard. Denis Burlap is a cruel portrayal of John Middleton

Murry, the editor of a literary magazine who makes a cult of his dead wife (Katherine Mansfield), advocates the poverty of St Francis, and seduces his female secretaries and contributors with a show of innocence. Mark Rampion, a painter and writer, is a version of D. H. Lawrence, and his wife Mary a version of Frieda; Maurice Spandrell who lives in squalor, advocates the devil, and deliberately corrupts an inexperienced young woman is an updated Baudelaire; Everard Webley and his Brotherhood of British Freemen (BBF) is loosely based on Sir Oswald Mosley and his British Union of Fascists (BUF). Other figures are more generic but may have particular models: Frank Illidge is the resentful working-class communist who advocates political murder but seeks upper-class company and resents his neglect; John Bidlake is a great painter of the 1890s now in decline and contemplating death: other figures are based on Huxley's own family. These identifications alone make the novel interesting for a student of the period, but as a novel of ideas, indebted to Dostoevsky and Gide, it is cumbersome. Moreover, its contrapuntal structure, which deploys a large cast of characters who are only slowly brought into relation, labours to maintain interest. The narrative and descriptive prose has little of the virtuosity and stylistic motivation of Wyndham Lewis, indeed the sentences are frequently banal, mechanical and lacking the enjoyable if overwritten glitter of the earlier novels. Moreover, the dialogue, in which each character elaborates her or his philosophy, is on the one hand long-winded, but on the other does little justice to the complexity of the ideas of figures such as Murry and Lawrence; indeed, Lawrence considered his own character a 'gas-bag'. The main interest of the novel lies in the final sections in which important narrative developments occur. Its structural problems are directly related to its ideological problems.

Huxley's 'Farcical History of Richard Greenow' in *Limbo* (1920) was a fable which depicted a brittle Oxford graduate, an internationalist and pacifist, who becomes increasingly absorbed in his own thoughts and for whom the real world becomes shadowy and unreal; his unconscious compensates, however, by launching him on a career as Pearl Bellairs, a successful novelist who actively supports the war – and denounces pacifism – in newspaper articles. Pearl Bellairs becomes Hyde to Greenow's Jekyll, and they pursue separate careers, until Greenow ends his life in an asylum. This story set out a dualistic opposition between mind and world, contemplation and action, and indeed between philosophy and the novel, which remained central to Huxley's work of the 1920s. *Point Counter Point* is thus set out in terms of an opposition between ideas and action, where action takes the form principally of sex and ends in death. The novel then is less a satire on the ideas of the period than on ideas in general, seeking to show how apparently high-minded characters are dominated by the desire for sex or murder. The action of the novel then consists of a series of resolutions; Lucy ends her relationship with Walter and he returns to his mistress; Quarles senior is exposed when his secretary turns up at the home he shares with his wife and announces that she is pregnant with his child; Denis Burlap finally seduces his latest assistant and sacks her predecessor; Illidge and Spandrell murder the Fascist Webley; Elinor Quarles, who has started an affair with Webley and plans to leave Phillip – whose intellectualism makes him a poor lover – returns home to find her son dying of meningitis; John Bidlake dies of cancer; and Spandrell is shot on his doorstep in a revenge attack by Fascists. Only Rampion escapes a negative outcome. In the narrow social range which it examines, the novel depicts a variety of marriages and affairs which are all deeply flawed, while the 'ideas' which characters espouse at length – a cross-section of the literary and political ideas of the period – are shown to be either irrelevant to lived experience or inadequate to it; or to be complex forms of hypocrisy or, in their apparent honesty, merely productive of suffering. The exception is Lawrence/Rampion, whose ideas, Huxley/Quarles concludes, are an antidote both to his own intellectualism and to the overheated sexuality of the times, a recipe for honest living. Rampion 'lives in a more satisfactory way than anyone I know. [...] The problem for me is to transform a detached intellectual scepticism into a way of harmonious all-round living' (Huxley, 1988: 326). That this opinion is so explicitly stated, rather than demonstrated, in the work tends to confirm Quarles/Huxley's problem. Quarles's frigidity alienates his wife, and her accusations about the consequence of his intellectualism for his art resemble unflinching autocritique on Huxley's part: 'If you were less of an overman', she tells him, 'what good novels you'd write' (84); 'I wish one day you'd write a simple straightforward story about a young man and a young woman who fall in love and get married and have difficulties, but get over them, and finally settle down' (200). Quarles cannot 'do' real life and love – whether in reality or in fiction. This is clearly Huxley's analysis of his own problem, self-reflexively built into the work, and one which the extensive documentation of character as well as the framework of action is designed to offset.

However, the problems of the work really lie in its intellectual detachment. Huxley vaguely seeks to borrow Lawrence's framework of ideas and mode of living to underpin his rejection of all other modes of thought – indeed, of thinking in general, as Quarles considers Rampion to belong to the rare species of the 'non-intellectual', the pre-Platonic thinker rather than the mere anti-intellectual, whose whole frame of reference is absolutely at odds with all of the intellectual activity of the present. Sex and death thus become the horizons which undermine all human meaning except that of the pre-Platonic thinker (Huxley draws on ideas which Lawrence used repeatedly and which are discussed in detail below).

Huxley's satire on his own age becomes itself detached: it is not a partisan analysis of the age so much as a rejection of it, which substitutes a simple moralism – your ideas are relative because you like sex, hurt yourself and others, and will die, whatever you say or think – for the kind of engagement with and commitment to reality which is found in the satire of Wyndham Lewis. It was left to Evelyn Waugh in the brilliantly confected satire of *Decline and Fall* and *Vile Bodies* to pick up Huxley's earlier manner, but it is Wyndham Lewis's engagement with a cultural project of negating specific social realities – however reprehensible his project – which leads him to create a satirical vehicle in *The Apes of God* and which makes Lewis, and not Huxley or Waugh, the great satirist of his age. Furthermore, as *Point Counter Point* frankly acknowledges, it is D. H. Lawrence who furnishes an alternative to Huxley's own trajectory from cynicism to sheer pessimism about human desire.

Realising Sex: The Utopian Alternative to the Jazz Age in Lady Chatterley's Lover

Writers as diverse as Lewis, Forster, Woolf and Joyce had attempted to modernise the presentation of sex within literature. The most comprehensive and complex view is that of *Ulysses*, which presents sex as a facet of consciousness and of everyday life, and uses the notion of the sexual fetish as a paradigm of symbolism in general, registering a terror of the *mise en abîme* of socially understood meaning, and of the banality of social practices which bind the average stunted consciousness in loveless unfreedom. This novel used to be read as an affirmation of flawed humanity, the product of genial middle age, but there is little cause for rejoicing in *Ulysses*. Although it details sexual acts and fantasies, and examines the role of sex in the most apparently casual relationships between the sexes, it does not really affirm the body in ways which its famous schema has led most readers to assume. Certainly it asserts that there are bodies and that these are a kind of irreducible presence: but in the same moment it goes further to show how the body occupies a kind of symbolic order and is from the outset already in some sense not there. Above all, the female body and clothing fetishistically point to something which is not there – the pun on whole/hole is repeatedly visited – while Molly's reversion to the phallic Boylan leaves her unfulfilled even when physically filled. Joyce shares with Lewis, Woolf and Forster a pessimism about sexuality which is now seen, in the company of Freud, as the determinant of an unhappy or fallen human consciousness. Consciousness would wish to escape this determination, but in a world without God renunciation of the flesh has no meaning: in the twentieth century, to turn your back on sex is to turn away from existence – from a consciousness which is deter- mined by it (Freud) and from a social evolution which depends on it (Darwin/Galton). Certainly, Joyce's novel asks along with its prota- gonist what place a notion of a sacred, disinterested love, *charitas*, can have in a secular world in which, as it turns out, all behaviour can be understood as biologically (Darwin) and psychologically (Freud) interested. In Joyce's world, the body inhabits the mind as the mind inhabits the body and the possibility of transcendence is dismissed, as is any idea of a healthy mind in a healthy body. Joyce's mapping of the unhappy consciousness owes much to a medieval world view even where its apparent assertion of the flesh seems to be offered as the antidote to Catholic renunciation.

Lawrence is more decisive than Joyce in his rejection of the Christian framework, more fundamentally Nietzschean in his desire to assert something, and less happy to follow a rationalism which can begin to see every aspect of human existence in terms of its social mediation, that is, of its determination by external necessities. Of course, many readers have judged Lawrence simply wrong or naïve in his assertion of sex and sexuality and his desire to 'realise' sex in literature, while others have followed Simone de Beauvoir in *The Second Sex* (1949) and Kate Millett in *Sexual Politics* (1970) in their rejection of his work for its apparent sexism. Certainly, *Lady Chatterley's Lover* (1928) has tended to be written off or disregarded for a number of reasons, and those few commentators who have chosen to defend it on what they consider are its own terms have seemed to apologise for some of its worst aspects. Because it is commonly taken as the simple expression of sexism or of sex, the novel has a tarnished reputation which makes it difficult to classify. It exists in any case in three significantly different published versions: *The First Lady Chatterley* [1926] and *John Thomas and Lady Jane* [1927] combine with the final version not so much as a series of options but as the articulation of a problem. The distance from the first to the final version of 1928 reveals changes of purpose, and Lawrence's famous note, 'A Propos of *Lady Chatterley's Lover*' (1929–30) cannot be taken as a true gloss on even the final version.

It is worth starting with 'A Propos' if only because it is so famously quoted by Foucault at the conclusion of the first volume of *The History of Sexuality* (1976), a connection which offers an opportunity to construct Lawrence as a proto-Foucauldian which should be resisted.[16] As is well known, Foucault uses the first volume of this work to reject the conventional view that in the modern world sex is repressed and to advance his theory that modernity has in fact witnessed an unprecedented discursive instrumentalisation of sex at all levels. In this model even Freud must not be seen as a hero revealing the role of a sexual repression which, once removed, might leave humanity in a state of greater liberty – remember that Foucault was writing at a time when sexual liberation was a central plank of a progressive youth agenda – but rather as a scientist advancing instrumental knowledge into a previously taboo domain. Sex is therefore being turned into a knowledge which is used by society to police and control its members. It is in the context of this analysis that Foucault quotes Lawrence, not as a hero of sexual liberation but as an ideologue of the discourse of sexuality, as someone who typifies the modern desire to bring sex into knowledge and thus submit it to administrative control. He quotes those words of Lawrence which appear to reflect this ambition:

> There has been so much action in the past, especially sexual action, a wearying repetition over and over, without a corresponding thought, a corresponding realisation. Now our business is to realise sex. Today, the full conscious realisation of sex is even more important than the act itself.[17]

Foucault follows this quotation with the remark:

> Perhaps one day people will wonder at this. They will not be able to understand how a civilization so intent on developing enormous

instruments of production and destruction found the time and the infinite patience to inquire so anxiously concerning the actual state of sex; people will smile perhaps when they recall that here were men – meaning ourselves – who believed that therein resided a truth every bit as precious as the one they had already demanded from the earth, the stars, and the pure forms of their thought. [...] And people will ask themselves why we were so bent on ending the rule of silence regarding what was the noisiest of our preoccupations. (Foucault, 1981: 157–8)

This remark certainly glosses over the status of *Lady Chatterley's Lover,* which hardly formed part of the official administrative machinery, as it could only be circulated covertly. Moreover, Lawrence's writing much more evidently belongs to what Foucault has earlier called 'a symbolics of blood' associated with earlier social forms and revived by Nazism, rather than the 'analytics of sexuality' which characterises modern administrative society. Indeed, in the discussion of marriage which occupies the bulk of his essay, Lawrence privileges the notion of 'blood' as he had frequently done throughout his work: 'blood is the substance of soul and of the deepest consciousness. It is by blood that we are [...]' (Lawrence, 1994b: 324). Yet, despite these notable divergences, an important element in Foucault's generalised account of the role of 'sex' in modern society has resonance in a description of Lawrence's work:

Through a reversal that doubtless had its surreptitious beginnings long ago [...] we arrive at the point where we expect our intelligibility to come from what was for many centuries thought of as madness; the plenitude of our body from what was long considered its stigma and likened to a wound; our identity from what was conceived as an obscure and nameless urge. (Foucault, 1981: 156)

Foucault concludes; 'The rallying point for the counterattack against the deployment of sexuality ought not to be sex-desire, but bodies and pleasure' (157).

Any attempt to place Lawrence as a proto-Foucauldian founders on the distinction that Foucault makes here, for Lawrence has no desire to relocate sex in terms of anything so contingent as bodies and pleasure. He retains the notion that sex can and must be central to identity, and persists in the belief that the body has become eclipsed by the mind, by sheer mentalism or will. His general stance may seem to match Foucault's description of the modern consciousness of sex, yet it is surely striking that among his contemporaries he remains relatively isolated in his insistent contrasting of a lost sexual wholeness with contemporary industrial reality.

To distinguish Lawrence's position in 'A Propos of *Lady Chatterley's Lover*' from the admittedly perfunctory use which Foucault makes of it, we should first note that the opening section of the essay aims to defend the novel's obscenity, and in particular its extensive use of explicit Anglo-Saxon terms and descriptions of sexual acts. Certainly, the language of sex is in question, and the dynamic of challenging or appearing to challenge a repressive censorious power which prohibits the use of such words certainly corresponds to that gesture of sexual liberation against which Foucault so vehemently polemicises. Yet Lawrence's terms do not suggest that he wishes to establish or rehabilitate any 'discourse' of sexuality, inasmuch as the term discourse implies an ordered, scientific form of knowledge. Lawrence writes: 'I want men and women to be able to *think* sex, fully, completely, honestly, and cleanly.' (Lawrence, 1994b: 308) What he means by 'think' is not 'represent', but rather what is indicated by the term 'realise' which Foucault does not query: 'our ancestors have so assiduously acted sex without ever thinking or realising it, that now the act tends to be mechanical, dull, and disappointing, and only fresh mental realisation will freshen up the experience.' This 'means being able to use the so-called obscene words, because these are a natural part of the mind's consciousness of the body. Obscenity only comes in when the mind despises and fears the body, and the body hates and resists the mind' (Foucault, 1981: 308–9). What Lawrence argues for, therefore, is not a discursive consciousness of sex, but a mental consciousness of the body, one which can be regained through a use of a 'natural' vocabulary. 'Realisation' is then literally a kind of making real of pleasure in a balanced relationship between mind and body; 'obscenity' is the dissociation or imbalance of the mental and physical.

I will return to the notion of the real implied by the term 'realisation' below, in connection with Lawrence's deployment of the phallus, which underpins it. In the remainder of his essay Lawrence outlines and defends his idea of marriage. Christianity in the form found in the South of Europe but not in the Protestant North is said to have preserved an ideal of marriage based on blood and on the cycle of the seasons, and therefore on authentic human feelings. It has been able to do so in spite of the sexual pessimism of official Christianity: the pagan rituals have been maintained within peasant culture and mapped on to the Christian festivals. In this environment, marriage can be based on 'real love'. Modern English society is characterised by 'counterfeit' love and emotions: 'Never was an age more sentimental, more devoid of real feeling, more exaggerated in false feeling than our own.' (Lawrence, 1994b: 312). The work culture of Protestantism has broken with the pagan past by abandoning its festivals and has made the body the 'trained dog' of the will. Radio, film, the press and literature all contribute to the culture of counterfeit. In particular, the tone of cynicism in writers such as Arlen (whom Lawrence does not name but who was a model for the cerebral and sexually modern Michaelis in the novel) contributes to a general 'mistrust' in human relations and does nothing to offset the tide of counterfeit:

> The Tragedy is, that in an age peculiarly conscious of counterfeit, peculiarly suspicious of counterfeit and swindle in emotion, particularly sexual emotion, the rage and mistrust against the counterfeit element is likely to overwhelm and extinguish the small, true flame of real loving communion, which might have made two lives happy. Herein lies the danger of harping only on the counterfeit and swindle of emotion, as most 'advanced' writers do. Though they do it, of course, to counter-balance the hugely greater swindle of the sentimental 'sweet' writers.
>
> (314)

The 'advanced' writers are those identified by Lewis as the 'sophisticated school', but the tenor of Lawrence's attack is quite different, for while these writers appear to be 'knowing' they in fact do not know the very thing which they appear to take for granted. Lewis's account defines the serious writer as the 'high-brow low-brow', an adjunct of the culture industry in spite of class pedigree and an ironic, antithetical stance. Lawrence similarly sees the potential of 'advanced' literature for authenticity suspended in a frozen dialectic with the popular culture which it appears to negate but to the effects of which it merely contributes.

It is an easy matter to open a critique of Lawrence's position in this essay. However, as with the work of Wyndham Lewis, the scope of the cultural intervention which Lawrence outlines here should not go unremarked. The question Lawrence asks about how happiness can be found in industrial mass society, a question about the possibility of the good life with its roots in Nietzsche, is not dismissible, even while Lawrence's solutions might appear to be mired in masculinism and family ideology. Critique there must be, however, and one which goes beyond the routine criticism of Lawrence's non-liberal personal 'values' to describe the problems in the structure of his thought, and to go on to relate these problems to the complex ambition of his art – to 'realise' something which, despite its apparent ubiquity, has become unreal.

Making real – an assertion of 'life' – takes the general form of a return to nature and the specific form of a celebration of the value of the phallus. The *locus classicus* of the critique of the role of nature in early-twentieth-century literature is Leo Lowenthal's essay on the Norwegian novelist Knut Hamsun, which was originally published in 1937.[18] Not every element identified by Lowenthal in Hamsun's writing is to be found in Lawrence, but there are several important conjunctures. Early in his essay, Lawrence asserts the real life of the body against the counterfeit sentiment of culture:

> The body's life is the life of sensations and emotion. The body feels real hunger, real thirst, real joy in the sun or snow, real pleasure in the smell of roses or the look of a lilac bush; real anger, real sorrow, real love, real tenderness, real warmth, real passion, real hate, real grief.　　(311)

Reality is to be found in the body, and the realities of the body can only appear in the general context of a 'regeneration' which involves a return to the cycles of nature:

> We *must* get back into relation, vivid and nourishing relation to the cosmos and the universe. The way is through daily ritual, and the re-awakening. We *must* once more practise the ritual of dawn and noon and sunset, the ritual of the kindling fire and pouring water, the ritual of the first breath, and the last. [...] For the truth is, we are perishing for lack of fulfilment of our greater needs, we are cut off from the great sources of our inward nourishment and renewal, sources which flow eternally in the universe. Vitally, the human race is dying. It is like a great uprooted tree, with its roots in the air. We must plant ourselves again in the universe.　　(329–30)

In his analysis of Hamsun's work, Lowenthal finds the following qualities:

> [T]he pagan awe of unlimited and unintelligible forces of nature, the mystique of blood and race, hatred of the working class and of clerks, the blind submission to authority, the abrogation of individual responsibility, anti-intellectualism, and spiteful distrust of urban middle-class life in general.　　(320)

Paganism and the mystique of blood are abundantly present in Lawrence, but the other elements would need careful qualification before being applied to him. If he shows a clear contempt for what working-class and lower-middle-class life have become it is because he does not accept the conditions of life as it is actually constituted under capitalism. While I am not in a position to evaluate Lowenthal's claim *vis-à-vis* Hamsun, it seems clear that the critical tradition of the

Frankfurt School with which Lowenthal aligns himself should be quite capable of distinguishing between the hatred of present conditions and a hatred of the people caught in those conditions, and of identifying the moment in which a critique of those conditions deviates from what is thinkable and subsequently becomes a simple class hatred and misanthropy. Lawrence, in his lucid moments at least, did not hate the working class, but rather hated what had befallen them, and he is dismissive of the whole pattern of class society. The other elements which Lowenthal identifies – blind submission to authority and anti-intellectualism have considerable resonance in Lawrence's work. Lowenthal's essay is concerned to identify the proto-Nazi elements in Hamsun's work, a tendency confirmed by Hamsun's allegiance during the Second World War. Hence the connection of submission to authority with the notion in Hamsun's work of Nature as a force to which the individual must submit: Nazism equated itself with nature via the notion of race and demanded submission to the rule of one man in whom nature and race mystically embodied itself. Certainly in the leadership phase of Lawrence's work, as embodied in *Aaron's Rod*, the notion of unquestioning submission of one man to another is the principal motif. What remains of the notion of submission in 'A Propos' is the claim that man must deny the separation of intellect and submit to the natural forces which are held to be those manifested in ritual and underwritten by the cycle of the seasons.

On the general shift in the notion of nature of which Lawrence's work partakes, Lowenthal writes:

> With the coming of doubt and even despair about personal fulfilment within society, the image of nature was no longer a basis for a new perspective, but became an alternative. Nature was increasingly envisaged as the ultimate surcease of social pressure. In this context, man could submit to nature and feel at peace. His soul, inviolable in ideology yet outraged in reality, could find solace in such a submission; frustrated in his attempt to participate autonomously in the societal world, he could join the world of nature. He could become a 'thing', like the tree or the brook, and find more pleasure in this surrender than in a hopeless struggle against manmade forces. (320–21)

Proceeding through a discussion of the use made by Nazism of vitalist philosophy (*Lebensphilosophie*), Lowenthal passes on to the function of the peasant in the anti-liberal schema common to Hamsun and Nazism:

The submergence of reason accompanied a glorification of the peasant, an integral part of anti-liberal undercurrents. The peasant is seen as not alienated from his work; unlike the industrial worker, he does not seem to violate nature but follows, so to speak, its true rhythm. Since his work is hard, healthy, meaningful and in harmony with natural processes, it is set forth as the model of true manliness, dignified and silent.   (322)

Many of the elements which Lowenthal identifies can be located in Lawrence's work, and the Nazi conclusion that a society must be based on instinctual blood kinship rather than on principles of autonomy and freedom is closely predicted by Lawrence in a model which would later serve the Leavises:

The sense of isolation, followed by a sense of menace and of fear, is bound to arise as the feeling of oneness and community with our fellow-man declines, and the feeling of individualism and personality, which is existence in isolation, increases. [...] Class hate and class-consciousness are only a sign that the old togetherness, the old blood-warmth has collapsed, and every man is really aware of himself in apartness. [...] In the old England, the curious blood-connection held the classes together. The squires might be arrogant, violent, bullying and unjust, yet in some way they were *at one* with the people, part of the same blood-stream.

(332–3)

A society in which class conflict is eliminated by recourse to a myth of national identity founded in 'blood and soil' (more literally 'blood and ground': *blut und boden* – a Nazi catchphrase) became central to Nazi political thinking. The cases of Lawrence and Hamsun are different, but the basis for a critique of Lawrence as a proto-Fascist can easily be developed. Clearly, for the critical theorists of the Frankfurt School, the critique of Nazi ideology was a matter of urgency. At the same time, a politics of human liberation which is precisely based on seeking the seeds of as yet unrealised and unimagined social possibilities must always be sensitive to the utopian moment which can be seized on in the unassimilable and resistant moments of art, even where these moments are bound up in regressive ideology. It is inevitable that they must be, and we need only consider the case of Anton Webern, on the one hand a composer of autonomous music of the kind which Adorno considered the last (and already heavily conflicted) site of utopian human freedom, and on the other hand an express Nazi sympathiser, to grasp that only a rigorous attention to the artwork rather than to explicit or implicit authorial ideology can uncover the sedimentation of resistance not only to existing social conditions and to the general ideology, but also to that critically constructed authorial ideology which remains a necessary but at times obstructive product of the reading process.[19]

I have focused on Lawrence's retrospective account of *Lady Chatterley's Lover* and the ideology critique which it invites in order to enable in what follows a bracketing of the question of authorial ideology, something which is more usually allowed in the analysis of poetry than fiction which, because of its prose nature, is often implicitly expected to yield categorical propositions. Indeed, prose fiction often deploys such statements in the narrative voice or in the dialogue or thought of characters, or sometimes in the undecidable space of third-person centre of consciousness narration. Such statements can often be directly associated with authorial statements made *in propria persona,* for example in essays or diaries, and the temptation to make such connections is often overwhelming. For this reason, authorial ideology remains a powerful presence even where bracketed. Nevertheless, it must be regarded as a component of the work rather than its content.

One final element of authorial ideology must be mentioned here: Lawrence's use of the term phallus, discussion of which appears in 'A Propos'. The body, the race and the couple are connected by the blood which engorges the phallus.

> Marriage is no marriage that is not a correspondence of blood. For the blood is the substance of the soul, and of the deepest consciousness. [...] In the blood, knowing and being, or feeling, are one and undivided [...]. The blood of man and the blood of woman are two eternally different streams, that can never be mingled. [...] Two rivers of blood, are man and wife, two distinct eternal streams, that have the power of touching and communing and so renewing [...]. And the phallus is the connecting link between the two rivers, that establishes the two streams in a oneness [...]. For the bridge to the future is the phallus, and there's the end of it. [...] For the new impulse to life will never come without blood-contact, the true, positive blood-contact, not the nervous negative reaction. (324–7)

The phallus can clearly be connected both to racial ideology and to Lawrence's widely noted phallocentrism. Either connection yields plausible but overwhelmingly negative accounts. In an attempt to confront the problems associated with the ideological connotations of the term, one commentator[20] seeks to associate the phallus in Lawrence with Lacan's treatment of the same in his now well-known introduction of linguistic theory into psychoanalysis. I will not attempt to summarise Lacan's crucial essay, 'The Meaning of the Phallus',[21] which is in an already condensed and occasionally enigmatic account of an argument which requires extensive commentary. The gesture of the essay, which it is useful here to isolate, is the distinction between need and desire, and between the penis and phallus, the penis being the real biological object, the phallus a signifier. Need can be met by an object, but desire is what remains of the demand for love once the appetite has been satisfied. Desire can never be satisfied, and is constitutive of the subject, henceforth defined as 'split'. The realm of desire is the symbolic, rather than the world of objects, and it is the phallus – as signifier – which is the object of both male and female desire. The phallus thus becomes the signifier *par excellence*, the mark of the split between the subject and signification in general. Hence it is something that both the male and the female subject desire, and which each seeks to posses – via a different logic – in the Other. So the phallus, far from being the penis which the male possesses and which the female must apparently envy, is now no longer a biological fact but the central symbolic fact of the unrealisability of desire *per se*. Expert Lacanians will excuse this clumsy summary, but the point is that the phallus in Lawrence, since it appears as signifier, can be glossed in Lacanian terms and understood in terms of a psychoanalytic problematic rather than as the simple expression of a male desire for domination. The male too desires the phallus which, as it is a sign, belongs to the realm of a permanently constituted, indeed foundational, desire which confirms the split and permanently incomplete nature of both male and female subjects. Lawrence, it can be argued, in a series of accounts of sexual encounters in *Lady Chatterley's Lover* where needs are met but desire remains, can be thought of as depicting this fundamental condition.

Lawrence is virtually a connoisseur of the varieties of dissatisfaction that remain after sexual encounters, and there is much scope for developing the Lacanian reading which I have outlined. The project of 'realising' sex as a making real of sex and uniting of psyche and language with the physical could easily be grasped as a quixotic attempt to overcome the splitting of the subject which fails to recognise that the subject is constituted by the very split which Lawrence's polemicising around the phallus seeks to overcome: thus, Lawrence's work, in its attempt to articulate the problematic of the phallus as he recognises it, generates an image – albeit an inverted one – of an authentic problematic which his drive towards 'realisation' accidentally uncovers and of which the author may be substantially unconscious.

It is very evident that references in Lawrence's work to the phallus are generally to the penis ('she saw the phallus rise under his clothing'[22]), although the symbolic role of the phallus in ancient Greece and in non-Christian religions certainly influenced his decision to privilege the term. However, inasmuch as the phallus in Lawrence generally functions as the symbol of human sexuality in general, it is the signifier of something which is absent in the sense of unreal. While in Lacan the phallus can never on any account become real, in Lawrence the possible reality of the phallus – that is, the possible reality of sex – is merely *historically* denied, so the phallus now is a symbol of an unreal, because unrealised, sexuality, and much of Lawrence's writing orbits around the potential presence of a real sex which is absent from the text in two ways. In one way it is absent because language cannot embody a phenomenon that belongs to the mind in relation with the body. In another way it is absent because it is altogether absent from the modern social reality of the industrialised world – specifically, from England. It is therefore doubly absent, and Lawrence's writing addresses its restoration in two ways. It has the potential to be restored to language through the use of dialect, which is assumed by Lawrence still to contain elements of a pagan or, as in the earlier quotation, 'natural' language. While modern and polite social discourse (which developed out of the intellect and will which drove Protestantism and the industrial revolution) has no access to the reality of the realised mind-body relationship, it may be that the resources of natural and pagan languages which hold themselves stubbornly apart from official discourse in working-class and dialect speech still hold the key to pagan realities. The question of restoring the phallus to reality may depend on social change (a thesis tested by *The Plumed Serpent*) or on individual choice (*Lady Chatterley's Lover*), but either way the task of the novelist becomes one of giving imaginative resonance to the phallus as symbol with the aim of preparing the restoration of its reality. This means that narratives must focus on the attempts of individuals to recover the reality of sex, and that textual surfaces must all veil this missing reality – for, if we were to follow Lacan, the phallus would be only the mark of signification and hence of textuality in general: 'For it is to this signified that is given to designate as a whole the effect of there being a signified.'[23]

It is better to view the missing reality as an achievable but unrepresentable social reality rather than as the unachievable (because always already represented) signified itself. The unrepresentability of this social reality would seem to be a moot point, for Lawrence will frequently place this unalienated condition in the past as well as in the future. Yet his examination of the political attempt to restore the pagan past in *The Plumed Serpent* (see below) seems not merely to query the regressive politics of Fascism, but to question the nostalgic view of the past as the site of real sex. It is this feature of Lawrence's work which is worth affirming. Lawrence identifies social alienation in terms of sexuality. Alienation is recognised in the dysfunction of mind and body at the most fundamental level, and is unequivocally grasped as a feature of capitalist development. Lawrence frequently embraces nostalgia and usually rejects communism, although in *The First Lady Chatterley* the working-class gamekeeper (called, in that version, Parkin) is an eloquent exponent of communism, a fact importantly related to his role as the sexual awakener of Constance Chatterley. Despite his more usual adherence to the nostalgic model, and his general refusal to consider human autonomy in terms of the liberation of labour power, Lawrence's sense that alienation in class society operates at the level of sex and sexuality coincides with the belief of Adorno, and the later and more elaborated theories of Marcuse, that social and sexual liberation were thoroughly entwined, and that psychoanalysis could be harnessed by Marxism to give an account of the psychosexual dynamic of class society. Adorno concentrated on the psychoanalysis of oppression – the 'jazz subject' and the 'authoritarian personality' – while Marcuse emphasised the liberative potential of 'polymorphous sexuality' in the present, emphasising the connection between class and sexual repression. They concurred in taking Freud's description of sexual normality as the starting point for thinking about what was involved in the processes of sexual normalisation and why certain forms of sexual normality were created by capitalist society. Without revisiting their accounts here, I would like simply to suggest that they display an important similarity with Lawrence's attempt to think about sexual liberation against the grain of a contemporary culture which told people that they were already sexually liberated because they were free to talk about and consume images of sex and to feel that in so doing they were 'expressing themselves'. For Lawrence, it is not simply the case that sex is always there, waiting to be discovered in language and in practice. Rather, as for Adorno and Marcuse, he considers that its reality is fundamentally absent, denied by class society, a fact which popular discourse about sex not only obscures but actively helps to bring about.

This at least is the conclusion that can be drawn from the role of class in *The First Lady Chatterley*, a feature of the work which is substantially in abeyance in the final version because of Lawrence's discomfort with his own logic. It is essential to see *Lady Chatterley's Lover* in terms of the relationship between the three different versions. Bakhtin tells us that we must consider the novel not as a discursively homogeneous entity like a lyric poem, but in terms of the 'distinctive links and inter-relationships' between the different types of 'utterances and languages' which it contains: this process of linking he calls dialogisation, and considers it to be the fundamental formal feature of the novel. He tends to see dialogisation as a formal feature of the work taken as a whole, and even refers to it as a 'higher unity', thus preserving a certain holy grail of formalism.[24] In this case we have three works which interdict each other's claims to unity, and others which can be regarded as belonging to them as satellites, but the notion of dialogisation usefully denotes the process by which different discursive types and different genres are brought into relation in this tripartite work. They are brought into relation, however, not in order to embody an existing socially heteroglossic reality, but in order to denote the absence and unreality of true human satisfaction.

Yet I have said that Lawrence's framing of the problem is immersed in ideology – to the point, in some of its aspects, of being delusional. My examination of *The Plumed Serpent* (Chapter Five) examines the most regressive components of his work in the context of class and gender politics in more detail, but another story from his Mexican phase can helpfully be discussed as a forerunner of *Lady Chatterley's Lover*. 'The Woman Who Rode Away' (written in 1924) is set in Mexico, and contrasts a white culture which has lost its connection with the cosmos with an imaginary native Indian culture which is in decline under pressure of the advance of white civilisation. The eponymous woman leaves her home and family to find an unsubordinated Indian tribe in the hills. What starts as a fascination with the impersonal or inhuman landscape turns into an encounter with members of a tribe who take her to their village where she is drugged and fed up for sacrifice at the winter solstice. The apparent ideology of the tale reproduces some of the terms which appear in 'A Propos', which describes personality as a modern nervous condition which gets in the way of a more authentic mode of being. In particular, the story associates the appearance of modern 'personality' with the new aspirations of women:

For hours and hours she watched, spell-bound, and as if drugged. And in all the terrible persistence of the drumming and the primeval, rushing deep singing, and the endless stamping of the dance of the fox-tailed men, the tread of heavy, bird-erect women in their black tunics, she seemed at last to feel her own death, her own obliteration. [...] Her kind of womanhood, intensely personal and individual, was to be obliterated again, and the great primeval symbols were to tower once more over the fallen individual independence of woman. (60)

More and more her ordinary personal consciousness had left her, she had gone into that other state of passional cosmic consciousness, like one who is drugged. The Indians, with their heavily religious natures, had made her succumb to their vision. (64)

She remains acquiescent in the plan of the Indians to sacrifice her, accepting her own death. At the moment of sacrifice at the end of the story, these final sentences appear:

Then the old man would strike, and strike home, accomplish the sacrifice and achieve the power.
The mastery that man must hold, and that passes from race to race.
(71)

Read as an expression of authorial ideology, the final sentence would seem simply to draw the moral of the whole tale: men must have mastery over women for the survival of the race; modern woman must sacrifice her 'personality' – that is, her claims to modern political autonomy – and submit impersonally to racial and cosmic destiny. We can certainly draw the conclusion that this is what Lawrence means. However, the final sentence returns us forcefully to a question of narrative point of view, which is in its turn a question of narrative genre and style. Who or what originates this final sentence?

This is a story cast in the impersonal mode of epic and folk tale. The narrative is indebted to the classic American captivity tale which Lawrence found in the work of James Fenimore Cooper. It also has elements in common with the desert romance (which I discuss below) and with the Sleeping Beauty story which informs *The Virgin and the Gipsy* and the *Chatterley* novels. The Sleeping Beauty story, of course, involves sexual awakening, and in Lawrence's versions involves personal renewal; here the awakening is not sexual and the renewal is to be the ceremonial renewal of a people, not that of an individual. In respect of sexual awakening there is no real inconsistency in terms of Lawrence's schema, since the woman discovers not sexuality in the Indians but chastity, and Lawrence in 'A Propos' equates true sexuality with chastity, the opposite of modern, nervous sexuality. This therefore remains a structural variation of the Sleeping Beauty story on the terms which Lawrence establishes elsewhere. The issue of renewal is a key difference, and embodies an evident shift in thinking from racial renewal in the Mexican phase to personal renewal in the Chatterley phase. The opposition between the personal and the impersonal need not be absolute, of course, but what Lawrence does here is to set up an inquiry into the possibility of impersonality understood as a return to a blind pagan past in which social forms are mechanical and unquestionable. As I outline below, he treats this at much greater length in *The Plumed Serpent.* The opposition of impersonal and personal is important in understanding the unfolding of the *Chatterley* novels because it is reproduced at the level of genre. The impersonal story form could never simply be expanded into the novel, which inevitably involves the personal, and the problem of shifting from the story of *The Virgin and the Gipsy* to the novel *The First Lady Chatterley* must be understood in these terms: it is a dialogic problem which arises from bringing different generic forms and the notion of the human which each projects into relation. The encounter generates problems which run through the three successive versions of the *Chatterley* novel.

This is the conflict which occurs at the level of genre, and it is reproduced at the level of style. What I have called the epic/folk style of 'The Woman Who Rode Away' is, of course, not an imitation of those styles but an invented synthetic medium. The impersonality of the style is advertised from the outset by the namelessness of the woman, although focalisation throughout is third-person centre of consciousness: we are shown this person's destiny through an account of her own perceptions. The thoughts and motives of the Indian are represented only in a few rudimentary conversations in which we learn that they despise whites for their lack of authentic relation to the cosmos – and we have no difficulty here in identifying the author's intrusions into these exchanges. Many important exchanges and events are entirely wordless. Descriptive passages which concentrate on the landscape or on the Indian people, their dwellings, attire and ritualistic behaviour, are the most obvious attempt to evoke beauty in the story, aiming to suggest a pristine ambience of elemental forces by deploying vivid colours and natural materials in simple, propositional sequences:

> It went on all day, the insistence of the drum, the cavernous, roaring, storm-like sound of the male singing, the incessant swinging of the fox-

skins behind the powerful, gold-bronze, stamping legs of the men, the autumn sun from a perfect blue heaven pouring in the rivers of black hair, men's and women's, the valley all still, the walls of rock beyond, the awful huge bulking of the mountain against the pure sky, its snow seething with sheer whiteness. (60)

This is the mountain where the woman will be sacrificed. Its whiteness gives us the clue that not all is as it seems in this apparently impersonal environment, for it recalls the whiteness of the whale in *Moby Dick,* and the whole pattern of white mischief which ended with Ahab sacrificing himself to the whale. The white woman and the white mountain may be destined then to meet not for reasons programmed by the (in any case imaginary) Indian culture, but for reasons emanating from white culture. While the story's final sentence may appear to belong to the impersonal consciousness of the implicitly male narrator, demanding female sacrifice, it may equally be that this is the woman's idea and not the moral of the tale at all. After all, the story ends in death, not renewal, and it may be the woman's sense of herself as being at the centre of an impersonal epic quest, the product of a Western Orientalist outlook, which is brought into question. The style of the descriptive passages reflects ideas about non-Western art in terms of its simple formal beauty and abstraction which were widely disseminated at this time. The story itself alludes to the logic of the desert romance which was organised around erotic female self-sacrifice. Narrative genre and style here are thus not simply the impersonal medium through which the story moves, but their deployment articulates an inquiry into the possibility of sexual renewal and asks whether it can be imagined, enacted or represented in other than a delusional fashion. Folk/epic impersonality is not an achieved generic fact, nor does it or can it reconstruct or rebuild the lost actuality of sex. The understanding of the woman and of the narrative style and genre are both defective, and are silenced, at the conclusion, turned back on themselves by their own faulty logic.

An understanding of the generic self-reflexivity of the inquiry into the possible realisation of sex is central to the most obvious predecessor of the *Chatterley* novels, *The Virgin and the Gipsy* (written in 1926). This is a Sleeping Beauty narrative, but the setting is removed from Mexico to England and the social setting is consequently much less fanciful. Although it remains a fable, more plausible social specifics must be concocted, and the result is the story of the daughter of a nonconformist minister who is saved during a flood (in which her grandmother, a 'wicked witch' figure, is drowned) by a Gipsy man with whom, for reasons of safety, she passes the night naked. By using a Gipsy, Lawrence is able to combine class and racial otherness as the source of renewal, and the highly specific social setting establishes English nonconformism rather than a generalised 'white' decadence as the culture requiring renewal. Yet the character of the Virgin, Yvette, remains fabular, incompletely delineated, and the state of renewal remains undescribed. The shift from folk impersonality to the personality of the novel remains incomplete. It is in *The First Lady Chatterley* that Lawrence completes the generic shift to the novel and to imagining renewal as a social reality. However, it is not the sex act but class difference which is the major topic of the first version.

We should immediately note that a reading of the *Chatterley* novels which sees them through the optic of Forster's *Maurice* in terms of the difficulties and attractions of sexual relationships between the classes falls very wide of the mark.[25] The first version of *Maurice* was completed in 1914 and, although it was not published until after Forster's death, it circulated in manuscript form and may have been known to Lawrence. It may even have prompted him to choose a gamekeeper as his sexual awakener. The point of *The First Lady Chatterley*, however, is to examine the ways in which authentic sex is denied in class society. The general plot outline, which remains constant if variable in all three versions, and concerns the affair of Constance Chatterley, married to the wheelchair-bound Sir Clifford, with the gamekeeper Parkin (later Mellors), is too well known to require reiteration. Lawrence probably blundered in having Sir Clifford impotent because of his war injuries, not only because the symbolism is rather too overt, but because it gives Constance a more or less pragmatic reason for leaving him, while Lawrence is actually more interested in the cultural motivation. These reasons shift between the first and final versions principally because of the change in class position of Parkin, of working-class origin, and Mellors, who is grammar school educated, served as an officer in the army, and has merely adopted dialect speech as a misanthropic strategy. Parkin identifies with his class and espouses communism, while Mellors hates working-class politics and sees Bolshevism merely as a further stage in the process of mechanisation. This contrast represents a fundamental shift from the first version which toys with the idea that working-class revolution may represent the alternative to capitalism and bring about the renewal of England, at the same moment that it

183

bestows the power of Constance's sexual renewal to a working-class man. In the later version, the seeds of sexual and social renewal are to be found only in a man who has abandoned class and lives on the margins, in the small and shrinking patch of wood on which the ravages of mining have not yet encroached. The class thematic is very much to the fore in the first version due to the general absence of sexual description – Lawrence had not yet in the first version set himself the task of discovering a language for sex. Instead, the first version takes the fable of the encounter with another race of 'The Woman Who Rode Away' and transposes it on to class. Thus, when Parkin is described as the 'black man of the woods' (Lawrence, 1973a: 44) this recalls not merely the folk-figure, but reinforces Constance's opinion that 'culturally, he was another race' (82). Much as the woman who rode away is stimulated by contact with the race that will destroy her and happily proceeds to her own death, so Connie experiences 'class fear':

> She felt a twinge of indefinite and awful dread, a dread of her own fellow-men and women, a special *class* fear. For a long time she would not believe where the strange twinge of fear-anguish came from. But at last, she had to admit, it was from her contact with the lower class.
> She had touched them, in actual passionate contact. And out of the touch came a twinge of wild, unknown fear. Perhaps they were her destroyers, the destroyers of her and her class! Perhaps even now the keeper was gloating over a certain subtle destruction of her. (93)

The process of renewal is always so poised between risk and possibility, that it is never merely a question of whether or not Constance gets good sex, but of the emergence of a new woman who has nothing in common with the intellectual 'new woman' of the pre-war whom Lawrence mostly parodies:

> She recognised the power that passion had assumed over her. She felt strange, different from herself. It was all very well entering on these voyages of new and passionate adventure, but they carried you away from yourself. They did not leave you where you were, nor what you were. No, she was aware of a strange woman inside herself, a woman wakened up and imperious. She was running now to get home to tea, but she was running also to get away from this new thing that had come upon her. She was running to escape from the woman inside herself, the woman who felt so fierce and so tender at the same time, so soft and boundless and gentle, but also so remorseless, like the sea. (77–8)

Of course, this and similar passages could be glossed as simply the representation of common passion. What seems important is that the moment of passionate experience is also the moment in which as yet unrealised human possibilities can be intuited: these are the moments in which a future social dispensation can be felt, in which a different humanity emerges. It is therefore very significant that Parkin, the agent of this change, belongs to the working class and endorses communism. Indeed, he is secretary of the local Communist league, a fact which he reveals not to Connie but to her friend the painter Duncan Forbes. It is Forbes, not Parkin, who sounds out Connie on the subject of communism. He has told Parkin that he is not a communist, so either in this conversation he is acting as the devil's advocate, or the conversation was devised as one between Parkin and Constance, and subsequently shifted to Forbes either for reasons of realism – Parkin is not so articulate and cannot like his successor Mellors abandon dialect and rudimentary speech – or because Lawrence already wished to diminish Parkin's communism. This can only ever remain guesswork, however, and moreover it is difficult to avoid the impression in this passage that Lawrence is reporting his own thoughts – the hatred of democracy and defence of natural aristocracy which Forbes repudiates had been Lawrence's own.[26]

'You're frightened of Communism?' he asked.

She looked up, and pondered herself.

'Yes!' she admitted slowly. 'I suppose I am. I'm afraid of anything which is materialism – wages and state ownership – and nothing else.'

'What is it but materialism today?'

[...]

'Anyhow,' she said, nettled. 'We aren't even then as materialistic, atavistically materialistic, as we should be if we were in Russia today. – Or do you believe in Russia?'

'No, I'm afraid I don't. [...] Yet I can see, the working people will *have* to do something about it sooner or later. And after all, England isn't Russia. A Tevershall collier isn't a Russian moujik. [...] Do you know what I think the English *really* want? [...] Contact! Some sort of passionate human contact among themselves. And perhaps if the Communists did smash the famous "system" there might emerge a new relationship between men: *really* not caring about money, *really* caring for life, and the life-flow with one another.'

[...]

'Why don't we start it now?'

'Because we know perfectly well we're all being carried round by the "system". [...] I believe the English, a sufficient quantity of them, are weary of materialism and weary of hardening their hearts to keep it going. – No, I've hated democracy since the war. But now I see I'm wrong calling for an aristocracy. What we want is a flow of life from one to another – to release some natural flow in us that urges to be released.'

(241–3)

It is in the nature of Lawrence's dialogic procedure that these opinions, although they may well represent his own thoughts in a given moment, are assigned to a character whose voice cannot be construed as authorial. Yet the sense remains that they give the clue to the political meaning of the novel which is mapped on to the format of 'The Woman Who Rode Away' and *The Virgin and the Gipsy*. This is the utopian moment in Lawrence which I have argued is always structurally implicit in the demand for the realisation of sex, even on those occasions when this demand takes the most regressive and proto-Fascist forms.

However, while a sophisticated theoretical framework can be imported to show what the meaning of this moment might be, it is difficult to claim that Lawrence himself was generally in possession of such a framework. His oppositions are generally binary – penis *vs* intellect; nature *vs* mechanism – a fact confirmed in the figure of Clifford who remains an implausible presence throughout all three versions precisely because he is weighed down by the ideological markers he bears – he stands for the upper class, for war-damaged England, for the will, for intellect without body, for technology and mechanical modernity, for classicism and detachment in literature, and for Platonic and Cartesian rationalism in philosophy. But it was the working-class and communist Parkin who had to go, Lawrence evidently regretting the flirtation with class politics into which his conversion of the earlier fable forms, as well as his visit to England during the strike, had led him. Mellors is situated on the margin of the English class system. The principal opposition is now between the false sexuality of Constance's relationship with the writer Michaelis, with whom she cannot achieve mutual orgasm, and the genuine sexuality of her relationship with Mellors, in which mutual orgasm and 'shameless' submission represent the absolutes of sexual possibility. The articulation of this theme requires the use of the explicit language which Lawrence rationalises in 'A Propos'. Despite the change of political emphasis incurred by the shift away from communism and towards an explicit language of sex, and despite the ideological reservations which it is scarcely necessary to emphasise further, the realisation of sex which the final version of the novel seeks to present can still be understood, when read through the first version, as the utopian moment which anticipates the potential for a more comprehensive negation of the distortion of sexuality under capitalism.

Notes

1. Wyndham Lewis, *The Art of Being Ruled*, p. 171.
2. Edward Carpenter, *The Intermediate Sex*, p. 19.
3. Quoted in Michael S. Howard, *Jonathan Cape, Publisher*, p. 104.
4. Douglas Goldring, *The Nineteen Twenties*, p. 225.
5. Lewis, *The Art of Being Ruled*, p. 181.
6. Wyndham Lewis, *Time and Western Man*, p. 30.
7. Wyndham Lewis (ed.), *The Enemy, II*, pp. 111–12.
8. Lewis's freewheeling use of 'inferiority complex' in the dialogue of his characters makes no reference to Freud, who himself pointed out that while the term appeared frequently in *belles lettres* with a show of explanatory force, it was scarcely used in psychoanalysis and had no simply graspable referent.
9. Lewis, *Time and Western Man*, pp. 56, 62.
10. See David Ayers, *Wyndham Lewis and Western Man* for one account of the structure in which Lewis's values are negotiated.
11. See Douglas Goldring, *Odd Man Out*, p. 147.
12. Goldring was present at the launch of *Blast*: see Goldring, *Odd Man Out*, p. 120.
13. In his recent account of this novel, John Lucas makes much of the background of labour radicalism and pacifism which the portrayal of Drummond and her activities evokes. See *The Radical Twenties*, pp. 53–4. This study was too recent for me to take it into account more fully in this book.
14. Goldring, *Odd Man Out*, p. 254.
15. 'Author's Note' to *The Façade*, p. 5.
16. Compare Lydia Blanchard, 'Lawrence, Foucault and the Language of Sexuality', in Michael Squires and Denis Jackson (eds), *D. H. Lawrence's 'Lady'*, pp. 17–35.
17. Lawrence, *Lady Chatterley's Lover*, p. 308. Quoted by Foucault, *Sexuality, I*, p. 157.
18. Leo Lowenthal, 'Knut Hamsun', in Andrew Arato and Eike Gebhardt (eds), *The Essential Frankfurt School Reader*, pp. 319–45.
19. On music, see Theodor Adorno, *Philosophy of Modern Music*. On the attempt to distinguish between general and authorial ideology, which I am here suggesting needs to be overcome, see Terry Eagleton, *Criticism and Ideology*, pp. 54–60.

20. See Ed Jewinski, 'The Phallus in D. H. Lawrence and Jacques Lacan', in *The D. H. Lawrence Review*, 21:1 (Spring 1989), 7–24.
21. Jacques Lacan, 'The Meaning of the Phallus', in Juliet Mitchell and Jacqueline Rose (eds), *Feminine Sexuality*, pp. 74–85.
22. Lawrence, 'The Sun' in *The Woman Who Rode Away and Other Stories*, p. 29.
23. Lacan, 'The Meaning of the Phallus', p. 80.
24. Mikhail Bakhtin, *The Dialogic Imagination*, p. 263.
25. For a detailed account of the possible connections see Frederick P. W. Powell, '"Moments of Emergence and of a New Splendour": D. H. Lawrence and E. M. Forster in Their Fiction', in Squires and Jackson (eds), *D. H. Lawrence's 'Lady'*.
26. See, for example, Lawrence's 1925 essay, 'Aristocracy', in *Phoenix II*, pp. 475–84.

5

England and its Other

Seduction and Friendship, Bodies and Ghosts

T HE FIRST WORLD WAR signalled the beginning of the end for the British Empire. In his memoir and survey of the period, Douglas Goldring distinguishes three areas of extreme reaction in British foreign policy: the opposition to Bolshevism, and the oppression of India and Ireland.

> Direction of foreign policy, subject to Mr. Lloyd George's improvisations and 'intuition', was entirely in the hands of the financial oligarchy which has retained control over it ever since. The suppression of the demo-cratic forces berated by the war, both at home an abroad, was – and remains [in 1945] – their paramount aim.   (Goldring, 1945: 6)

Winston Churchill railed against 'the foul baboonery of bolshevism' and with the help of the press created a climate in which 'in the middle and upper classes, the word "Bolshevik" became the worst term of abuse which could in decency be applied to any human being'. Counter-revolution in Russia became a priority of Britain and the USA, and 'over a hundred million pounds of British money was wasted in supporting the ex-Czarist generals Denikin, Wrangel, Yudenitch and Admiral Koltchak', the leaders of the 'White' armies who fought against the Revolution and Trotsky's Red Army (7). Not only huge sums of money, but also 'British troops, enlisted to fight for "Democracy", were sent to Archangel and the Caucasus, and secret agents were let loose to blow up bridges and otherwise hinder the establishment of the new régime' (7). If Marx had called Com-munism a 'spectre' haunting Europe, the Russian Revolution of 1917 had given the spectre bodily form, and the fight against Bolshevism

189

abroad was undertaken as an insurance against the threat of socialism at home. The Government arrived at the point of threatening
the Soviets with war in 1920, a threat headed off by the intervention
of the Labour Party and trade union leaders in a meeting in the
Commons in August of that year, where they threatened to organise
for a general strike if the Government attempted to prosecute the
war.

'The folly and ineptitude of the Government's treatment of Russia
was surpassed by their brainless brutality in India and Ireland.' (8).
The failure of British policy in India was exemplified most clearly in
the actions of General Dyer in the Amritsar massacre (which forms
an important part of the context for E. M. Forster's *A Passage To
India*) which is invoked by Goldring as further evidence for the
illiberalism of the British regime:

> General Dyer, the soldier responsible for firing on a crowd which had
> illegally gathered in the Jallianwala garden at Amritsar – also for leaving
> the killed and wounded without succour, and compelling Indians to
> crawl on their hands and knees past a spot where some roughs had
> beaten up a woman missionary – was a type of military fanatic which we
> are now inclined to regard as exclusively the product of Nazi Germany,
> Fascist Italy and Franco Spain.   (8)

While the 'British Public' showed some indignation at the Massacre,
and the Cabinet moved to court-martial Dyer, Goldring also notes the
support for Dyer of the House of Lords and the campaign of support
for Dyer in the *Morning Post* whose readers 'subscribed to present
him with a tip of £26,000, to console him for the abrupt end of his
military career'.

Equally scathing comment is reserved for 'the typically "Nazi"
methods which characterized the rule of the British Conservative
class in India in 1919' which 'were applied – with no backing from
the British people – in the attempt to hold down Southern Ireland'.
Goldring is here referring to the activities of the Black and Tans, a
paramilitary force which committed a series of atrocities which are
now well known and well documented. Goldring compares the man
who organised them, Sir John Anderson, to Mussolini, and concludes
that without a political solution, which he considers was forced on
the British by the United States, nothing would have ended the
slaughter:

> Had opinion in the United States permitted the continuance of the Irish
> guerilla war, there is little doubt that the Black-and-Tans would have

crushed the Sinn Feiners, made a wilderness of Southern Ireland, and called it peace. The full story of the Black-and-Tan activities was told, soon after the struggle ended, by General F. P. Crozier, Henry W. Nevinson and other eye-witnesses. Their books – painful reading to those who believed that even the horrors of war could not turn an English 'gentleman' into savages [sic] – reveal how the 'methods of barbarism', later associated with Mussolini, Hitler and Franco, originated.   (9)

The General Election of December 1918 had seen the election of seventy-three Members of Sinn Féin to the House of Commons. None of them took their seats, but instead they formed an independent parliament, the Dáil Éireann, based in Dublin, which published a declaration of independence in January 1919. This was ignored, and the newly-formed Irish Republican Army began a series of guerilla actions against the police. The response of the British Government was to create squads of ex-servicemen, to become known as the Black and Tans, which attempted to suppress the Republicans with a series of atrocities, among which is the famous Bloody Sunday – 21 November 1920 – when the Black and Tans opened fire on a crowd at a sports event which had been surrounded with the intention of searching for weapons. Fourteen people were killed and sixty injured. The attack was in itself the response to the assassination of a number of policemen and Secret Service officers by the IRA the night before and was only one of a number of instances when the Black and Tans behaved as if they had a license to kill at will, which for nearly all practical purposes they did. Graves and Hodge, who as former combatants had some insight into the thinking of the disillusioned British soldier, furnish one possible explanation for the extremism of these former soldiers: '[They] showed remarkable savagery – for to them the Irish were traitors who had stabbed England in the back in the Easter Week rebellion of 1916, and deserved no mercy' (Graves and Hodge, 1985: 28). Be this as it may, support in Britain for the war came chiefly from Conservative politicians, but as information about the activities of the Black and Tans became public, the press and some politicians criticised the undeclared war, and the USA demonstrated full support of Irish independence. An undeclared war which was so clearly unjustified – the First World War had been fought, in propaganda terms at least, around the right to independence of small nations such as 'brave little Belgium' – and which was fought using atrocities of a type which had previously been credited only to the 'Bosch', would never win popular support, and was in any case ultimately unwinnable. In

December 1920 the Government of Ireland Act gave Ireland two separate parliaments, separating the six counties of Unionist Ulster from the rest and creating the potential for further conflict; in July 1921 a truce was called between the British Army and the Irish Republican Army, and in December 1921 the Irish Free State was created.

These facts are part of a history which, even as it happened, England was trying to forget. The impact of the Irish War on the English literature of the period is negligible, but the war and the history which determined it is clearly central to the work of Joyce and Yeats, and the 'troubles' form the backdrop to *Last September* (1929) by the Anglo-Irish author, Elizabeth Bowen. Unlike the conflict in India, it attracted no Forster, and its resolution, according to Collier and Lang, made it seem quickly remote. They note that already, in 1922, 'to England the Irish troubles were coming to assume something of the remoteness of a Balkan imbroglio' (Collier and Lang, 1932: 100). Moreover, intellectuals, while repudiating the war, had been unable to take sides with Irish independence:

> The Irish struggle placed English intellectuals in a dilemma. The lingering tradition of nineteenth-century Liberalism was on the side of the Irish [...]. But if libertarian sentiment was made uneasy, the disturbance never became a genuinely emotional response; there was nothing comparable to the enthusiasm of nineteenth-century poets for Greece, Hungary and Italy – not so much as one song before sunrise. [...]. Even Liberals were beginning to doubt the sufficiency of nationalist idealism. Little nations might be – in the phrase of Mr. Lloyd George's sonorous nineteenth-century echo – divinely chosen vessels for particularly potent wines, but 1921 was the morning after a heavy night of that particular intoxication.   (Collier and Lang, 1932: 102)

This is a generous gloss on what has turned out to be a more sustained English indifference to Irish affairs.

No analysis of the relation of the Western subject with the racial other would be complete without a discussion of anti-Semitism. The 'Jew' has been burdened with representing the ultimate contamination of Western male identity with his geographical transgressiveness and putatively feminine characteristics and feminising agenda. However, since I have treated this subject at length elsewhere in relation to the anti-Semitism of Wyndham Lewis, I will not reiterate those arguments here.[1] Instead, this chapter begins with a treatment of one only possibly more benign aspect of 1920s Orientalism, the popular desert romance, which transformed the culturally other into the nexus of sexual fantasy, and which shares the feature of seduction with the two works which are next examined. The analysis of D. H. Lawrence's *The Plumed Serpent* details the complexity of Lawrence's response to the crisis of the West and the search for an alternative beyond the frame of colonialism; and is viewed here in terms of its infrequently acknowledged utopian potential. The final section concludes this book with the claim that E. M. Forster's *A Passage to India* must be understood in terms of its attempt to negotiate the limits of English culture and politics on a fictional map which, contrary to the usual claims, posits a ground in which identity and difference are no longer the determining terms of mutual cultural invisibility.

Seduced by Difference: The Sheik *and* Desert Love

Tarzan of the Apes, the hero of a series of novels by the American Edgar Rice Burroughs, was, Graves and Hodge claim, 'the most popular fictional character among the low-brow public of the Twenties; though the passionate Sheik of Araby, as portrayed by E. M. Hull and her many imitators, ran him pretty close' (Graves and Hodge, 1985: 51). Tarzan was, of course, English, even if his author was not, and owed much to Kipling's *Jungle Tales.* An analysis of Tarzan and his popularity would tell us something about received notions of Englishness in this period, although the American mediation makes the topic a complex one. The domestic products of Hull and her imitators in the 'Desert Romance' genre are more directly relevant.

The Desert Romance[2] was a sub-genre of romantic fantasy which achieved widespread popularity in the 1920s, first as fiction and subsequently in the cinema. The most celebrated are *The Sheik* (1919) by E. M. Hull and *Desert Love* (1920) by Joan Conquest, the authors' names being pseudonyms for female writers who aimed their works at the growing market of bestsellers for women. Hull and Conquest produced a string of novels in the same generic vein, the titles of which leave the casual browser in no doubt as to their content. Conquest's novels include *The Hawk of Egypt* (1922), *Zarah the Cruel* (1923), *Forbidden* (1927), *An Eastern Lover* (1928) and *Harem Love* (1930), while Hull takes credit for *The Shadow of the East* (1921), *The Desert Healer* (1923) and *The Sons of the Sheik* (1925). Desert fans could also turn to a string of works by Kathlyn Rhodes which included *The Relentless Desert* (1920), *Under Desert Stars* (1921), *Desert Lovers*

(1922) and *Desert Justice* (1923). The works of Hull and Conquest represent a form of pornography which was freely and frankly aimed at women. While their language is inexplicit, they describe extreme and implausible situations involving the rape or seduction of a European woman who has been transported into the desert by an Arab 'Sheik'. Hull's *The Sheik*, while not representing the founding moment of the genre, can nevertheless be seen as its archetype. Conquest's *Desert Love* already contains the seeds of decadence: the novel can (and indeed must) be read 'straight', but it also contains elements of pastiche which can be read humorously by those with a knowledge of the genre. The pastiche element may well be an acknowledgement that the readership was becoming more critical, but rather than attribute any form of postmodern knowingness to Conquest's texts,[3] it is better to see this apparent form of distantiation as a feature of genre fiction, which is inevitably pastiche as a consequence of being generic, and which is as unable to renew itself as it is unable to resist letting the consumer in on the joke that they have been sold the same thing again. Unable to renew itself, the fiction dresses its repetitiousness as a joke which solicits the complicity of the consumer in purchasing once again the same thing that they have already previously purchased. The breathtaking unreflectingness of Hull's novel and the apparent self-awareness of Conquest's do not represent opposing forces, although the celebration of irony and appropriation in the most lacklustre versions of contemporary cultural studies might lead us to see them this way. Rather, Conquest's texts deploy a rhetoric of self-awareness, of alerting the reader to the fictionality of the text and to the absurdity of the genre conventions, only in order to press the titillating fantasies further, as if to repress further the question of what might be the relationship between this fantasy and any actually possible life.

With or without the rhetoric of fictional self-awareness, the novels of Hull and Conquest cultivate fantasies which are similar, although they diverge interestingly. They have a common narrative structure which features a sexually unawakened female protagonist who is abducted by (*The Sheik*) or chooses to travel alone with (*Desert Love*) a powerful Arab who is characterised by the power which he holds over others and by the single-mindedness of his pursuit of her love. The symbolic journey begins in the safety of a larger town with a colonial presence (Biskra in Algeria, Ismailia in Egypt), but once in the desert the civilising force of colonial power is absent, and the elementary masculinity of the Sheik figure represents the only power; the Arab becomes the protagonist's protector and at the same time the only real threat to her. The journey concludes at an oasis where the protagonist, initially deprived of human contact other than with the Arab and his servants, learns to love her captor/guardian after repeated seductions or rapes, which are only represented euphemistically. The protagonist is now thoroughly sexually awoken, according to the logic of the genre, in the context of a relationship in which the polarisation of sexual roles is understood to be far more complete than in the relative sexual confusion of European society. When given a chance to return to European civilisation she refuses, preferring her life as the lover of her Arab Sheik.

In Lawrence's equation, non-Western cultures offered an alternative of authentic existence to Europeans whose culture had become jaded and degenerate under the influence of industrialisation and civilisation. In particular, he regrets the loss of heavily polarised gender relations in modern society. In *The Plumed Serpent* the opposition between the European and the primitive non-Western is shown to be an ambivalent one for Lawrence's protagonist who, as a woman, must choose whether to submit to the will of a man who derives his power from pre-Christian sources. For all his aversion to the masses and to popular culture, it cannot have escaped Lawrence that the very framework in which he wrestled with questions of gender identity was essentially similar to that found in the popular desert romance.

The romances represent English upper-/middle-class society as sexually repressive, disapproving spontaneity and appetite and any hint of the improper. *The Sheik* frames its protagonist on the opening page in the commentary of one Lady Conway, whose role is merely to define the unusualness of the heroine and the transgressiveness which is to follow:

> I consider that even by contemplating such a tour alone into the desert with no chaperon or attendant of her own sex, with only native camel drivers and servants, Diana Mayo is behaving with a recklessness and impropriety that is calculated to cast a slur not only on her own reputation, but also on the prestige of her country. I blush to think of it.
> (Hull, 1921: 5)

The speaker is only interested in issues of propriety and national prestige, and does not consider the possibility of genuine sexual endangerment which might be the occasion of more than a mere socially correct blush. That the native can be other than a servant or driver and subsequently emerge as a sexual force is more than this particular upper-class speaker can contemplate. However, the reader is not immediately invited to identify with the protagonist against her society. Diana Mayo is portrayed as a denatured young woman. She is the product of an upper-class upbringing at the hands of an uncle who has raised her as a boy, to hunt, shoot and fish, an education said to have made her incapable of love. The men consider her the 'coldest little fish in the world, without an idea in her head beyond sport and travel'(6). That she is 'clever' and 'plucky' identifies her with the tomboy heroines of schoolgirl adventure fiction, a figure inevitably irritating to the more adult reader of romance who might happily expect this character to be riding for a fall. Praised for her dancing by a man who clearly appreciates its erotic effect, Diana explains that it is easy 'if you have been in the habit of making your body do as you want' (Hull, 1919: 10), a physical self-possession which will later be overthrown when her knees buckle before the erotic onslaught of the Sheik. Diana claims she has never loved, has never been kissed, and has never obeyed anybody in her life. It is above all her capacity for obedience and her potential for surrender to the will of a man which are in question. According to the values of the novel, these traits are essential to a femininity which Diana lacks.

Diana Mayo's coldness is not calculated to make her either sympathetic or antipathetic to the reader, but to create a distance of interested observation akin to the voyeuristic. Yet although the novel appears to be dealing with the sexual repression of upper-class society as manifested in the asexuality of the gender misidentified adventure heroine, the massive popularity of this novel and its many avatars indicate a specific connection with the 1920s. Of course, narratives of sexual awakening with a titillating content are always likely to find an audience, yet these novels seem to address a feeling that the decline of patriarchal power has led to a depolarisation of the sexes which tends to culminate in asexual androgyny or in the role reversal of so-called 'inverts' and lesbians. It might be more accurate to say that these fictions do not so much address this feeling as attempt to create it, attaching an anti-feminist ideological agenda to the more straightforward business of selling sex. After all, the widely advertised new sexual morality of 'Bloomsbury' seemed more likely to promise sexual gratification than submission to tyrannous monogamy, even though it is submission as a lover rather than as a wife which *The Sheik* celebrates.

Before she is abducted by the Sheik the heroine considers that the Oriental pattern of marriage, in which she believes women are so subordinate as to barely count as people, would be completely unacceptable to her. After her capture, she learns the erotic meaning of this subordination, which she ultimately cannot resist, an event which the novel interprets as the emergence of a natural femininity which has been suppressed by an unnatural upbringing. The Sheik himself is similarly construed as the natural expression of masculinity, a masculinity which emerges not from civilised European culture, but which can only exist as an Oriental 'other', mixing sexual threat and colonialist myth. The language used to describe him when he initially appears owes little to the canons of European realism:

> It was the handsomest and cruellest face that she had ever seen. Her gaze was drawn instinctively to his. He was looking at her with fierce burning eyes that swept her until she felt that the boyish clothes that covered her slender limbs were stripped from her, leaving the beautiful white body bare under his passionate stare. (52)

The Sheik's power to subordinate a woman with his gaze and expose her true femininity, making her feel naked, is allied to his power over his followers and over nature. His power over nature, and his own sheer brutality, is manifested in an episode in which he breaks an unruly colt, through 'savagery and determination' (90),[4] a manifestation of the will which is also used to break Diana Mayo through repeated rape in captivity. Emotionally she capitulates: 'He was a brute, but she loved him [...] for his very brutality and superb animal strength' (116); 'the feminine weakness that she had despised and fought against had triumphed over her unexpectedly with humiliating thoroughness' (164). This Sheik is revealed to be ultimately of European origin, and has chosen to take his place in pre-civilised culture, but it is the 'real man' with the 'thin layer of civilisation stripped from him' (197) which the novel presents as its thrilling spectacle.

Conquest's *Desert Love* mocks its own conventions along lines that the more sophisticated reader will easily spot. Thus, in the opening pages, the passivity of the heroine, Jill, is described in terms that flaunt their implausibility (and even jeopardise the logic of the novel itself, as such a heroine would be unlikely to resist her sheik even for a chapter):

> Jill's ideas on franchise and suffrage, and a 'good time' as seen from the standpoint of the average society girl or woman were absolutely nil.

> She wanted first of all a master, then a home, and then children, many
> of them.
> Her idea of love was utter submission to the man she should love.
>
> (Conquest, 1920: 15)

As this submission is something that the heroine must learn it is
inconsistent to describe it as a trait which she already possesses, but
the very object of this passage is to make explicit the absurd assumption which underlies Hull's novel – that such submissiveness can be
learnt. As a fictional rhetoric this passage also points to the paradox
that while the narrative must possess a causal logic it need not
possess plausibility. The chapter describing Jill's character and background from which this passage is taken concludes with an apology
to the reader for having in effect wasted her time with a futile exercise
in providing a bedrock of realism which is in practice unwanted and
has served only to defer the sexual action. The pretence of narrative
causality is stretched to the limit when the heroine makes the
decision to ask Hahmed, her sheik (actually a trader), to take her to
the nearest oasis on the basis of tossing a coin. In case we doubt the
hyper-masculinity of Hahmed his love speech before the journey
begins makes matters clear:

> Allah! To think that I, the worst feared man in Egypt, whose word is law,
> who condemns to death by the lifting of a finger, of a race who looks on
> women as a useful plaything, at the most as a potential mother of sons, *I*
> crave to serve you.   (67)

Although Hahmed's form of service involves building her a big
house, it does also involve a significant element of enforced isolation
and a warning about what happened to his previous wife, who was
discovered on the day of their wedding in a passionate lesbian
embrace with her servant. The marriage was not consummated, but
the wife was stripped naked, given a hundred lashes and then stoned
to death by the other wedding guests (108). Conquest mocks the
masochistic aspect of the fiction through hyperbole, at least for those
readers who are not simply more deeply thrilled, yet the narrative
game continues in spite of occasional metafictional lapses: 'Everything, as you will note if you have the patience to get through to the
end of this book, happened to Jill in the light of the full moon'
(149). Indeed.

Beyond the Reach of Empire: D. H. Lawrence's
The Plumed Serpent

Post-colonial theory presents us with a number of ways of thinking about the relationship of Western literature to the sites of colonial conquest – to the colonial 'subject' or the colonial 'other'. Edward Said, in *Orientalism*, famously identifies Orientalist discourse as a monolithic structure which manifests itself across official, creative and popular writing – for example, in Oriental scholarship, travel writing and fiction. The concepts of Said's account of Orientalism have come to suffuse post-colonial theory in general, although subsequent commentators have suggested that his account is absurdly monolithic and undialectical. It makes a mystery of the colonised 'other' which is always located beyond knowledge, and makes no allowance for the way in which the Orientalist account must necessarily be contradictory or dissonant, a fact which may become apparent even to the Western subject and which is absolutely apparent to the colonised subject, whose own account of colonial reality conflicts immediately with the Orientalist or imperialist version. Homi Bhabha's work uses Freud to suggest that the colonial subject is a conflicted site for the Western onlooker, not merely the static object of a discourse but the site of fantasy and desire in which the Westerner uncannily recognises himself and is returned to the dissonances of his own account of the world.[5]

D. H. Lawrence's Mexican novel *The Plumed Serpent* (1926), which deals with the culture of pre-conquest Mexico and elaborates a fantasy of the revival of Aztec religion, has aroused negative commentary and defensive or ambivalent responses on the part of many commentators precisely because it deals with a post-colonial topic – a colonial subject people treated in terms of Lawrence's own attempt to overcome the limitations, as he perceived them, of English or Western society. There is, as always in Lawrence, much that invites a querulous response from the reader. However, recent developments in post-colonial criticism give the clue not so much to how Lawrence might be placed as part of the machinery of colonial subjection, but to how he himself recognised that the process of colonisation – the Spanish completed their conquest of the Aztecs in 1521 – was itself an extended process of obliterating social alternatives which carried Western forms and values to almost every corner of the world. What his work attempts to deal with cannot be understood in terms of the subjection of the colonised by the coloniser, for the England which he rejected was even more throughly colonised by its own values than any colonised country. Rather, Lawrence asks where an alternative to the West can be found, whether the alternative can be re-established in colonised nations where the traces of pre-colonial societies have survived slightly more intact than have the forms of pre-capitalist societies in the West, and whether or how the Western subject can escape the frameworks which shape her or his existence and enter into any kind of dialogue with the alternative. As we might expect, Lawrence finds this question to be almost intractable, for although I have used the term dialogue to characterise this exchange, the notion of the subject and of inter-subjective communication which this implies is already highly problematic for Lawrence, who considers the dialectic and the notion of the subject as far back as the dialogues and dialectic of Plato (greatly admired by Clifford Chatterley) to be the very feature of Western society which has closed it off from the non-discursive realities of the body and of physical community. Dialogue and dialectic, while central to Lawrence's very method, as critics who have used Bakhtin to analyse his work have noted, are also part of the horizon which he wishes to transgress.[6] The kind of exchange which Lawrence is therefore postulating is not merely an exchange of ideas, but involves a fundamental change of attitude in the Western subject which he characterises as 'submission'. The idea of submission, of one man to another whom he accepts as leader, or of a woman to a man she accepts as her husband, does of course invite anti-Fascist and feminist critique. However, such critique is premature if it does not recognise that the role which submission plays in Lawrence's work is not merely that of reasserting established male prerogatives, but a question about how a new and utopian social form is to emerge. Dialogue in Lawrence belongs to the superficial Western world of 'spirit' rather than to the inner reality of 'soul' or 'blood'; submission then is the mode of spirit's acquiescence to blood, the mode by which the false individual of the West can rejoin the collective, whether as the mass of people or as the couple:

> Now, must she admit that the individual was an illusion and a falsification?
> – There was no such animal. Except in the mechanical world. In the world of machines, the individual machine is effectual. The individual, like the perfect being, does not and cannot exist, in the vivid world. We are all fragments. Or at best, halves. The only whole thing is the Morning Star. Which can only lie between two: or between many. (Lawrence, 1995e: 390)

'There has to be a return to an older vision of life', Lawrence wrote in a letter in 1924. 'It needs some welling up of religious sources that have been shut down in us: a great *yielding* rather than an act of will.'[7] Marriage in Lawrence fills a utopian role: the possibility of the connection of a man and a woman in marriage anticipates and predicts in a utopian fashion the reconnection of an individual with a people and thereby with nature. So Lawrence's work recognises the alienation of Western industrial society and wonders aloud how it might be overcome. We need to recognise the affirmative and utopian moment even where it is framed in a manner which seems dogmatically patriarchal and authoritarian – or simply fanciful.

The problem for Lawrence is therefore a kind of cross-cultural and inter-gender exchange which cannot be purely subjective since it is the nature of the 'subject' in general with which the exchange is concerned. Moreover, the state of the human being after subjectivity can only dimly anticipate itself by looking back to pre-modern, pre-subjective, social forms for its model. Although Lawrence is sometimes assumed to be merely asserting the validity of the pre-modern society of pre-Conquest Mexico in this novel, it is more accurate to see the novel as an exploration of what it might mean to revive these social forms, inasmuch as they can be understood, and the novel especially tries to imagine what it might mean for a subjectively convinced religious leader to bring these ideas to the unconvinced who do not share his intuitions. The closure of the modern and the hazy ungraspability of a genuinely post-modern social existence are what concern Lawrence here.

The problem of what it means to have an exchange of this nature is closely tied to a question about the identity of the agents or actors involved in the exchange. In the first, and until recently unpublished, version of this novel, *Quetzalcoatl* (completed 1923; published 1995), the question of the exchange had not been the focus of the narrative. The figure of Kate Leslie had been present merely as a convenient repository for the explanations of Ramón Carrasco about the nature of his new religion. Kate does not marry Ramón's ally General Cipriano Viedma, nor does she assume the role of the goddess Malintzi in the revived Aztec pantheon. The final version of the novel has her take a more complete role, and, crucially, the question of the nature and status of the new religion is now one for her and hence for the reader.[8] However, it would be a mistake to assume that Lawrence's development of Kate Leslie is simply an attempt to create a more developed window on the world of

Quetzalcoatl, or to redress the gender balance. In the terms which I have already suggested, Lawrence significantly complicates his original project – the portrayal of the imagined realisation of a return of the old gods – by emphasising the prospects for actual social mediation of the new religion. In raising the question of communication, he is able to go further in registering his own ambivalence towards the project. In simple terms, he had already rejected all existing forms of mass politics and religion, and it is fairly clear that as soon as he begins to contemplate an alternative based on his own intuitions about what the nature of a true mental/ physical health might be, the dangers of the other forms which he has rejected quickly surface in his ideal form: the religion of Quetzalcoatl soon moves from bloodless iconoclasm, in the episode in which a church is stripped of its Christian symbols with the collaboration of the priest, to the ritualised execution of traitors. The use of Kate Leslie allows Lawrence to explore his own distance from the project of Ramón, for while Ramón in his theorising can be thought of as a Lawrence surrogate, it is certain that Kate, as a curious but unassimilated traveller, is allocated many of her author's own habitual thoughts. The development of Kate's role further allows Lawrence to link his two major concerns – the future of mass society and the future of marriage.

Mexico itself functions as the site of a condensed world history. There is the remnant of an indigenous people which has lost its pre-Christian culture, often interbred with the descendants of the Christian colonisers, themselves reduced to apathy in a post-Christian order which, on Lawrence's reckoning, offers no real avenue of social renewal. The Mexican Revolution of 1910 which lasted for twenty years bequeathed a situation of political instability which gave Lawrence the background to his novel. The Revolution represented an amalgam of left- and right-wing interests: Lawrence maps Mexico as a country ravaged by socialist revolution and threatened by what he considers to be American values from across the border: in other words, just as he had found in Europe, the values of industry, whether in communist or capitalist form, here serve to deny human possibility. It is against this background that Ramón asserts his credo, connecting the situation of Mexico to that of Kate's Ireland, also recently partly liberated by a revolution which has cost Kate's second husband his life:

> 'Mexico is another Ireland. – Ah no, no man can be his own master. If I
> must serve, I will not serve an idea, which cracks and leaks like an old

wine-skin. I will serve the God that gives me my manhood. There is no liberty for a man apart from the God of his manhood. Free Mexico is a bully, and the old, colonial-ecclesiastical Mexico was another sort of bully. When man has nothing but his *will* to assert – even his good-will – it is always bullying. Bolshevism is one sort of bullying, capitalism another: and Liberty is a change of chains.' (Lawrence, 1995e: 73)

Behind the politics of Mexico is the American land itself, the constant possibility, represented most often in Kate's thought, that the inhuman land itself returns people to a fundamental instinct which is merely a kind of death-drive, a complete negation of human possibility, rather than the Edenic site of a new start and a rebirth which the colonisers' concept of the New World had always sought to present:

> And sometimes she wondered whether America really was the great death-continent, the great *No!* To the European and Asiatic and even African *Yes!* Was it really the great melting pot, where men from the creative continents were smelted back again, not to a new creation, but down into the homogeneity of death? Was it the great continent of the undoing, and all its peoples the agents of the mystic destruction? Plucking, plucking at the created soul in a man, till at last it plucked out the growing germ, and left him a creature of mechanism and automatic reaction, with only one inspiration, the desire to pluck the quick out of every living, spontaneous creature. [...] And would the great negative pull of the Americas at last break the heart of the world? [...]
>
> These handsome natives! Was it because they were death-worshippers, Moloch-worshippers, that they were so uncowed and handsome? Their pure acknowledgement of death, and their undaunted admission of nothingness kept them so erect and restless. [...]
>
> The strange, soft flame of courage in the black Mexican eyes. But still it was not knit to a centre, that centre which is the soul of a man.
>
> And all the efforts of white men to bring the soul of the dark men of Mexico into final clinched being had resulted in nothing but the collapse of the white men. (77–8)

The words heart and darkness recur frequently in this text and, at a late stage, are in the narrative brought together – affirmatively – in the phrase 'heart of darkness' (382), as if to acknowledge the presence of Joseph Conrad's meditation on the vocabulary of colonialism in *Heart of Darkness*, a fable which locates the nature of a colonialist fantasy that equates white skin with light and religious/ intellectual truth, black skin with darkness and the destructive instincts, and asks whether the benightedness of the colonised so frequently evoked as a justification for the colonial enterprise is not more truly found at the centre of the civilising impulse. Lawrence's depiction of the Mexicans as reduced to purposeless torpor closely resembles Conrad's depiction of native Africans deprived by slavery of all meaningful life-functions. Yet while Conrad is content to play with the paradoxes of the light/dark metaphor, Lawrence is concerned to analyse the notion of colonial darkness and to ask whether there is indeed some vital aspect of human existence, which can rightly be understood as dark precisely because it does not belong to the world of light, to the world of revealed, visible truth, to the Western subject and its discourse, and which should not therefore be understood as mere projection, a mere imposition of the colonial value system on the colonised world which is made possible simply by the accident of skin colour.

There are many discursive passages in the novel which resemble the one quoted above, and they do not quite add up to a consistently developed essay on the topic which I have outlined. In this passage, as in others, is found a combination of 'sentimental primitivism' (Bell, 1991) and curiously resonant commentary. Why should Mexicans be understood as generically courageous merely because their eyes are dark and they appear somehow assured in their bearing? This is surely the projection of a traveller who himself lacks assurance in a strange country and finds in some way enigmatic the intentions, indeed the actual look, of people he encounters and who probably consider his presence enigmatic or intrusive. Lawrence's writing often reflects a discomfort with travelling and a hostility to the people that he encounters which, although it arises simply from the fact of travel, is often accompanied by spurious commentary on cultural difference. All of this can be found in the extract above. Yet there remains a resonant question which is carefully shaped. Lawrence proposes, through the thoughts of his character, that Western civilisation – what he calls at one point 'spirit' (116) – may be based on a denial of death, and hence on a denial of physical nature. At the same time, although Kate/Lawrence finds an acceptance of death in the attitude of the Mexican man, s/he also refuses to attribute to him any kind of idealised completeness of being. In other words, the Mexican, so construed, is not simply the site of a human possibility which Europe has eclipsed, an intact and available alternative. Moreover, Kate/Lawrence goes on to suggest that the very incompleteness of the Mexican – representing the colonised in all of her or his identities – has provided the motive to the European to impose his own standard of 'clinched being' – the finalised form of industrial/Christian identity which Lawrence rejects. Thus, in a complex gesture, Lawrence defends the cultural difference of the colonised other not in terms of what it is, but in terms of the human possibility which it represents, and which his 'own' culture, which he has dis-owned, seeks to obliterate.

It would be a falsification of the novel to pretend that less ambivalent passages than the above do not reflect a more uncritical absorption of the white supremacist map of the world, for example, when the narrator, again elucidating Kate's thoughts, comments on the wavering of white supremacy in the modern world:

> While the white man keeps the impetus of his own proud onward march, the dark races will yield and serve, perforce. But let the white man once have a misgiving about his own leadership, and the dark races will at once attack him, to pull him down into the old gulfs. To engulph him again.
>
> Which is what is happening. For the white man, let him bluster as he may, is hollow with misgiving about his own supremacy.
>
> Full speed ahead, then, for the débâcle. (148)

If this passage represents Lawrence's own understanding, then it reflects little of the complexity of viewpoint which I am attributing to the structure of the novel. The thoughts are, in their context, attributed to Kate, although the narrative 'voice' seems less like a disciplined example of third-person centre of consciousness narration than an intrusive authorial attempt to express yet more essayistically conceived insights – here the tag 'leadership' alerts us to a character-istically Lawrentian theme. Yet almost every thought attributed to whatever character in this novel seems to belong to the Lawrentian thematic, and my claim is that, despite the limitations of the con-ceptual framework which I have begun to explore, it is the dramatic and intersubjective structure of the novel that remains of interest.

What can be understood as the limitations of Lawrence's under-standing are dramatised in the novel to become the limitations of understanding itself. To grasp Lawrence's novels in Bakhtinian terms as dialogic because they are polyphonic and eschew closure falls some way short of accounting for the specific nature of the dramatic situations which Lawrence develops and the utopian impulse which drives his interest in social and cultural exchange. In other words, while an analysis of Lawrentian polyphony seems to serve admirably in locating Lawrence as a novelist of the stature of Dostoevsky, or a 'master of language',[9] it tends to ignore the specifi-city of the situation of communication in Lawrence in favour of a formal emphasis on 'the continuous struggle between competing interests and ideas'.[10] So while it has become orthodox to claim that the Lawrentian novel remains dialogically 'open' in the same way that the future remains open, the ways in which the social situation of what I have preferred to call exchange are themselves thematised as neglected, and this is of especial importance in *The Plumed Serpent*, which presents us not merely with a mixture of characters and points of view, but with a model designed to foreground the problems of cultural exchange itself as something supra-dialogic and of extreme and immediate urgency for the future.

If the structure of Lawrence's novel is grasped in this way, then the purpose of developing the role of Kate Leslie in the published version begins to become more apparent. Kate's Irishness may owe something to Matthew Arnold's famously romantic typology, but is better understood as a structural device which enables Lawrence to signal his protagonist as both insider and outsider: she is a white European as far as the Mexicans are concerned, but her nation is on the fringes of modern, industrial Europe. Not only is Ireland much less industrialised than England, it has until recently been an English colony and is only now partially liberated from England by the revolutionary war which cost Kate's second husband his life. So, while in one frame of reference Kate has moved from imperial and industrial Europe to the colonies, in another and more important sense she has moved from one revolution to another – Lawrence makes no effort to differentiate between national revolution and socialist revolution because he discounts the value of modern revolution altogether, registering it as a mere change of rulers rather than a change in the nature of rule and therefore of the human order itself. It is in the colonies, less completely harnessed to the logic of industrialism, that the residue of 'soul' – the pre-industrial way of being – survives:

> Sometimes, in America, the shadow of that old pre-Flood world was so strong, that the day of historic humanity would melt out of Kate's consciousness, and she would begin to approximate to the old mode of consciousness, the old, dark will, the unconcern for death, the subtle, dark consciousness, non-cerebral, but vertebrate. [...]
>
> The Mexicans were still this. That which is aboriginal in America still belongs to the way of the world before the Flood, before the mental-spiritual world came into being. In America therefore the mental-spiritual life of white people suddenly flourishes like a great weed let loose in Virgin soil. Probably it will as quickly wither. A great death come.

> And after that, the living result will be a new germ, a new conception of human life, that will arise from the fusion of the old blood-and-vertebrate consciousness with the white man's present mental-spiritual consciousness. The sinking of both beings into a new being.
>
> Kate was more Irish than anything, and the almost deathly mysticism of the aboriginal Celt or Iberian peoples lay at the bottom of her soul. It was a residue of memory, something that lives on from the pre-Flood world, and cannot be killed. Something older, and more everlastingly potent, than our would-be fair-and-square world. (415)

This is how Lawrence describes the cultural meaning of the racial configuration which he has selected. My argument concerns not so much the ideas expressed here, which have been loosely glossed as a version of second-hand German *lebensphilosophie* and an intuitive anticipation of Heidegger,[11] but the mode of intersubjectivity in which these ideas strive for realisation.

Not only is Kate a culturally mixed proposition, but her two principal informers, Ramón and Cipriano, are themselves of mixed cultural allegiance, with a European and Christian education and degrees from Columbia and Oxford respectively (68). The fact that they are culturally informed by modernity, and the fact that their cult is also directed towards the pragmatic end of political dominance as well as that of spiritual renewal, already creates doubt as to the meaning and authenticity of their activities. Indeed, the whole dynamic of the novel is arranged around Kate's doubts as to its validity, doubts which it crucially frames as ontological, not epistemological. That is to say that the judging subject, Kate, knows that to shift her allegiance to the cult means not only changing her ideas but changing her whole mode of being. The problem which such a shift entails is that it involves going against or overcoming the judgement of the mind, which on the one hand cannot make a detached intellectual judgement of the validity of the cult, since it is the grounds of such a judgement which the cult seeks to put into question, but at the same time has no option but to resist the surrender of its subjectivity to external force. These forces are abundantly present, for while the first version of the novel concentrated on explanation, the second concentrates on Kate's experiences of interaction.

I have already said that the idea of intersubjectivity does not begin to grasp the nature of the exchanges in which Kate is involved. Moreover, Lawrence was acutely aware of how the coercion of the mass can impact on the individual from his wartime experiences – the immediate source of his own dissatisfaction with mass politics.

So, from the outset, the reader is instructed in the sadism of the mass – the opening chapter discovers Kate in Mexico at a bull fight. This chapter at one level serves to distinguish Kate as a soul-searcher from the Americans who take her to the fight and believe that they are experiencing 'real life' – that this is an ontologically authentic experience rather than a sadistic spectacle for the masses. Lawrence accomplishes many things in this opening chapter, not least answering in anticipation Hemingway, whose *Fiesta; or, The Sun Also Rises* (1927) it uncannily predicts and pre-empts. It is not only that the chapter deals decisively with modern, and here specifically 'American', readings of non-white culture. It also demonstrates the inherent danger of human interactions which are not intersubject-ive but are based on force and on a language of the body. While Kate and her group interact with each other intersubjectively, that is to say as conversing individuals, the crowd interacts with them by bullying and teasing them, sitting on their feet or throwing things at them, in a way which the non-white crowd considers harmless but which the whites find menacing. That they are right to detect menace is confirmed by the gory nature of the bull fight. The chapter locates sadism and blood lust in the crowd and sets up a question which remains in force throughout the text about the dangers of non-discursive interactions – both as the direct confrontation of bodies and as the indirect confrontation of modes of being, which Lawrence consistently incorporates in descriptions of physical posture, or bearing. If other of Lawrence's tales, such as 'The Woman Who Rode Away' and 'The Princess', use the myth of Sleeping Beauty to explore an ambiguous notion of (female) sexual awakening, *The Plumed Serpent* inverts the model by examining a protagonist who is asked to fall asleep, who is to be bludgeoned *out* of consciousness, to surrender the world of the eye and of know-ledge to the world of darkness and pre-intellectual being. 'Who sleeps – shall wake!' intone the singers in one of Ramón's rituals (175), but Kate's own meditations reveal that this religious awaken-ing involves putting part of herself to sleep: 'Let me close my eyes to him, and open only my soul. Let me close my prying, *seeing* eyes, and sit in dark stillness along with these two men.' (184).

What brings her to contemplate a surrender which she can never make nor renounce – the novel's open-ended conclusion – is a series of encounters which act on something other than her knowing mind, although this mind is always itself well in evidence, and often in its crotchety resistance to other people resembles what we know of the author's own mind. What I have called bearing, the stance of a body understood as relationship to others, is present in the often commented episode in which Kate is rowed across Lake Sayula by a Charon-like boatman, whose body as he rows, even though his posture is marred by a birth defect, signals to Kate the elusive and other mode of being which the novel will continually tempt her with: 'Then she noticed he was a cripple, with inturned feet. But how quick and strong! [...] She felt he was naturally truthful, honest and generous.' (89). Kate's intuitions about native natures will vary, however, as she is drawn into difficult relationships first with her house servant, Juana, and her family, then with Teresa, the wife of Ramón. Superficially, these Mexican women seem to be developed as stereotypes, but in fact the text looks closely at the ways in which Kate's hostility to them is based not on what liberal thought now regards as 'prejudice' – that is, a refusal to accept others as equal if different – but on an understanding that cultural difference is precisely not a matter of equality, that fundamental and possibly irreducible differences are involved, and that the dislikes which develop and are mutual in the situations depicted are necessary forms of cultural confrontation.

> An insignificant little thing, humble, Kate thought to herself.
> But she knew that really Teresa was neither insignificant nor humble. Under that soft brown skin, and in that stooping female spine was a strange old power to call up the blood in a man, and glorify it, and, in some way, keep it for herself. (401)

This is a confrontation between Western feminism, which in Lawrence's optic is *the* levelling effect of mass society, the creation of an ultimate in-difference at the heart of social and psychic life, and a 'traditional' because dependent femininity which can make its only gains in deference and self-effacement. Kate's reading of the situation in the quoted passage signals her own ambivalence about feminism and femininity; her hostility to Teresa is both interested – based on sexual rivalry – and disinterested – based on an a feminist intellectual evaluation of her role. Throughout their confrontation aspects of posture, gesture and tone are of as much importance as the verbal exchanges. They make clothes, ride, and in general bond silently in work, so their tension is a complex one in which each identifies with the other's difference and becomes ambivalent about her own nature, although each is unable to become the other.

In Lawrence's schema, such exchanges – incomplete and irreducible confrontations of individuals and cultures – are necessary to the emergence of the future, and they are about far more than verbal and rational exchange. Lawrence, of course, always specialised in depicting relationships in terms of extradiscursive confrontations of difference, whether of gender difference or of racial difference, as is much evidenced in *The Rainbow.* Here that interest is brought to a canvas which now asks what is the importance of difference in terms not of individual but of global function. Moreover, the unusual story of *The Plumed Serpent* means that a great variety of extradiscursive forms of interaction can be brought into play – not merely lethal violence, both random and targeted, but drumming, ritual and especially the famous poems, the hymns of Quetzalcoatl, as well as a series of interactions with the non-human, animals and landscape, all of which tend to seduce and coerce by acting on the non-rational mind. While Lawrence's ideas remain idealistic to the point of being regressive, the literary form in which they are deployed aims to be true both to world history and to Lawrence's personal experience, is highly attentive to nuance, and achieves a degree of coherence in its shaping of a problematic which has continued to return in post-colonial debate.

The Politics of Friendship in A Passage to India

Although it seems to be removed in every significant respect from the culture of the desert romance, it is striking that E. M. Forster's *A Passage to India* (1924) shares with this more popular and considerably less critical genre a focus on seduction and rape. The rape in question is the molestation of the young English woman, Adela Quested, which she alleges to have taken place at the hands of a young Indian doctor, Aziz, on a journey which he has organised to the Marabar Caves outside Chandrapore, locations modelled on the Barabar Hills and on Bankipore, a suburb of Patna in the north-east of India. The alleged attempted rape is the subject of a trial which polarises the hostility of Muslims and Hindus to the British Raj, and it is only when on the witness stand that Adela acknowledges that she did not see Aziz enter the cave with her, and admits to herself that the event may have been an 'illusion'. On the one hand, the term 'illusion' suggests a Freudian reading: Adela's feeling that she has been molested in the dark may be a hysterical projection related to her own sexual repression, amply documented in terms of her relationship with her prospective husband, the young administrator Ronny Heaslop. On the other hand, this reading belongs to a rationalism which the novel attempts to exceed. The term 'illusion' is itself part of a series of terms which suggest the importance of the suprarational: ghost, God, telepathy and Friend ('a Persian expression for God' [Forster, 1989: 273]) being the key terms in this respect. The suprarational in all of its aspects belongs to the concept of seduction. Seduction is the mode in the novel in which non-rational communication takes place, and it is the mode *par excellence* of friendship, by which the novel sets a great deal of store. The principal and key friendships are that between Aziz and Mrs Moore, the mother of Ronny Heaslop who has voyaged to India in order to arrange their marriage, and that between Aziz and Cyril Fielding, the principal of the local school who is a maverick outsider with respect to the British administration and who represents a version of Forster himself – albeit a deliberately limited one – inasmuch as he embodies the hope of cross-cultural friendship and communication. Although these are the friendships which are most heavily thematised in the novel, friendship and association are examined under a variety of forms. Friendship is, of course, the mode of relation of individuals and small groups, and other important friendships which are examined include that between the small Muslim group around Aziz, the friendship between Adela and Ronny as it develops before the expedition to the caves, and that between Adela and Fielding as it develops after the breakdown of the trial and her consequent alienation from the British community. The other form of friendship which the novel examines is group association; the British enclave is the main focus for this examination, although Forster also examines the nature of Muslim self-constitution as a group as manifested in a prejudice against Hindus, and also looks at the mechanisms by which Muslims and Hindus are united in anti-British sentiment after the trial – a reflection of the historical convergence of the two groups after the Amritsar (Punjab) Massacre in 1919 and the trial of the Ali brothers (founders of the Khilafat movement) in 1921, events which created unity around the movement for independence under the leadership of Mahatma Gandhi and which led to independence in 1947.

A conventional reading of the novel suggests that Forster, as what is often called (with insufficient regard for the history and ambivalence of the terms) a 'liberal humanist', valorises individual friendship and disdains the group. Certainly, the novel places individual identity above group identity and examines the difficulty of the individual in defying the power, and indeed the seductiveness, of the group. However, the basis of individual friendship and collective association is shown to be similar, each being based on the hope inspired by sympathetic illusion; seduction, or what the novel calls love, is based on an openness to the irrational which is also and more simply a way of receiving difference, and acknowledgement of the differend[12] which enters all communicative acts, be they intra- or inter-cultural, and a commitment to the simple truth of otherness.

It is important in this regard to notice the feebleness of the 'otherness' model which is so often brought to this and other 'Orientalist' writing, based as it is on a binary opposition which assumes the transparency and identity of a given 'culture' and the absolutely alien nature of any other 'culture'. Forster more scrupulously locates otherness everywhere, and this is something seen in the attempted friendship of Fielding and Adela, an important and sometimes overlooked moment in the novel. In this friendship, Fielding is initially seduced by a feeling of identity with Adela. She belongs to his background and shares some of his liberal intellectual ideas. She is a modern woman and a feminist, and differs quite as much from the reactionary women of Anglo-India as Fielding does from the men. However, in the course of their conversation, in which a sympathy is elicited which Fielding initially rejects out of loyalty to Aziz and a disdain for the whole process which Adela has inaugurated, there arises a sympathy and apparent coincidence of outlook. The subject on which they eventually most profoundly agree and which in the very moment of agreement creates the profoundest split is telepathy and the rejection of love, an only apparently curious conjunction. 'I was bringing to Ronny nothing that ought to be brought', confesses Adela:

> 'I didn't feel justified. Tenderness, respect, personal intercourse – I tried to make them take the place of –'
> 'I no longer want love,' he said, supplying the word.
> 'No more do I. My experiences have cured me. But I want others to want it.'   (261)

The conversation switches to the topic of what happened in the cave. Adela does not know, but believes that Mrs Moore did:

> 'How could she have known what we don't?'
> 'Telepathy, possibly.'
> The pert, meagre word fell to the ground. Telepathy? What an

explanation! Better withdraw it, and Adela did so. [...] Were there worlds beyond which they could never touch, or did all that is possible enter their consciousness? They could not tell. They only realised that their outlook was more or less similar, and found in this a satisfaction.

(261)

In the moment of their parting their friendship is seen in an optic not of transparent communication and shared identity but of irreducible difference, the value and meaning of the liberal, rational interchange not merely relativised but put decisively into question:

> A friendliness, as of dwarfs shaking hands, was in the air. Both man and woman were at the height of their powers – sensible, honest, even subtle. They spoke the same language, and held the same opinions, and the variety of age and sex did not divide them. Yet they were dissatisfied. When they agreed, 'I want to go in living a bit', or 'I don't believe in God', the words were followed by a curious backwash, as though the universe had displaced itself to fill up a tiny void, or as though they had seen their own gestures from an immense height – dwarfs talking, shaking hands and assuring each other that they stood on the same footing of insight. [...W]istfulness descended on them now, as on other occasions; the shadow of the shadow of a dream fell over their clear-cut interests, and objects never seen again seemed messages from another world. (262)

This passage combines several motifs from the novel which it is worthwhile to separate, because they do not add up to a consistent view. On the one hand, there is the motif of scale. Adela and Fielding are 'dwarfs' – that is, they possess less than the stature which the human measure gives to the human. The use of the term dwarf is highly specific and embodies a paradox – if these humans are not as important on a universal scale as they believe themselves to be, they can nevertheless imagine a perspective from which to see themselves as dwarfs, a perspective which must in its turn be human and which implies even an infinite regress of human perspectives which see the preceding perspective as that of dwarfs. This is, in other words, a thoroughly human measure of the non-human, the suggestion of a vast perspective which is only the human imagining of such; it is a trope of scale which is one of the unsatisfactory features of the novel. The novel constantly offers the simple geography of India as something which exceeds the human. Moreover, the Hindu faith is, in one respect, identified with India as adequate to its non-human perspectives – in another respect it will be merely asserted that Hinduism embodies a certain lightness, a capacity for humour, which Christianity lacks. The equation of the religion with the landscape is a fundamental conceptual flaw. The very ancientness of the Hindu religion is invoked as its truth – it thus is identified with scale in a certain respect – while Christianity and Islam are the modern monotheistic religions which do not acknowledge the vastness of time and of space. India, as a place which is both temporally and geographically vast cannot be seized either by Muslim conquerors or their British successors. Such an act would be akin to seizing the fabric of space and time which we are assured so exceeds the human. Hinduism therefore has a certain sort of truth in this perspective, even if Forster will enter all the usual liberal caveats – it is another case of 'I want other people to want it' – a sentence which reads as a candid admission of Forster's own part and on the part of the liberal atheism for which he speaks. Indeed, it is an excellent paradox that liberalism and Hinduism become so entwined in this novel, each confirming the truth and untruth of the other, and leaving Christianity and Islam entirely stranded. However, I suggest that the way in which Infinity is wheeled in by Forster to dwarf human perspectives is itself a perspectival trick which mistakes the nature of the real and fails to locate Hinduism in a social history as a human culture; instead, its alleged archaic origins are merely invoked to testify to its truth, a truth already falsified by the perspective of the modern atheism from which its polytheism is viewed.

In other words, to represent the infinite in terms of extension and argue that it is sheer extension which eludes human perception reveals itself to be a paradox in the moment in which it is a human metaphor – the 'dwarf' – which is used to invoke it. The 'backwash', the 'tiny void', the 'wistfulness' and the 'shadow of a shadow of a dream' suggest a more interesting line of inquiry, however. Fielding and Adela, renouncing love and any finality within thought are frozen in that state which Hegel calls the Unhappy Consciousness:

> This *unhappy, inwardly disrupted* consciousness, since its essentially contradictory nature is for it a *single* consciousness, must for ever have present in the one consciousness the other also; and thus it is driven out of each in turn in the very moment when it imagines it has successfully attained to a peaceful unity with the other. [...] The Unhappy Consciousness itself *is* the gazing of one self-consciousness into another, and itself *is* both, and the unity of both is also its essential nature. But it is not as yet explicitly aware that this is its essential nature, or that it is the unity of both.[13]

I invoke this model of the Unhappy Consciousness here partly because Hegel's *Phenomenology* is the source of so much of the discussion of otherness and difference which has characterised theoretical debate in recent times; and also because, while Hegel's discussion is here taken out of context, it appears to me, taken as a whole, to characterise the stalled state of the liberal consciousness which is certainly shared by Fielding and Adela, and which has resonance for more contemporary forms of liberalism which, because they doubt the possibility of the universality of reason, doubt the meaning of their own capacity to engage the other and, while ardently wishing that others will continue to want love, renounce it for themselves. Finally, I invoke it because it is on this point – the potential of spirit for absolute knowledge – that post-Hegelian thought has had so much to say since Nietzsche. In particular, while Hegel will develop a model of reason as the zone in which purely internalised differences are subsumed, Forster's text will anticipate current demands in postmodern philosophy for a recognition and negotiation of difference in terms of love or friendship.[14]

While his liberals are unhappy, Forster's Hindus have something of the unity with what Hegel calls the 'Unchangeable' which his atheist rationalists lack. Their specific unhappiness in the above exchange arises from an acknowledgement not of an external infinite, but of the infinite within thought even where reason appears identical with itself – that is, where they agree. This internal infinite is the 'tiny void' to which the text refers. Its recognition evokes from them 'wistfulness' – a nostalgia for the love which they have renounced – and they feel themselves haunted by the 'shadow of a shadow of a dream' which belongs to another world which falls over their rationally conceived and apparently self-transparent 'interests'. This is not the place to engage the confrontation between Hegel and a series of post-differential thinkers – here I include Deleuze, Derrida and Lyotard. It is enough to state, without seeking to adjudicate, that post-differential thinking has roundly rejected the series of arguments which allow Hegel to claim that 'Reason is Spirit when its certainty of being all reality has been raised to truth, and it is conscious of itself as its own world, and of the world as itself.'[15] I wish instead to note two things. First, that the possible emergence of spirit as a sufficient adequation between reason and reality is present in *Passage to India* in a merely nostalgic form: it is not something which reason moves towards through modern thinking but is present merely as a moment in a Hinduism characterised by Forster as childish and irrational, as if genuine spirit were a lost, childlike state which the progress of reason has merely served to deny to the modern. The irrationalism is less that of Hinduism than of the rationalist who valorises a moment for others which he has himself outgrown: Fielding in his middle age represents the middle age of a culture which has only the old age of Mrs Moore and nihilistic vision to look forward to – hence Fielding's limited affirmation that 'I want to go on living a bit' (262). It is death itself which is invoked as the limiting horizon of reason, and a childlike innocence of death which is nostalgically evoked as the already undermined affirmation of an earlier cultural and developmental model. 'We are subdued to what we work in', remarks Fielding *a propos* a discussion of death, but this subdual amounts to a rejection of thinking itself as not worthwhile in an objectivity which denies the communication and ultimate human happiness on which thought is predicated (262).[16] This liberal disillusion is certainly one moment in the logic of *A Passage to India*. However, the second thing which I wish to note in this regard is the novel's suggestion of a model which works against the limitation of reason and against finitude, and suggests the possibility of a transcendence of spirit in a newly optimistic version that accords with what Derrida claims in his now well-known essay, 'Différance': 'From the vantage of this laughter and this dance, from the vantage of this affirmation foreign to all dialectics, the other side of nostalgia, what I will call Heideggerian *hope*, comes into question',[17] the hope of giving a proper name to the 'essential nature of being'. It is probable that this hope is in its turn a substitution for Hegelian optimism based now not on the claims of reason, but on the acknowledgement of *différance* as it is designated by Derrida. *Différance* corresponds in *A Passage to India* to the infinite 'void' which lies even in agreement, that is, the difference inherent even to agreement. What can cross, or tend to cross, difference as understood culturally, even, in Derrida's essay, the notional opposition between life and death, is in the above passage from the novel a shadow – elsewhere in the novel, the ghost or, as elsewhere in Derrida's work, the spectre.

The idea of rational exchange presupposes the possibility of exchange between subjects, subjects who themselves have mastered the rules: subjects who are 'at the height of their powers' and who 'speak the same language'. The ghost and its relation telepathy – or telepoesis – do not rest on presence but rather on absence, indeed, on the absence of the dead. 'Imagine us both as addressing you from another and happier world' (33), Aziz's friend Hamidullah tells him jokingly in the very first exchanges of the novel, a remark which not only announces the concern with the voice of the dead, but connects the possibility of a voice without presence to a possible Utopia, a happier world which the sceptical, English-educated Hamidullah here invokes ironically.

The suggestion that friendship transcends death, and may even transcend actual acts, recurs throughout the novel. Accounts of *A Passage to India* most usually see the concern with friendship as a very English intellectual ideal, one inculcated in Forster by the Apostles circle at Cambridge. Certainly, Fielding's hope for friendship with Aziz is based on Forster's own relationship with Syed Ross Masood, on whom Aziz is largely based.[18] It is often remarked that the concluding passage of the novel reflects this relationship, and Forster's desire for love within it, a possibility which is denied in the novel by the history which divides their respective nations – although biographically the impossibility was a more straightforward matter of Masood's unresponsiveness to Forster's love. However, it is important to recognise that the notion of friendship is extended by the novel beyond Fielding's conception of it via the notion of the ghost, and that the point(s) of view of the novel cannot simply be identified with those of one of its characters, even where Fielding's views were echoed by Forster speaking *in propria persona* in lectures and essays. This is most clearly visible *vis-à-vis* the whole issue of the politics of friendship where Fielding's views closely resemble Forster's own:

> The world, he believed, is a globe of men who are trying to reach one another and can best do so by the help of goodwill plus culture and intelligence – a creed ill-suited to Chandrapore, but he had come out too late to lose it. (80)

> [Fielding's 'manifesto':] 'I believe in teaching people to be individuals, and to understand other individuals. It's the only thing I do believe in.' (132–3)

Fielding's beliefs certainly represent a classic liberal pose, but the absence of cultural relativism in his views is surely meant to be remarkable in relation to the cultural relativism of the text: this is a doomed ideal, and the model of friendship as ghost which the logic of the text advances offers an alternative. In an account published only after Independence, Forster seems to agree in seeing the politics of friendship advanced by Fielding as the core of the book, and attempts to justify it in relation to the political situation which subsequently overshadowed Fielding's more individual concerns:

> we were paying for the insolence of Englishmen and Englishwomen out here in the past. I don't mean that good manners can avert a political

upheaval. But they can minimize it [...]. But it's too late. Indians don't long for social intercourse with Englishmen any longer. They have made a life of their own.[19]

Again, this view had been explicitly offered by Fielding: 'Indians know whether they are liked or not – they cannot be fooled here. Justice never satisfies them, and that is why the British Empire rests on sand.' (258).

Yet it seems to me that Forster's novel goes further than many of his subsequent glosses on it, and that his later quasi-diplomatic role in a context in which his novel was seen by some as having been instrumental in modifying the British attitude to Independence played a part in leading him to interpret his own work conservatively. As part of an excellent and scrupulous account of the historical and intellectual backgrounds of Forster's novel, Adwaita P. Ganguly shows precisely how the question of manners informed the whole context of Indo-Anglian relations in the period of Forster's two visits to India in 1912 and 1922.[20] Ganguly's account confirms Forster's own sense that personal relations were important for both sides, and were even a matter of conscious political decision for the Raj. The brief visit of the Lieutenant-Governor of the Province after the trial, in which he condones Fielding's behaviour in defending the inno-cence of Aziz at the cost of alienation from his own community, criticises the local administration and insists on Fielding's readmis-sion to the Anglo-Indian club, is only one confirmation of the role which policy played in these matters. The bigotry of the local Anglo-Indian outpost, at which Forster directs so much satirical venom, simply reflects the inability of the lower officials to interpret the policy of the government for which they work: their own ideology of Empire is by no means identical with that of the higher Imperial administration, a disparity brutally reflected in the actions of General Dyer in the Amritsar Massacre, the inhumanity of which remains difficult to believe – the massacre was provoked by a peaceful gathering, was begun without warning, and at the cessation of fire Dyer simply marched his troops away without attending to the two thousand dead and injured men, women and children he left behind.

Forster's own account of this action is found in his description of the attitudes in the Club after the alleged rape of Adela, a mood which is shown to be hysterical – I use the term advisedly and in all of its associations, for Forster will find in the Anglo-Indian women, rather than the men, the most intemperate forms of intolerance: so it is the wife of the Collector who is most outspoken in her denunciation of the Indians, while: 'Her friends kept up their spirits by demanding holocausts of natives.' (200). Although he does not depict the massacre – his novel is historically 'suspended' between the dates of his two visits to India in 1912 and 1922 – Forster wrote, of course, knowing that such a demand had been answered. Like Conrad, who had located the Victorian elevation and cocooning of women as a key element in the brutality of imperialism in *Heart of Darkness,* Forster finds the old-fashioned Victorian attitude to women behind the reaction to the rape of Adela, a reaction which makes Adela herself uncomfortable: she is a modern woman who has changed with the times in England, while the colonials have been here in most case twenty years or more and their ideas reflect an earlier dispensation, unaffected by the cultural shifts in England in the post-war. Adela is thus ashamed of her tears and uneasy that they inspire such a fierce reaction: 'Although Miss Quested had not made herself popular with the English, she brought out all that was fine in their character' is the narrative's ironic gloss on this situation (187).

There is a politics of friendship and a reality of hatred in the Indian situation of 1912–22 which Forster's novel reflects fairly accurately. Certainly, a pragmatic evaluation of the role of manners is part of Forster's account, as is an equally careful documenting of the psychology of friendship and of group association. The novel's deployment of the ghost seems initially to suggest straightforward opposition between Western rationalism, in the form of the justice dispensed by the British in India, and Oriental irrationalism, with the Oriental being granted the upper hand. I suggest, though, that the ghost is exactly that presence which bridges the gap between (absent) speaker and (absent) audience, bridging the void within discourse not only when there is a differend based on cultural difference or simple misrecognition, but also, as in the case I have outlined above, where there is apparent discursive agreement. Thus, friendship acquires a metaphysical frame in the novel which goes beyond, or attempts to suggest a beyond to, the pragmatics of politics and even of individual psychology. Derrida's *Politiques de l'amitié* is a series of meditations on a quotation attributed by Montaigne to Aristotle: 'O mes amis, il n'y a nul ami'. Linking friendship to the ideals of the Revolution, Derrida argues that friendship is based on a principle of hope:

'L'amitié, l'être-ami, donc, qu'est-ce que c'est que ça? Eh bien, c'est aimer *avant* d'être aimé. Avant même de penser ce que veut dire *aimer, l'amour, l'aimance*, il faut savoir qu'on ne le saura qu'en interrogeant d'abord l'acte et l'expérience d'aimer plutôt que l'état ou la situation de l'être aimé. [...] L'argument paraît simple en effet: il est possible d'être aimé (voix passive) *sans le savoir*, mais il est impossible d'aimer (voix active) *sans le savoir*. [...] L'ami, c'est celui qui aime avant d'être l'être-aimé [...].'

(Derrida, 1994: 25)

Aimer comes before *savoir*, and one loves/likes without being loved/liked. Fielding's remark that 'Indians know whether they are liked or not [...]. Justice never satisfies them', is cast into perspective by this passage, and (British) justice aligned with the valorisation of knowledge over love. Without pursuing the logic of Derrida's series of texts, it is possible here to claim that it is the ghost in Forster's novel which makes possible a friendship based precisely on loving/ liking before knowing. This is the type of friendship between Aziz and Mrs Moore after their accidental meeting in the Mosque. Although their acquaintance is slight, each is committed to the other without knowing the other. This is an *event* which breaks the rules, and for a moment, perhaps an unrepeatable moment, shatters the overdetermined framework of civil space which dictates what friendship (*amitié*) or love (*amour*) must be – a framework which is in the context of British India of an extreme rigidity. It is the moment of what Derrida calls '*aimance*', a form of loving which goes beyond the socially determined forms of love and friendship, and beyond the existing cultures and traditions of love.[21] It is the *aimance* of Aziz and Mrs Moore which survives the history which the novel presents, rather than the attempted homosocial *amitié* of Fielding and Aziz or the heterosexual *amour* of Adela and Ronnie.

Although their friendship is imbroiled in disaster, and although the novel in one of its aspects announces a scepticism towards the illusions of superstition, it seems to be this form of love without knowledge, a love which opens the future as risk – what Derrida, following Nietzsche, calls the *peut-être* – on which the emergence of the future must be based. 'I like Aziz. Aziz is my real friend' states Mrs Moore (Forster, 1989: 111). The component of election and divinity in this friendship is quite as important as the exploration of the psychological motivations which lead each character to idealise the friendship, although Forster keenly documents the psychological predispositions which lead each character into this relationship. 'God is here', says Mrs Moore to Aziz when he finds her in the

Mosque (42), a phrase which appeals to Aziz's sentimentality but which, as the novel continues to show, is the basis on which individual and cultural differends must appear – although they cannot be 'recognised' or 'overcome', but only 'appear' and 'be negotiated'. If I connect the individual and cultural differend here it is because the differend cannot in any case be categorised – it arises precisely when categories are exceeded, when the void within and between discourses appears in its irreducibility. This is why the model of 'otherness' so often applied from a perspective of post-colonial theory to a discussion of this novel so radically mistakes its object. For while otherness suggests the possibility of a realm of self-transparent communication and sameness as within a given culture, Forster more accurately locates the differend in and between all individuals, so that which divides – in spite of the novel's conclusion – is not merely culture and geography, and the notion of otherness, which implies an identity B concealed from an identity A which has no access to it, is quite inadequate to a reality which is based on infinite difference, on endless non-identity. Mrs Moore instantly identifies the animal which has upset her son's carriage as a 'ghost', aligning herself not merely with India, nor with an abstract notion of transcendence, but more fundamentally with a recognition of the principles on which friendship – that is, any form of democratic human association – must be based.

After her death Mrs Moore remains a ghostly presence herself, a symbol of hope even as her name echoes, distorted in the mouths of people who have no idea who she is: 'Esmiss Esmoor'. Of course, there is much in the novel which mitigates against this optimistic reading. Thus, while I have characterised the ghost as being in some way an echo, I am equally aware that the echo itself – the 'bou-oum' of the Marabar caves – is also offered as a symbol of the ultimate emptiness of human meaning, at least in the final vision of Mrs Moore: 'She had come to that state where the horror of the universe and its smallness are both visible at the same time' (212). However, no one in this novel should be allowed the final word, and the pessimism of Mrs Moore is offset by the optimism of the final ceremony of the birth of Krishna. It remains my conclusion that Forster's novel will, in certain of its moments, go beyond what Derrida has called a merely 'adolescent' model of friendship – 'why can't we be friends'[22] – into a modelling of the nature of friendship in terms of a genuinely utopian effort to imagine how a future beyond the schemata of the present might emerge. This is more, I think, than what Derrida calls an 'erotic of race', even though the novel's homoeroticism is rightly queried – as he shows in *Politiques de l'amitié*, friendship is customarily modelled in the gendered terms of *fraternité*, the democratic ideal of the French Revolution (Derrida, 1994: 12–13). Moreover, the access of women, especially of subaltern women, to the exchanges of *fraternité* remains an urgent question in the novel, and is bracketed with some irony by Forster in his decision to make Aziz's poetic project 'The Indian lady as she is and not as she is supposed to be' (Forster, 1989: 268); 'His poems were all on one topic – oriental womanhood. "The purdah must go," was their burden, "otherwise we shall never be free"' (290). It is important in this regard that the *aimance* of Aziz and Mrs Moore is neither homo-social nor heterosexual, nor is it mono-cultural: its 'madness' is that it exceeds all cultural categories.

I began by saying that the novel shared with the desert romance an emphasis on seduction, on what I have generalised as an openness to the irrational or the differend. It proposes seduction rationally as a principle of hope which goes beyond the limitations and imperialistic claims of subjective reason. While *A Passage to India* cannot be granted a coherence which is in any case impossible for it, its attempt to negotiate an impossible situation remains rational in its commitment to the thinking through of the role of reason, and this thought, more apparent in the novel than in the author's subsequent commentary, emerges as a stronger and more progressive current than the much slighter and more questionable liberal comprehensiveness which an earlier generation of critics have affirmed.[23]

*

A Passage To India occupies a unique position among the literature examined in this study, since it raises urgent critical questions in the context of its Indian reception relatively independently of its reception in Britain. In respect of the other works here examined, the attempt to locate the fiction of the 1920s in its general social context returns us to the question of our own relationship to the decisions and choices which were made by writers at that time, specifically with regard to the priorities of the models of 'Modernism' and 'English Literature', a question which cannot be properly articulated when English literature is annexed to American literature and appropriated by the American academy. It is a matter of recognising that this writing remains an English literature, not simply one literature in English amongst others. What follows from this recognition is the necessity of conducting a criticism which goes beyond the insights of the now internationally orthodox version of ideology critique to disengage the moments in this literature which exceed ideological incoherence to pose questions of a persistent urgency about the cultural norms of modern capitalism in the declining British state. This study has found much to query in the work of the Modernist Virginia Woolf, of the anti-Modernist Modernist Wyndham Lewis, and of the modern critic of modernity, D. H. Lawrence. Yet, without returning these writers to a generalised notion of formal Modernism, it has been possible to highlight the negative and critical moment in their works which set them apart from their contemporaries and which, despite the deep-seated flaws and ideologically objectionable components which their works contain, continues to demand our attention. Other works – those of Radclyffe Hall and Ford Madox Ford – take their place alongside them as the site of interesting but less thoroughgoing critique. The critical modes adopted have not simply defended the capacity of formally more complex works to supply the negative moment which committed works in their relative neglect of formal questions fail to address, thereby assimilating themselves in the most damaging manner possible to existing circumstances.[24] These accounts have also sought to discover a critical thinking in and behind these works which is as much part of their meaning as their form, even where thought and form appear to diverge. However, the articulation of critique certainly depends on this attention to received forms and contents, and this is why, for example, the radical reaction of Wyndham Lewis continues to claim our attention in ways which the communist fervour of Douglas Goldring does not. In all of this, then, this study retains an extended notion of Modernism as the critical literature of modernity, and recommends an attention to the 1920s not with the project of reclaiming a series of lesser authors in the New Historicist manner, but in the spirit of articulating the limits of works which are critically formulated in order to clarify that within them which speaks of a disillusion with a modernity that is continuous with our own.

Notes

1. In Ayers, *Wyndham Lewis and Western Man*.
2. Compare the discussion in Billie Melman, *Women and the Popular Imagination in the Twenties*, pp. 89–104.
3. Following the noted argument about postmodernism and pastiche as presented and exemplified in Fredric Jameson, *Postmodernism*, pp. 16–19.
4. The Sheik is implicitly linked to the figure of Gerald in *Women in Love*, who uses his own overpowering of a horse to exemplify his theory of the will. See Lawrence, *Women in Love*, pp. 110–13 and p. 139. Gerald's horse is an Arab which he has bought in Constantinople.
5. This necessarily condensed exposition is drawn from Robert Young, *White Mythologies*, pp. 119–56.
6. See Avrom Fleishman, 'He Do the Polis in Different Voices: Lawrence's Later Style', in Balbert and Marcus (eds), *D. H. Lawrence*, pp. 162–79; Avrom Fleishman, 'Lawrence and Bakhtin: Where Pluralism Ends and Dialogism Begins', and David Lodge, 'Lawrence, Dostoevsky, Bakhtin: Lawrence and Dialogic Fiction', both in Keith Brown (ed.), *Rethinking Lawrence*, pp. 92–119; for confirmation of the appositeness of the Dostoevsky connection, see Philip Sicker, 'Lawrence's Auto da fe: The Grand Inquisitor in *The Plumed Serpent*', *Comparative Literature Studies*, 29:4 (1992), 417–40.
7. Lawrence, *Letters, V*, p. 68.
8. See Kimberley Van-Hoosier Carey, 'Struggling with the Master: The Position of Kate and the Reader in Lawrence's "Quetzalcoatl" and *The Plumed Serpent*', in the *D. H. Lawrence Review*, 25:1–3 (1993–4), 104–18.
9. Fleishman, in Brown (ed.), *Rethinking Lawrence*, p. 110.
10. Lodge, in Brown (ed.), *Rethinking Lawrence*, p. 96.
11. See Michael Bell, *D. H. Lawrence: Language and Being*, and Anne Fernihough, *D. H. Lawrence: Aesthetics and Ideology*. Each writer is aware that while the parallels with German thought are discernible, it is difficult to assign Lawrence to an intellectual history of which he simply does not form a direct part. This is especially true in relation to Heidegger, whose thought is based on carefully articulated encounters with all of the important texts of ancient and modern philosophy, and who offers highly nuanced models of a type which are anathema to Lawrence's whole mode of proceeding, even where the parallels are superficially striking. This is one of the reasons I have preferred to identify the meaning of Lawrence's work as literature, even where this involves going through his ideas, rather then attempting to locate him as a thinker in a tradition of which he knew almost nothing.
12. The use of the term 'differend' follows that of Jean-François Lyotard in *Le Différend* (Paris: les Éditions de Minuit, 1983): 'A la différence d'un

litige, un différend serait un cas de conflit entre deux parties (au moins) qui ne pourrait pas être tranché équitablement faute d'une règle de jugement applicable aux deux argumentations. Que l'une soit légitime n'impliquerait pas que l'autre ne le soit pas.' (p. 9) Lyotard frames the question of his work in the following way: 'Un genre de discours fournit par sa règle un ensemble de phrases possibles, chacune relevant d'un régime de phrases. Mais un autre genre de discours fournit un ensemble d'autres phrases possibles. Il y a un différend entre ces ensembles (ou entre les genres qui les appellent) parce qu'ils sont hétérogènes. [...] En l'absence d'un régime de phrases ou d'un genre de discours jouissant d'une autorité universelle pour trancher, n'est-il pas nécessaire que l'enchaînement, quel qu'il soit, fasse un tort aux régimes ou aux genres dont les phrases possibles restent inactualisées?' (p. 10)

13. Hegel, *The Phenomenology of Spirit*, p. 126.
14. See Thomas Docherty, *Alterities*, for varieties of the claim that the ethical now 'requires a specifically postmodern philosophy of love' (p. 12). On the subject of friendship, I will refer specifically in the text to Derrida's *Politiques de l'amitié*.
15. Hegel, *The Phenomenology of Spirit*, makes the following claim: 'Reason is Spirit when its certainty of being all reality has been raised to truth, and it is conscious of itself as its own world, and of the world as itself.' (p. 263).
16. Again, there is a close correspondence with Hegel's discussion of Unhappy Consciousness: 'as regards the contradictory relation in which consciousness takes its own *reality* to be *immediately a nothingness*, its actual doing becomes a doing of nothing, its enjoyment a feeling of wretchedness. Work and enjoyment thus lose all their *universal content* and *significance* ...' (p. 135). I would however need to introduce many more stages to this argument to confirm that my use of Hegel's discussion is so germane and space prohibits a revaluation of the relationship between Hegel and the post-differential philosophy which should follow from the juxtaposition with Derrida et al.
17. Derrida, 'Différance', in *Margins of Philosophy*, p. 27.
18. See Rustom Barucha, 'Forster's Friends', in *Raritan*, 4 (Spring 1986), 105–22, and reproduced in Jeremy Tambling (ed.), *E. M. Forster*, pp. 115–32.
19. Forster, *The Hill of Devi*, p. 153.
20. Adwaita P. Ganguly, *India: Mystic, Complex and Real*, pp. 33–60.
21. Derrida, *Politiques de l'amitié*, p. 88.
22. Compare Sara Suleri, *The Rhetoric of English India*, pp. 132–48.
23. Although I have no space to discuss them here, the most influential early writing on Forster includes Lionel Trilling, 'A Passage to India' (1948) and Malcolm Bradbury, 'Two Passages to India: Forster as a

Victorian and Modern' (1969), reproduced in Harold Bloom (ed.) *E. M. Forster's* A Passage To India. For a more recent account which examines Forster's liberalism in terms of the reading of other cultures and differences of character point of view, with reference to Rorty and Habermas, see Paul B. Armstrong, 'Reading India: E. M. Forster and the Politics of Interpretation,' in *Twentieth Century Literature* 38: 4 (Winter 1992), 365–85.

24. The model is that of Adorno. See, for example, 'Commitment', in Arato and Gebhardt, *The Essential Frankfurt School Reader*, pp. 300–18, which defends 'autonomous art' against Sartre's advocacy of 'committed art' in *What is Literature?*

Bibliography

Primary Sources

Aldington, Richard, *The Colonel's Daughter*. London: Chatto and Windus, 1931.

— *D. H. Lawrence*. London: Chatto and Windus, 1930.

— *Death of a Hero*. (1929, unexpurgated edition 1965.) London: Sphere, 1968.

— *A Dream in the Luxembourg*. London: Chatto and Windus, 1930.

— *A Fool i' the Forest. A Phantasmagoria*. London: Allen & Unwin, 1924.

— 'Introduction' to D. H. Lawrence, *Kangaroo*. Harmondsworth: Penguin, 1950.

— *Roads to Glory*. London: Chatto and Windus, 1930.

Arlen, Michael, *The Green Hat*. (1924) London: Clark, 1991.

Blunden, Edmund, *Undertones of War*. London: Cobden-Sanderson, 1928.

Bowen, Elizabeth, *The Collected Stories of Elizabeth Bowen*. Introduction by Angus Wilson. London: Cape, 1980.

— *The Hotel*. (1927) London: Jonathan Cape, 1981.

— *The Last September*. (1929) Harmondsworth: Penguin, 1982.

Brittain, Vera, *Testament of Youth: An Autobiographical Study of the Years 1900–1925*. London: Gollancz, 1933.

Carpenter, Edward, *The Intermediate Sex: A Study of Some Transitional Types of Man and Woman*. London: George Allen and Unwin, 1908.

Clephane, Irene, *Ourselves: 1900–1930*. London: John Lane The Bodley Head, 1933.

Cocteau, Jean, *Les Enfants Terribles*. Paris: Grasset, 1929.

Collier, John, and Iain Lang, *Just The Other Day: An Informal History of Great Britain Since the War*. London: Hamish Hamilton, 1932.

Conquest, Joan, *Desert Love*. London: T. Werner Laurie, 1920.

Deeping, Warwick, *Sorrell and Son.* (1925) London: Cassell, 1984.

Eliot, T. S., *Selected Prose of T. S. Eliot.* Edited with an Introduction by Frank Kermode. London: Faber & Faber, 1975.

Ellis, Havelock, *Studies in the Psychology of Sex*, Volume II. (1910) New York: Random House, 1936.

Firbank, Ronald, *Valmouth and Other Novels.* (1919, 1924, 1926) Harmondsworth: Penguin, 1961.

Ford, Ford Madox, *The Bodley Head Ford Madox Ford.* Edited and introduced by Grahame Greene. In four volumes. London: Bodley Head, 1962–3.

— *The English Novel: From the Earliest Days to the Death of Joseph Conrad.* London: Constable, 1930.

— *Joseph Conrad: A Personal Reminiscence.* London: Duckworth, 1924.

— *Parade's End.* (1924–8) Introduction by Robie Macauley. London: Penguin, 1982.

Forster, E. M., *The Hill of Devi: Being Letters from Dewas State Senior.* London: Arnold, 1953.

— *A Passage to India.* (1924) Edited by Oliver Stallybras. London: Penguin, 1989.

Galsworthy, John, *The Forsyte Saga.* London: Heinemann, 1922.

Gerhardie, William, *Futility: A Novel on Russian Themes.* (1922) Preface by Michael Holroyd. Harmondsworth: Penguin, 1974.

Gide, André, *Les Faux-Monnayeurs.* Paris: Gallimard, 1925.

— *Si le grain ne meurt … .* Paris: Gallimard, 1920.

Goldring, Douglas, *The Black Curtain.* London: Chapman and Hall, 1920a.

— *Cuckoo: A Comedy of Adjustments.* London: Chapman and Hall, 1925.

— *Dublin: Explorations and Reflections.* By an Englishman. Dublin and London: Maunsel, 1917a.

— *The Façade.* London: Jarrolds, n.d.

— *The Fight For Freedom: A Play in Four Acts.* Plays for a People's Theatre I. London: C. W. Daniel, 1919.

— *The Fortune: A Romance of Friendship.* Dublin and London: Maunsel, 1917b.

— *The Merchant of Souls.* London: Jarrolds, n.d.

— *The Nineteen Twenties: A General Survey and Some Personal Memories.* London: Nicholson and Watson, 1945.

— *Nobody Knows.* London: Chapman and Hall, 1923.

— *Odd Man Out: The Autobiography of A Propaganda Novelist.* London: Chapman and Hall, 1935.

— *Pacifists in Peace and War.* London: Wishart, 1932.

— *Reputations: Essays in Criticism.* London: Chapman and Hall, 1920b.

— *South Lodge: Reminiscences of Violet Hunt, Ford Madox Ford and the English Review Circle.* London: Constable, 1943.

— *A Stranger in Ireland.* By an Englishman. Dublin; London: Talbat Press: Fisher Unwins, 1918.

Graves, Robert, *Goodbye to All That.* (1929) Harmondsworth: Penguin, 1960.

Graves, Robert and Alan Hodge, *The Long Week-End: A Social History of Great Britain 1918–1939.* (1940) London: Hutchinson, 1985.

H.D., *Bid Me To Live.* (1960) London: Virago, 1984.

Hall, Radclyffe, *The Well of Loneliness.* (1928) Introduction by Alison Hennegan. London: Virago, 1992.

Hibberd, Dominic and John Onions (eds), *Poetry of the Great War: An Anthology.* London: Macmillan, 1986.

Holtby, Winifred, *Anderby Wold.* London: John Lane The Bodley Head, 1923.

— *The Crowded Street.* London: John Lane The Bodley Head, 1924.

— *South Riding.* London: Collins, 1936.

Hueffer [Ford], Ford Madox, *The Critical Attitude.* London: Duckworth & Co., 1911.

Hull, E. M. *The Sheik.* (1919) London: Newnes, 1921.

Hulme, T. E., *Speculations: Essays on Humanism and the Philosophy of Art.* (1924) Edited by Herbert Read with a Foreword by Jacob Epstein. London, Henley and Boston: Routledge and Kegan Paul, 1977.

Hutchinson, A. S. M., *If Winter Comes.* London: Hodder and Stoughton, 1921.

Huxley, Aldous, *Antic Hay.* (1923) London: Triad Grafton, 1990.

— *Brief Candles: Stories.* London: Chatto and Windus, 1930.

— *Crome Yellow.* (1921) St. Albans: Triad/Panther, 1977.

— *Leda.* London: Chatto and Windus, 1920.

— *The Letters of Aldous Huxley.* Edited by Grover Smith. London: Chatto and Windus, 1969.

— *Limbo: Six Short Stories and a Play.* (1920) London: Chatto and Windus, 1946.

— *Mortal Coils.* London: Chatto and Windus, 1928.

— *Point Counter Point.* (1928) London: Triad Grafton, 1988.

— *Those Barren Leaves.* London: Chatto and Windus, 1925.

Joyce, James, *Dubliners.* (1914) Introduction and Notes by Terence Brown. London: Penguin, 1992.

Kaye-Smith, Sheila, *Joanna Godden.* London: Cassell, 1921.

Kennedy, Margaret, *The Constant Nymph.* (1924) Introduction by Anita Brookner. London: Virago, 1986.

Klaus, H. Gustav (ed.), *Tramps, Workmates and Revolutionaries: Working Class Stories of the 1920s.* London: Journeyman, 1993.

Lawrence, D. H., *Aaron's Rod.* (1922) Edited by Mara Kalnins with an Introduction and Notes by Steve Vine. London: Penguin Books, 1995a.

— *Apocalypse.* (1931) Edited with an Introduction and Notes by Mara Kalnins. London: Penguin, 1995b.

— *The Complete Poems of D. H. Lawrence.* Edited by Vivian de Sola Pinto and Warren Roberts. Harmondsworth: Penguin, 1977.

— *The Complete Short Novels.* Edited with an Introduction and Notes by Keith Sagar and Melissa Partridge. London: Penguin, 1987. [Includes *The Virgin and The Gipsy* and *The Escaped Cock.*]

— *England, My England and Other Stories.* (1922) Edited by Bruce Steele with an Introduction and Notes by Michael Bell. London: Penguin, 1995c.

— *Fantasia of the Unconscious; Psychoanalysis and the Unconscious.* (1922; 1921) Harmondsworth: Penguin, 1971.

— *The First Lady Chatterley: The First Version of Lady Chatterley's Lover.* [1926] Foreword by Frieda Lawrence. Harmondsworth: Penguin, 1973a.

— *The Fox; The Captain's Doll; The Ladybird.* (1923) Edited by Dieter Mehl with an Introduction and Notes by David Ellis. London: Penguin, 1994a.

— *John Thomas and Lady Jane: The Second Version of Lady Chatterley's Lover.* [1927] Harmondsworth: Penguin, 1973b.

— *Kangaroo.* (1923) Edited by Bruce Steele with an Introduction and Notes by Macdonald Daly. London: Penguin, 1997a.

— *Lady Chatterley's Lover. A Propos of 'Lady Chatterley's Lover'.* (1928) Edited with an Introduction and Notes by Michael Squires. London: Penguin, 1994b.

— *The Letters of D. H. Lawrence.* Edited by James T. Boulton et al. Seven volumes. Cambridge and New York: Cambridge University Press, 1979–93.

— *The Lost Girl.* (1920) Edited by John Worthen with an Introduction and Notes by Carol Siegel. London: Penguin, 1995d.

— *Mornings in Mexico.* London: Secker, 1927.

— *Mr Noon.* Edited with Notes by Lindeth Vasey and an Introduction by Peter Preston. London: Penguin, 1996a.

— *Phoenix: The Posthumous Papers of D. H. Lawrence.* (1936) Edited by Edward D. McDonald. London: Heinemann, 1967.

— *Phoenix II: Uncollected, Unpublished and Other Prose Works by D. H. Lawrence.* Collected and Edited with an Introduction and Notes by Warren Roberts and Harry T. Moore. London: Heinemann, 1968.

— *The Plumed Serpent.* (1926) Edited with an Introduction and Notes by L. D. Clark and Virginia Crosswhite Hyde. London: Penguin, 1995e.

— *Quetzalcoatl: The Early Version of* The Plumed Serpent. (1923) Edited by Louis L. Martz. Redding Ridge, CA: Black Swan, 1995f.

— *The Rainbow.* (1915) Edited by Mark Kinkead-Weekes with an Introduction and Notes by Anne Fernihough. London: Penguin, 1995g.

— *Reflections on the Death of a Porcupine and Other Essays.* (1925) Edited by Michael Herbert. Cambridge: Cambridge University Press, 1988.

— *Sea and Sardinia.* (1923) Edited by Maria Kalnins. Cambridge: Cambridge University Press, 1997.

— *Sketches of Etruscan Places and Other Italian Essays.* (1932) Edited by Simonetta de Filippis. Cambridge: Cambridge University Press, 1992.

— *St. Mawr and Other Stories.* (1925) Edited by Brian Finney with an

Introduction and Notes by Charles Rossman. London: Penguin, 1997c. [Includes *The Overtone* and *The Princess.*]

— *Studies in Classic American Literature.* London: Secker, 1924.

— *Study of Thomas Hardy and Other Essays.* Edited by Bruce Steele. Cambridge: Cambridge University Press, 1985.

— *The Woman Who Rode Away and Other Stories.* (1928) Edited by Dieter Mehl and Christa Jansohn with an Introduction by N. H. Reeve. London: Penguin, 1996b.

— *Women in Love.* (1920) Edited by David Farmer, Lindeth Vasey and John Worthen with an Introduction and Notes by Mark Kinkead Weekes. London: Penguin, 1995h.

Lawrence, D. H. and Molly Skinner, *The Boy in the Bush.* (1924) Edited with an Introduction and Notes by Paul Eggert. London: Penguin, 1996.

Leavis, F. R., *Culture and Environment: The Training of Critical Awareness.* London: Chatto and Windus, 1933a.

— *Education and the University: A Sketch for an 'English School'.* London: Chatto and Windus, 1943.

— *For Continuity.* Cambridge: Minority Press, 1933b.

— *New Bearings in English Poetry: A Study of the Contemporary Situation.* London: Chatto and Windus, 1932.

Leavis, Q. D., *Fiction and The Reading Public.* (1932) Reissued London: Chatto and Windus, 1965.

Lehmann, Rosamond, *Dusty Answer.* (1927) Harmondsworth: Penguin, 1936.

Lewis, Wyndham, *The Apes of God.* (1930) Afterword by Paul Edwards. Santa Barbara: Black Sparrow Press, 1981.

— *The Art of Being Ruled.* (1926) Edited with Afterword and Notes by Reed Way Dasenbrock. Santa Rosa: Black Sparrow Press, 1989.

— *The Childermass.* London: Chatto and Windus, 1928a.

— *The Complete Wild Body.* Edited by Bernard Lafourcade. Santa Barbara: Black Sparrow Press, 1982.

— *Doom of Youth.* London: Chatto and Windus, 1932.

— (ed.), *The Enemy: A Review of Art and Literature.* London: Arthur Press, 1927–9

— *Hitler.* London: Chatto and Windus, 1930a.

— *The Letters of Wyndham Lewis.* Edited by W. K. Rose. London: Methuen, 1963.

— *Paleface: The Philosophy of the 'Melting Pot'.* London: Chatto and Windus, 1929.

— *Satire and Fiction: Preceded by the History of a Rejected Review by Roy Campbell.* London: Arthur Press, 1930b.

— *Tarr.* (1918) Revised edition. London: Chatto and Windus, 1928b.

— *Time and Western Man.* (1927) Edited with Afterword and Notes by Paul Edwards. Santa Rosa: Black Sparrow Press, 1993.

— *The Wild Body.* London: Chatto and Windus, 1928c.

Mansfield, Katherine, *The Stories of Katherine Mansfield.* Edited by Anthony Alpers. Auckland and Oxford: Oxford University Press, 1984.

Masterman, C. F. G., *England After the War.* London: Hodder and Stoughton, 1922.

Montague, C. E., *Disenchantment.* London: Chatto and Windus, 1922.

Mottram, R. H., *The Spanish Farm Trilogy.* London: Chatto and Windus, 1927.

Murry, John Middleton, *Fyodor Dostoevsky: A Critical Study.* (1916) London: Secker, 1923.

— *Keats and Shakespeare: A Study of Keats' Poetic Life from 1816 to 1820.* London: Oxford University Press, 1925.

— *The Necessity of Communism.* London: Cape, 1932.

— *The Problem of Style.* (1922) London: Oxford University Press, 1960.

— *Reminiscences of D. H. Lawrence.* London: Cape, 1933.

— *Son of Woman: The Story of D. H. Lawrence.* London: Cape, 1931.

Postgate, R. W., Ellen Wilkinson MP and J. F. Horrabin, *A Workers' History of the Great Strike.* London: The Plebs League, 1927.

Powys, T. F., *Mr Weston's Good Wine.* London: Chatto and Windus, 1927.

Private 19022 [Frederic Manning], *Her Privates We.* London: Davie, 1930.

Proust, Marcel, *Sodome et Gomorrhe* (1921, 1922). Preface by Antoine Compagnon. Paris: Gallimard, 1989.

Reilly, Catherine (ed.), *Scars Upon My Heart: Women's Poetry and Verse of the First World War.* London: Virago, 1981.

Richardson, Dorothy M., *Pilgrimage.* Four volumes. Introduction by Gill Hanscombe. London: Virago, 1979.

Rickword, Edgell, *Essays and Opinions: 1921–1931.* Edited by Alan Young. Manchester: Carcanet, 1974.

Russell, Dora, *Hypatia: or, Woman and Knowledge.* London: Kegan Paul, Trench, Trubner, 1925.

[Sassoon, Siegfried], *Memoirs of an Infantry Officer, by the Author of Memoirs of a Fox-Hunting Man.* London: Faber and Faber, 1930.

Sinclair, May, *Life and Death of Harriet Frean.* London: Collins, 1922.

Stephen, Martin (ed.), *Never Such Innocence: A New Anthology of Great War Verse.* London: Buchan and Enright, 1988.

Strachey, Lytton, *Eminent Victorians.* (1918) Harmondsworth: Penguin, 1948.

Strachey, Ray, *'The Cause': A Short History of the Women's Movement in Great Britain.* London: Bell, 1928.

Swinnerton, Frank, *The Georgian Literary Scene.* (1925) Reissued, London: Dent, 1938.

Tate, Trudi (ed.), *Women, Men and the Great War: An Anthology of Stories.* Manchester and New York: Manchester University Press, 1995.

Townsend Warner, Sylvia, *Mr Fortune's Maggot.* (1927) London: Virago, 1978.

— *Lolly Willowes: or, The Loving Huntsman.* (1926) London: Women's Press, 1979.

— *The True Heart.* (1929) London: Virago, 1978.

Trotsky, Leon, *Leon Trotsky on Britain.* Introduction by George Novak. New York: Monad Press, 1973.

Trotter, W., *Instincts of the Herd in Peace and War.* London: Fisher Unwin, 1916.

Vansittart, Peter (ed.), *Voices From the Great War.* London: Jonathan Cape, 1981.

Ward, A. C. *The Nineteen-Twenties: Literature and Ideas in the Post-War Decade.* London: Methuen and Co. Ltd., 1930.

Waugh, Alec, *The Loom of Youth.* London: Cassell, 1917.

Waugh, Evelyn, *Decline and Fall.* (1928) Harmondsworth: Penguin, 1937.

— *Vile Bodies.* London: Chapman and Hall, 1930.

Wells, H. G., *The World of William Clissold: A Novel at a New Angle.* Three volumes. London: Benn, 1926.

West, Rebecca, *D. H. Lawrence.* London: Secker, 1930.

— *Harriet Hume: A London Fantasy.* London: Hutchinson, 1929.

— *The Judge.* (1922) New Introduction by Jane Marcus. London: Virago, 1980.

— *The Return of the Soldier.* (1918) Introduction by Victoria Glendinning. London: Virago, 1980.

— *The Strange Necessity: Essays and Reviews.* (1928) Introduction by G. Evelyn Hutchinson. London: Virago, 1987.

Wilkinson, Ellen, *Clash: A Novel.* London: Harrap, 1929.

Williamson, Henry, *The Patriot's Progress: Being the Vicissitudes of Pte. John Bullock.* Related by Henry Williamson and drawn by William Kermode. London: Bles, 1930.

Woolf, Virginia, *The Diary of Virginia Woolf.* Five volumes. Edited by Anne Oliver Bell. London: Hogarth Press, 1975–80.

— *The Essays of Virginia Woolf.* Four volumes. Edited by Andrew McNeillie. London: Hogarth Press, 1986–94.

— *Jacob's Room.* (1922) Edited with an Introduction and Notes by Sue Roe. London: Penguin Books, 1992a.

— *The Letters of Virginia Woolf.* Six volumes. Edited by Nigel Nicolson and Joanne Trautmann. London; Hogarth Press, 1975–80.

— *Mrs Dalloway.* (1925) Edited by Stella McNichol with an Introduction and Notes by Elaine Showalter. London: Penguin, 1992b.

— *Night and Day.* (1919) Edited with an Introduction and Notes by Julia Briggs. London: Penguin, 1992c.

— *Orlando.* (1928) Edited by Brenda Lyons with an Introduction and Note by Sandra M. Gilbert. London: Penguin, 1993a.

— *A Room of One's Own and Three Guineas.* (1929, 1938) Edited and with an Introduction and Notes by Michèlle Barrett. London: Penguin, 1993b.

— *To the Lighthouse.* (1927) Edited by Stella McNichol with an Introduction and Notes by Hermione Lee. London: Penguin, 1992d.

— *The Waves.* (1931) Edited with an Introduction and Notes by Kate Flint. London: Penguin, 1992e.

Zangwill, Edith Ayrton, *The Call.* London: George, Allen and Unwin, 1924.

Secondary Sources

Abel, Elizabeth, *Virginia Woolf and the Fictions of Psychoanalysis.* Chicago: University of Chicago Press, 1989.

Adorno, Theodor W., *Philosophy of Modern Music.* Translated by Anne G. Mitchell and Wesley V. Blomster. London: Sheed and Ward, 1987.

Alberti, Johanna, *Beyond Suffrage: Feminists in War and Peace.* London: Macmillan, 1989.

Arato, Andrew, and Eike Gebhardt (eds), *The Essential Frankfurt School Reader.* New York: Continuum, 1982.

Armstrong, Paul B., *The Challenge of Bewilderment: Understanding and Representation in James, Conrad, and Ford.* Ithaca: Cornell University Press, 1987.

Ayers, David, *Wyndham Lewis and Western Man.* London: Macmillan, 1992.

Bakhtin, Mikhail, *The Dialogic Imagination: Four Essays.* Austin: University of Texas Press, 1981.

Balbert, Peter and Phillip L. Marcus (eds), *D. H. Lawrence: A Centenary Consideration.* Ithaca and London: Cornell University Press, 1985.

Baldick, Chris, *The Social Mission of English Criticism: 1848–1932.* Oxford: Clarendon, 1983.

Bazin, Nancy Topping, *Virginia Woolf and the Androgyous Vision.* New Brunswick: Rutgers University Press, 1973.

Beauman, N., *A Very Great Profession: The Woman's Novel 1914–39.* London: Virago, 1983.

Beddoe, Deirdre, *Back to Home and Duty: Women Between The Wars 1918–1939.* London: Pandora, 1989.

Bedford, Sybille, *Aldous Huxley: A Biography.* Two volumes. London: Chatto and Windus, 1973–4.

Beer, Gillian, *Virginia Woolf: The Common Ground. Essays by Gillian Beer.* Edinburgh: Edinburgh University Press, 1996.

Bell, Michael, *D. H. Lawrence: Language and Being.* Cambridge: Cambridge University Press, 1991.

Berman, Marshall, *All That is Solid Melts Into Air: The Experience of Modernity.* London: Verso, 1983.

Birnbaum, M., *Aldous Huxley's Quest For Values.* Knoxville, Tennessee: Tennessee University Press, 1971.

Bloom, Clive (ed.), *Literature and Culture in Modern Britain. Volume I: 1900–1929.* London and New York: Longman, 1993.

Bloom, Harold (ed.), *E. M. Forster's* A Passage to India. New York and Philadelphia: Chelsea House, 1987.

Blythe, Ronald, *The Age of Illusion: England in the Twenties and Thirties 1919–1940.* London: Hamish Hamilton, 1963.

Bowlby, Rachel, *Feminist Destinations and Further Essays on Virginia Woolf.* Edinburgh: Edinburgh University Press, 1997.

— (ed.), *Virginia Woolf.* London and New York: Longman, 1992.

Brabon, Gail, *Women Workers of the First World War: The British Experience.* London: Croom Helm, 1981.

Bradbury, Malcolm and James McFarlane (eds), *Modernism: A Guide to European Literature: 1890–1930.* London: Penguin, 1991.

Branson, Noreen, *Britain in the Nineteen Twenties.* London: Weidenfeld and Nicolson, 1975.

Bridson, D. G., *The Filibuster: A Study of the Political Ideas of Wyndham Lewis.* London: Cassell, 1972.

Britton, Derek, *Lady Chatterley: The Making of the Novel.* London: Unwin Hyman, 1988.

Brown, Keith (ed.), *Rethinking Lawrence.* Milton Keynes and Philadelphia: Open University Press, 1990.

Buitenhuis, Peter, *The Great War of Words: Literature as Propaganda 1914–1918 and After.* London: Batsford, 1987).

Butler, Christopher, *Early Modernism: Literature, Music and Painting in Europe: 1900-1916.* Oxford: Clarendon Press, 1994.

Cadogan, Mary and Patricia Craig, *Women and Children First: The Fiction of Two World Wars.* London: Victor Gollancz Ltd., 1978.

Caramagno, Thomas C., *The Flight of the Mind: Virginia Woolf's Art and Manic Depressive Illness.* Afterword by Kay Redfield Jamison. Berkeley; Los Angeles; London: University of California Press, 1992.

Carey, John, *The Intellectuals and the Masses.* London: Faber and Faber, 1992.

Cassavant, Sharon Greer, *John Middleton Murry: The Critic As Moralist.* Alabama: The University of Alabama Press, 1982.

Cassell, Richard A. (ed.), *Critical Essays on Ford Madox Ford.* Boston, Mass.: G. K. Hall & Co., 1987.

— (ed.), *Ford Madox Ford: Modern Judgements.* London: Macmillan, 1972.

Clark, L. D., *Dark Night of the Body: D. H. Lawrence's* The Plumed Serpent. Austin: University of Texas Press, 1964.

Cockburn, Claud, *Bestseller: The Books That Everyone Read, 1900–1939.* London: Sidgwick and Jackson, 1972.

Colls, Robert and Philip Dodd, *Englishness: Politics and Culture 1880–1920.* London: Croom Helm, 1993.

Craig, Cairns (ed.), *The History of Scottish Literature. Volume IV: Twentieth Century.* Aberdeen: Aberdeen University Press, 1987.

Delany, Paul, *D. H. Lawrence's Nightmare: The Writer and his Circle in the Years of the Great War.* Sussex: Harvester Press, 1979.

Derrida, Jacques, *Margins of Philosophy*. Hemel Hempstead: Harvester, 1982.
— *Politiques de l'amitié suivi de L'oreille de Heidegger*. Paris: Galilée, 1994.
DeSalvo, Louise, *Virginia Woolf: The Impact of Childhood Sexual Abuse on her Life and Work*. London: Women's Press, 1989.
DiBattista, Maria, *Virginia Woolf's Major Novels: The Fables of Anon*. New Haven and London: Yale University Press, 1980.
Dick, Susan, *Virginia Woolf*. London: Edward Arnold, 1989.
Docherty, Thomas, *Alterities: Criticism, History, Representation*. Oxford: Oxford University Press, 1996.
Dowling, David, *Bloomsbury Aesthetics and the Novels of Forster and Woolf*. New York: St. Martin's, 1985.
Doyle, Charles, *Richard Aldington: A Biography*. London: Macmillan, 1989.
Eagleton, Terry, *Criticism and Ideology*. London; Verso, 1978.
— *The Function of Criticism: From The Spectator to Post-structuralism*. London: Verso, 1984.
Ellis, David, *D. H. Lawrence: Dying Game. 1922–1930*. Cambridge: Cambridge University Press, 1998.
Ellmann, Maud, *The Poetics of Impersonality: T. S. Eliot and Ezra Pound*. London: Harvester Press, 1987.
Fernihough, Anne, *D. H. Lawrence: Aesthetics and Ideology*. Oxford: Clarendon Press, 1993.
Ferrer, Daniel, *Virginia Woolf and the Madness of Language*. London: Routledge, 1990.
Firchow, P., *Aldous Huxley: Satirist and Novelist*. Minneapolis: Minnesota University Press, 1972.
Foucault, Michel, *The History of Sexuality. Volume I: An Introduction*. (1976) Translated from the French by Robert Hurley. Harmondsworth: Penguin, 1981.
— *Power/Knowledge: Selected Interviews and Other Writings 1972–1977*. Edited by Colin Gordon. London: Harvester Wheatsheaf, 1980.
Freud, Sigmund, *The Pelican Freud Library: Volume 11. On Metapsychology: The Theory of Psychoanalysis. Beyond the Pleasure Principle; The Ego and the Id; and Other Works*. Translated from the German under the general editorship of James Strachey. Compiled and edited by Angela Richards. Harmondsworth: Penguin, 1984.
Fussell, Paul, *Abroad: British Literary Traveling Between the Wars*. Oxford: Oxford University Press, 1980.
— *The Great War and Modern Memory*. New York and London: Oxford University Press, 1975.
Ganguly, Adwaita P., *India: Mystic, Complex and Real. A detailed study of E. M. Forster's A Passage to India: his treatment of India's Landscape, History, Social Anthropology, Religion, Philosophy, Music and Art*. Foreword by John Beer. Delhi: Motilal Banarsidass Publishers, 1990.
Gates, Norman T. (ed.), *Richard Aldington: an Autobiography in Letters*.

University Park, PA.: Pennsylvania State University Press, 1992.

Gervais, David, *Literary Englands: Versions of 'Englishness' in Modern Writing*. Cambridge: Cambridge University Press, 1993.

Gilbert, Sandra M. and Susan Gubar, *No Man's Land: The Place of the Woman Writer in the Twentieth Century. Volume 1: The War of the Words; Volume II: Sexchanges*. New Haven and London: Yale University Press, 1988; 1989.

Goldman, Dorothy, *Women and World War I: The Written Response*. London: Macmillan, 1993.

Hanson, Clare, *Virginia Woolf*. Basingstoke and London: Macmillan, 1994.

Harman, Claire, *Sylvia Townsend Warner: A Biography*. London: Chatto and Windus, 1989.

Harris, Janice Hubbard, *The Short Fiction of D. H. Lawrence*. New Brunswick, NJ: Rutgers University Press, 1984.

Hegel, G. W. F., *Introductory Lectures on Aesthetics*. London: Penguin, 1993.

— *The Phenomenology of Spirit*. Translated by A. V. Miller with analysis of the text and foreword by J. N. Findlay. Oxford: Oxford University Press, 1977.

Hewitt, Douglas, *English Fiction of the Early Modern Period: 1890–1940*. London and New York: Longman, 1988.

Holderness, Graham, *D. H. Lawrence: History, Ideology and Fiction*. Dublin: Gill and Macmillan, 1982.

Howard, Michael S., *Jonathan Cape, Publisher: Herbert Jonathan Cape; G. Wren Howard*. London: Jonathan Cape, 1971.

Hussey, Mark, *The Singing of the Real World: The Philosophy of Virginia Woolf's Fiction*. Columbus: Ohio State University Press, 1986.

— (ed.), *Virginia Woolf and War: Fiction, Reality and Myth*. Syracuse, New York: Syracuse University Press, 1992.

Hynes, Samuel, *A War Imagined: The First World War and English Culture*. London: Bodley Head, 1990.

Jameson, Fredric, *Fables of Aggression: Wyndham Lewis; The Modernist as Fascist*. Berkeley; Los Angeles; London: University of California Press, 1979.

— *Postmodernism, or, The Cultural Logic of Late Capitalism*. London: Verso, 1991.

Jarvis, Simon, *Adorno: A Critical Introduction*. Cambridge: Polity, 1998.

Jeffreys, Sheila, *The Spinster and Her Enemies: Feminism and Sexuality 1880–1930*. London: Pandora, 1985.

Joannou, Maroula, *'Ladies, Please Don't Smash These Windows': Women's Writing, Feminist Consciousness and Social Change 1918–1938*. Oxford/Providence: Berg, 1995.

Johnstone, J. K., *The Bloomsbury Group: A Study of E. M. Forster, Lytton Strachey, Virginia Woolf and their Circle*. New York: The Noonday Press, 1963.

Jones, Stephen J., *Workers at Play: A Social and Economic History of Leisure 1918–1939*. London; Routledge and Kegan Paul, 1986.

Judd, Alan, *Ford Madox Ford*. Cambridge, Massachusetts: Harvard University Press, 1991.

Kenner, Hugh, *The Pound Era: The Age of Ezra Pound, T. S. Eliot, James Joyce and Wyndham Lewis.* London: Faber and Faber, 1972.

— *Wyndham Lewis.* London: Methuen, 1954.

Kime Scott, Bonnie, *Refiguring Modernism. Volume I: The Women of 1928; Volume II: Postmodern Feminist Readings of Woolf, West and Barnes.* Bloomington: Indiana University Press, 1995.

King, James, *Virginia Woolf.* London: Penguin, 1995.

Kinkead-Weekes, Mark, *D. H. Lawrence: Triumph to Exile. 1912–1922.* Cambridge: Cambridge University Press, 1996.

Leavis, F. R., *D. H. Lawrence, Novelist.* London: Chatto and Windus, 1955.

Leavis, F. R., *Thought, Words and Creativity: Art and Thought in D. H. Lawrence.* London: Chatto and Windus, 1976.

Lee, Hermione, *The Novels of Virginia Woolf.* London: Methuen, 1977.

— *Virginia Woolf.* London: Chatto and Windus, 1996.

Leed, Eric J., *No Man's Land: Combat and Identity in World War One.* Cambridge: Cambridge University Press, 1979.

Leer, Norman, *The Limited Hero in the Fiction of Ford Madox Ford.* Michigan: Michigan University Press, 1966.

Levenson, Michael H., *A Genealogy of Modernism: A Study of English Literary Doctrine 1908–1922.* Cambridge: Cambridge University Press, 1984.

Light, Alison, *Forever England: Femininity, Literature and Conservatism between the Wars.* London: Routledge, 1991.

Lindberg-Seyersted, Brita (ed.), *Pound/Ford: The Story of a Literary Friendship. The Correspondence between Ezra Pound and Ford Madox Ford and Their Writings about Each Other.* London: Faber & Faber Ltd., 1982.

Lockett, Terence Anthony, *Three Lives: Samuel Bamford, Alfred Darbyshire, Ellen Wilkinson.* London: University of London Press, 1968.

Lucas, John, *The Radical Twenties: Aspects of Writing, Politics and Culture.* Nottingham: Five Leaves Publications, 1997.

Lukács, Georg, *The Meaning of Contemporary Realism.* Translated from the German by John and Necke Mander. London: Merlin Press, 1963.

MacKillop, Ian D., *F. R. Leavis: A Life in Criticism.* London: Allen Lane, 1995.

MacShane, Frank (ed.), *Critical Writings of Ford Madox Ford.* Lincoln: University of Nebraska Press, 1934.

— *Ford Madox Ford: the Critical Heritage.* London: Routledge and Kegan Paul, 1972.

Marcus, Jane, *Virginia Woolf and the Languages of Patriarchy.* Bloomington: Indiana University Press, 1987.

Marwick, Arthur, *The Deluge: British Society and the First World War.* (1965) Second edition. Basingstoke and London: Macmillan, 1991.

— *The Explosion of British Society 1914–62.* London: Macmillan, 1965.

— *Women at War 1914–18.* London: Fontana, 1977.

Marx, Karl and Friedrich Engels, *The German Ideology: Part One. With selections from Parts Two and Three, together with Marx's 'Introduction to a*

Critique of Political Economy'. Edited and with an Introduction by C. J. Arthur. London: Lawrence and Wishart, 1977.

Materer, Timothy, *Wyndham Lewis the Novelist*. Detroit: Wayne State University Press, 1976.

McAleer, Joseph, *Popular Reading and Publishing in Britain 1914–1950*. Oxford: Clarendon Press, 1992.

McLeod, Sheila, *D. H. Lawrence's Men and Women*. London: Heinemann, 1985.

McNichol, Stella, *Virginia Woolf and the Poetry of Fiction*. London: Routledge, 1990.

Meisel, Perry, *The Absent Father: Virginia Woolf and Walter Pater*. New Haven and London: Yale University Press, 1980.

Melman, Billie, *Women and the Popular Imagination in the Twenties: Flappers and Nymphs*. London: Macmillan Press, 1988.

Meyers, Jeffrey, *The Enemy: A Biography of Wyndham Lewis*. London and Henley: Routledge and Kegan Paul, 1980.

— *Wyndham Lewis: A Revaluation. New Essays*. London: Athlone Press, 1980.

Miller, C. Ruth, *Virginia Woolf: The Frames of Art and Life*. Basingstoke: Macmillan, 1988.

Miller, Jane Eldridge, *Rebel Women: Feminism, Modernism and the Edwardian Novel*. London: Virago, 1994.

Milton, Colin, *Lawrence and Nietzsche: A Study in Influence*. Aberdeen: Aberdeen University Press, 1987.

Minow-Pinkney, Makiko, *Virginia Woolf and the Problem of the Subject*. Brighton: Harvester Press, 1987.

Mitchell, Juliet and Jacqueline Rose (eds), *Feminine Sexuality: Jacques Lacan and the* école freudienne. New York and London: Norton, 1982.

Modleski, Tania, *Loving with a Vengeance: Mass Produced Fantasies for Women*. London: Methuen, 1982.

Montefiore, Janet, *Men and Women Writers of the 1930s: The Dangerous Flood of History*. London: Routledge, 1996.

Montgomery, John, *The Twenties: An Informal Social History*. London: George Allen and Unwin, 1957.

Moore, Harry T., *The Priest of Love: A Life of D. H. Lawrence*. Harmondsworth: Pelican, 1976.

Moore, Madeline, *The Short Season between Two Silences: The Mystical and the Political in the Novels of Virginia Woolf*. Boston: George Allen and Unwin, 1984.

Morris, Margaret, *The General Strike*. London and West Nyack: Journeyman Press, 1976.

Mowat, Charles Loch, *Britain Between The Wars: 1918–1940*. London: Methuen, 1968.

Mulhern, Francis, *The Moment of 'Scrutiny'*. London: NLB, 1979.

Naremore, James, *The World Without a Self: Virginia Woolf and the Novel*. New Haven and London: Yale University Press, 1973.

Newbury, Maggie, *Picking Up Threads: The Complete Reminiscences of a Bradford Mill Girl.* Edited by James Ogden. Bradford: Bradford Libraries, 1993.

Nicholls, Peter, *Modernisms: A Literary Guide.* London: Macmillan, 1995.

Nixon, Cornelia, *Lawrence's Leadership Politics and the Turn Against Women.* Berkeley: University of California Press, 1986.

Ouditt, Sharon, *Fighting Forces: Writing Women: Identity and Ideology in the First World War.* London and New York: Routledge, 1994.

Parfitt, George, *Fiction of the First World War: A Study.* London: Faber and Faber, 1988.

Partlow, Robert B. and Harry T. Moore (eds), *D. H. Lawrence: The Man Who Lived.* Carbondale: Southern Illinois University Press, 1980.

Phillips, Kathy J., *Virginia Woolf Against Empire.* Knoxville: University of Tennessee Press, 1994.

Pichardie, Jean-Paul, *D. H. Lawrence: La Tentation utopique: de Rananim au Serpent au plumes.* Rouen: Université de Rouen, 1988.

Pinkney, Tony, *D. H. Lawrence.* Brighton: Harvester Wheatsheaf, 1990.

Poole, Roger, *The Unknown Virginia Woolf.* (1978) Fourth edition. Cambridge: Cambridge University Press, 1996.

Preston, Peter and Peter Hoare (eds), *D. H. Lawrence in the Modern World.* London: Macmillan, 1989.

Radford, Jean, *The Progress of Romance: The Politics of Popular Fiction.* London: Routledge, 1986.

Raitt, Suzanne and Trudi Tate (eds), *Women's Fiction and the Great War.* Oxford: Clarendon, 1997.

Read, Donald (ed.), *Edwardian England.* London and Canberra: Croom Helm, 1982.

Roe, Sue, *Writing and Gender: Virginia Woolf's Writing Practice.* Hemel Hempstead: Harvester Wheatsheaf, 1990.

Rosencrance, Barbara, *Forster's Narrative Vision.* Ithaca and London: Cornell University Press, 1982.

Rowbotham, Sheila and Jeffrey Weeks, *Socialism and the New Life: The Personal and Sexual Politics of Edward Carpenter and Havelock Ellis.* London: Pluto Press, 1977.

Ruderman, Judith, *D. H. Lawrence and the Devouring Mother: The Search for a Patriarchal Ideal of Leadership.* Durham, NC: Duke University Press, 1984.

Said, Edward, *Orientalism.* London: Routledge and Kegan Paul, 1978.

Samson, Anne, *F. R. Leavis.* London: Harvester Wheatsheaf, 1992.

Saunders, Max, *Ford Madox Ford: A Dual Life.* Two volumes. Oxford: Oxford University Press, 1996.

Scheckner, Peter, *Class, Politics and the Individual: A Study of the Major Works of D. H. Lawrence.* Rutherford, NJ: Farleigh Dickinson University Press, 1985.

Showalter, Elaine, *The Female Malady: Women, Madness and English Culture 1830–1980.* London: Virago, 1987.

— *A Literature of Their Own: British Women Writers from Brontë to Lessing.* London: Virago, 1978.

Silkin, Jon, *Out of Battle: The Poetry of the Great War.* (1972) Oxford: Oxford University Press, 1978.

Simpson, Hilary, *D. H. Lawrence and Feminism.* London: Croom Helm, 1982.

Smith, Anne (ed.), *Lawrence and Women.* London: Vision Press, 1978.

Snitow, Ann Barr, *Ford Madox Ford and the Voice of Uncertainty.* Baton Rouge: Louisiana State University Press, 1984.

Spengler, Oswald, *The Decline of the West.* Two volumes, 1918, 1922. Translation with notes by Charles Francis Atkinson. London: Allen & Unwin, 1926, 1926.

Spivak, Gayatri C., 'Unmaking and Making in *To The Lighthouse*', in *In Other Worlds: Essays in Cultural Politics.* London: Methuen, 1987.

Squier, Susan Merrill (ed.), *Women Writers and The City: Essays in Feminist Literary Criticism.* Knoxville: University of Tennessee Press, 1984.

Squires, Michael and Denis Jackson (eds), *D. H. Lawrence's 'Lady': A New Look at* Lady Chatterley's Lover. Athens, GA: The University of Georgia Press, 1985.

Stang, Sondra J. (ed.), *The Ford Madox Ford Reader.* Foreword by Graham Greene. Manchester: Carcanet Press, 1986.

— William Trevor and Edward Crankshaw (eds), *The Presence of Ford Madox Ford: A Memorial Volume of Essays, Poems, and Memoirs.* Philadelphia: University of Pennsylvania Press, 1981.

Stevenson, Randall, *Modernist Fiction: An Introduction.* New York and London: Harvester Wheatsheaf, 1992.

Suleri, Sara, *The Rhetoric of English India.* Chicago: Chicago University Press, 1992.

Tambling, Jeremy (ed.), *E. M. Forster.* London: Macmillan, 1995.

Taylor, Barbara, *Socialism and Feminism in the Nineteenth Century.* London: Virago, 1983

Theweleit, Klaus, *Male Fantasies. Volume I. Women; Floods; Bodies; History.* Translated by Stephen Conway. Foreword by Barbara Ehrenreich. *Volume II. Male Bodies: Psychoanalysing the White Terror.* Translated by Chris Turner and Erica Carter. Foreword by Jessica Benjamin and Anson Rabinhach. Minneapolis: Minnesota University Press, 1987, 1989.

Tratner, Michael, *Modernism and Mass Politics: Joyce, Woolf, Eliot and Yeats.* Stanford, California: Stanford University Press, 1995.

Trotter, David, *The English Novel in History: 1895–1920.* London and New York: Routledge, 1993.

Tylee, Claire M., *The Great War and Women's Consciousness: Images of Militarism and Womanhood in Women's Writings, 1914–64.* Basingstoke and London: Macmillan, 1990.

Vernon, Betty D., *Ellen Wilkinson: 1891–1947.* London: Croom Helm, 1982.

Wagner, Geoffrey, *Wyndham Lewis: A Portrait of the Artist as the Enemy*. London: Routledge & Kegan Paul, 1957.

Waites, Bernard, *A Class Society at War: England 1914–1918*. Leamington Spa, Hamburg and New York: Berg, 1987.

Weiss, Timothy, *Fairy Tale and Romance in the Works of Ford Madox Ford*. Lanham, New York, London: University Press of America, 1984.

Widdowson, Peter (ed.), *D. H. Lawrence*. London and New York: London, 1992.

Wiltsher, Anne, *Most Dangerous Women: Feminist Peace Campaigners of the Great War*. London: Pandora, 1985.

Winter, J. M., *The Great War and the British People*. Basingstoke and London: Macmillan, 1985.

Worthen, John, *D. H. Lawrence and the Idea of the Novel*. London: Macmillan, 1979.

Young, Robert, *White Mythologies: Writing History and the West*. London: Routledge, 1990.

Zilboorg, Caroline (ed.), *Richard Aldington and H.D.: The Early Years in Letters*. Bloomington and Indianapolis: Indiana University Press, 1992.

Zwerdling, Alex, *Virginia Woolf and the Real World*. Berkeley: University of California Press, 1986.

Index